DIGITAL FUTURES FOR LEARNING

Digital Futures for Learning offers a methodological and pedagogical way forward for researchers and educators who want to work imaginatively with "what's next" in higher education and informal learning. Today's debates around technological transformations of social, cultural and educational spaces and practices need to be informed by a more critical understanding of how visions of the future of learning are made and used, and how they come to be seen as desirable, inevitable or impossible. Integrating innovative methods, key research findings, engaging theories and creative pedagogies across multiple disciplines, this book argues for and explores speculative approaches to researching and analysing post-compulsory and informal learning futures – where we are, where we might go and how to get there.

Jen Ross is Senior Lecturer in Digital Education in the Moray House School of Education and Sport, Co-Director of the Centre for Research in Digital Education and an Edinburgh Futures Institute Fellow at the University of Edinburgh, UK.

DIGITAL FUTURES FOR LEARNING

Speculative Methods and Pedagogies

Jen Ross

Cover image: © Getty images/lightpainting single exposure – by julian marshall

First published 2023
by Routledge
605 Third Avenue, New York, NY 10158

and by Routledge
4 Park Square, Milton Park, Abingdon, Oxon, OX14 4RN

Routledge is an imprint of the Taylor & Francis Group, an informa business

© 2023 Jen Ross

The right of Jen Ross to be identified as author of this work has been asserted in accordance with sections 77 and 78 of the Copyright, Designs and Patents Act 1988.

All rights reserved. No part of this book may be reprinted or reproduced or utilised in any form or by any electronic, mechanical, or other means, now known or hereafter invented, including photocopying and recording, or in any information storage or retrieval system, without permission in writing from the publishers.

Trademark notice: Product or corporate names may be trademarks or registered trademarks, and are used only for identification and explanation without intent to infringe.

ISBN: 978-1-032-06405-5 (hbk)
ISBN: 978-1-032-05812-2 (pbk)
ISBN: 978-1-003-20213-4 (ebk)

DOI: 10.4324/9781003202134

Typeset in Bembo
by SPi Technologies India Pvt Ltd (Straive)

CONTENTS

List of Illustrations	*ix*
Acknowledgements	*x*

PART 1
Understanding learning futures   **1**

1 Introduction   **3**
A learning future 3
Educational technology and learning futures 6
The future, multiple futures and critical futures 10
Speculative methods and pedagogies 12
My commitments and position 14
Structure of this book 15
Notes 17
References 17

2 How learning futures are made   **22**
Introduction 22
Sociotechnical and edtech imaginaries 23
Anticipation and mobilising the future in the present 26
*Futures that count: promissory organisations and data-driven
    future-making 28*
Futures work as a site of critical engagement 31
Notes 34
References 34

vi Contents

3 **Complexity, emergence and learning futures**   38
Introduction 38
Understanding the world as complex 39
Learning as relational, indeterminate and contingent 42
From causality to complexity: digital education research 44
Not-yetness 46
Becoming, complexity and learning futures 49
Notes 51
References 51

4 **Speculative approaches to research and teaching**   56
Introduction 56
Temporality and speculative method 59
Epistemology and speculative method 61
Engagement, performativity and speculative method 63
Speculation in practice: examples from research and teaching 66
Notes 74
References 74

PART 2
Speculative objects to think with   79
Objects-to-think-with 80
Ten years of speculation: introducing the case studies 80

5 **Teaching at scale, automation and a speculative
teacherbot**   83
Introduction 83
*Online teaching at scale and automation: a short history of
EDCMOOC 85*
*"We welcome our robot colleagues": teacherbot and
automated teaching 87*
Glitches as speculative interruptions: teacherbot goes live 90
Speculation beyond the glitch 93
Teacherbot futures 95
Notes 99
References 100

6 **Working with digital futures for learning through
student–generated open educational resources**   104
Introduction 104
*Open educational resources, practices and a continuum
of openness 105*

Contents **vii**

The Digital Futures for Learning course 107
Co-creating futures: the OER assignment 109
Speculative pedagogy through student-generated OERs 117
Notes 120
References 121

7 **Artcasting and digital cultural heritage engagement
futures**   **124**
Introduction 124
Digital engagement, digital cultural heritage 126
*Value and evaluation: measuring engagement
   with cultural heritage 130*
The Artcasting project 131
Artcasting as a speculative method 136
Artcasting and heritage engagement futures 139
Notes 142
References 142

8 **Telling data stories to explore the future of surveillance 148**
Introduction 148
Surveillance in the digital university 149
Higher education after surveillance and the Data Stories project 152
Making a speculative Data Stories Creator 154
Stories about surveillance futures 157
*Resisting resignation: participatory speculative fiction and surveillance
   futures 161*
Notes 163
References 163

PART 3
Keeping learning futures moving   **167**

9 **Speculative methods and digital futures research**   **169**
Introduction 169
Asking questions about the future 170
Objects-to-think-with 171
Participation in a speculative encounter 173
Capturing and analysing speculative data 175
The ethics of speculative approaches 177
Speculative research and truth claims 178

viii Contents

An example speculative project: inventive self-presentation 179
Conclusion 182
Notes 183
References 183

10 Speculative pedagogies and teaching   **187**
Introduction 187
Speculative course design 188
Supporting futures work 190
Participation, ethics and assessment 191
Informal learning, speculatively 192
Futures teaching case study: culture, heritage and
  learning futures 194
Conclusion 196
Note 197
References 197

11 Keeping learning futures moving   **200**
Key messages from this book 200
What next? 204
Hope for the future in challenging times 205
References 206

Index   *209*

ILLUSTRATIONS

Figures

6.1	Rationale for Murphy's "How to Adult" speculative scenario.	113
6.2	Peckham's "surviving entanglement" machine.	116
7.1	Text of artcast of Mapplethorpe's *Nick Marden*. Sent to the year 1997, to the sender's school in Ireland.	132
7.2	Artcasting banner at the Bowes Museum, November 2015.	134
7.3	Drop-in artcasting session at the National Galleries of Scotland, January 2016.	135
7.4	Artcasting Dialectogram, Mitch Miller, 2016.	139

Tables

6.1	Digital Futures for Learning course structure, 2020	111
8.1	Prompt questions for the data stories creator	155

ACKNOWLEDGEMENTS

This book tells the story of more than a decade of research and teaching collaborations, and I am grateful for the collegiality, friendship, support and insights of the many people I've been fortunate enough to work and learn alongside during that period.

I am extremely fortunate to have found a home in a university with such an amazing community of talented, smart, imaginative and kind people. In particular, the people associated with the Centre for Research in Digital Education and the MSc in Digital Education at the University of Edinburgh have been incredibly supportive and inspiring. Thank you to Digital Education students, mentors, friends and colleagues, with special mention of Hamish Macleod, Lydia Plowman, Philippa Sheail and James Lamb. And for her brilliance, leadership and friendship, thank you to Siân Bayne, whose work has always been foundational to my understanding of what digital education could be.

The projects and approaches I discuss in the book happened as they did because of the incredible insights and energy of co-investigators, co-authors and co-tutors: Amy Collier (kindred spirit and the spark for many good adventures over the past decade), Claire Sowton, Chris Speed, Jeremy Knox, Chris Barker, Christopher Ganley, Christine Sinclair, Hamish Macleod, Siân Bayne, Stuart Allan, Huw Davies, Shawn Bodden, Jane McKie, Pat Lockley and Anna Wilson.

Beyond the people involved in these projects, a heartfelt thanks to those who have helped me to think about and value the ideas that are expressed in this book and set an example for inquisitive and critical approaches to education and cultural heritage, including George Veletsianos, Vel McCune, Melissa Terras, Tim Fawns, Angelina Russo, Koula Charitonos, Anne-Marie Scott and Màiri Lafferty. Thanks also to the members of the Higher Education After Surveillance network, the Digital Cultural Heritage research cluster, and colleagues at the Edinburgh Futures Institute.

The period of writing this book has seen its share of struggle, but also of music, laughter, walks, great chats, gardens, food and sunny days. I am so thankful for the love and support of friends and family near and far, who have believed in and cared about what I was doing and provided welcome distractions when needed. Thank you for the small and large acts of affection and friendship that have sustained me. Finally, my love and gratitude to Louise: always ahead of your time.

PART 1

Understanding learning futures

1
INTRODUCTION

A learning future

In the future, a technology called "the Ledger" will be used by a billion people to track their learning and income. "Edublocks", which represent one hour of learning in any subject, will be earned from formal institutions, apps, individuals or informal community groups. Ledger profiles will be read by potential employers and used to offer a job or a short "gig". The value of income earned will be tracked through the ledger system and used to help people select subjects to study based on the income they have generated for others, or to trade a percentage of future income to investors in exchange for free learning hours. Distinctions between formal and informal learning, teacher and student, and work and study will be fully erased, and the ability to track, verify and accredit learning and skills will be coordinated through an advanced and ubiquitous digital platform.

Stop for a moment to consider this future. How do you feel: excited, worried, hopeful, annoyed? What questions do you have? Maybe you are thinking about how this would affect you, your family, your students, your community or workplace, or other people, communities or workplaces. Perhaps you are homing in on some issues of concern or wondering about the technical or policy developments that could produce this future. Possibly the nature of the prediction itself interests you. Or maybe there is something else on your mind now, sparked by your reaction to the Ledger.

This scenario comes from a video, *Learning is Earning 2026*, which was produced for an event held as part of the South x Southwest Education conference in Austin, Texas, in 2016. The event was co-designed by the Institute for the Future (IFTF), a foresight organisation, and the ACT Foundation. ACT is a non-profit organisation best known for the ACT test, a standardised test widely

DOI: 10.4324/9781003202134-2

4 Understanding learning futures

used in the US and Canada to measure college readiness and underpin college admissions (for scale, 1.67 million high school graduates took the test in 2020).[1] The seven-minute video was created as a prompt for players to immerse themselves in a "36-hour interactive forecasting experience" (Institute for the Future, n.d.). To date, according to public YouTube statistics, the standalone video has been viewed about 11,000 times.

In a series of six "stories from the Ledger", the video illustrates possible use cases for Ledger technology. In them, Edublock records become a permanent part of the global blockchain and serve as a "growing public record of our collective learning and working" (Institute for the Future (IFTF), 2016). People describe earning Edublocks by listening to audiobooks while driving, being taught by other members of peer learning groups, playing online science games, completing tasks at work and verifying skills through real-world tests. One story involves a recent college graduate describing how they paid off their student loans through a "pay it forward" programme, where "whatever blocks you earned in school, you can teach them to others... I'm pre-approved to teach any subject I passed". The implications of the Ledger system are far-reaching, including the disappearance of entry-level jobs in favour of gig- or project-based employment offered to people based on credentials searchable in the Ledger. Temporary roles and projects benefit workers because they earn Edublocks through them as well, increasing their employability for their next gig.

Learning is Earning is one of my favourite examples of a vision of a digital future for learning – not because I like the vision, but because it is such an excellent illustration of how such futures can be framed. It captures a moment in time in the mid-2010s, when the rise in interest in the use of blockchain ledger technologies intersected with intense debates about the value and cost of higher education (especially in the US), contributing to an educational imaginary that has been growing in influence in recent years.[2]

In 2018, Means characterised *Learning is Earning* as part of a speculative discourse of platform learning (2018, p. 327), one that frames learning as "a prescriptive process, rooted in efficiency and calculation, and powered by artificial intelligence, mobile apps, cloud services, and data processing" (p. 329). He points to other work done by IFTF on the theme of integration of on-demand work and learning in a "learning economy" (p. 331), and argues that this works "anticipat[es] the digitalization of learning as economic currency" (ibid) and ushers in an orientation to education that is shaped by "radical customization and optimization". These orientations are made explicit in the *Learning is Earning* video, and the video does normative work in shaping debate about learning futures, permitting some possibilities and closing off others as it sets up the terms of debate that the "players" of the 2016 experience – and anyone who encounters the video afterwards – can engage with.

The following year, Tapscott and Kaplan (2019) included the video as one of three examples of "initiatives exploring ways to credential students for everything they learn, no matter the setting" (p. 11) in their report for the IBM Institute for Business Value. The other two examples they give are Open Badges and blockchain certificates – both of which were existing, if not mainstream, digital technologies in 2019. Combining existing and imaginary initiatives, the authors build their case for the potential of blockchain in education, and its implications for identity, data rights and privacy, funding models and most of all transformation and disruption of education systems.

In *Learning is Earning*, high production values, idealistic framing of an emerging technology, rhetoric of "disruption" and stated purpose as part of a participatory design process combine to shed light on the ways that learning futures are made. It also demonstrates some of the intended and unintended consequences of producing learning futures, including how some visions of the future persist, while others are subordinated or even erased. At some point after the 2016 event, the web site that originally accompanied the *Learning is Earning 2026* video disappeared. The web site was the location of the input from the players of the 2016 conference experience, capturing the "positive" and "shadow" imaginations sparked by the video, prompted by a set of questions:

> What could be different? What would you change... in your school, in your work, in your company, in your life? What amazing things could happen in your community? What new challenges would we face – and how could we solve them?
>
> *(IFTF, 2019)*

Players' imaginings were expressed in the form of brief textual responses, and a selection was shared anonymously on the home page of the game site. There, a few objections to the video's message, now publicly accessible only through the Internet Archive's Wayback Machine,[3] offer a glimpse at the concerns this vision raised:

> Won't some edublocks have greater value than others?
>
> There will be elites of people with permanent jobs (those that require really knowing the organizations) and people with transient jobs.
>
> Why would I want to monetize learning I do to feed my soul?

Because of the accessibility of the video, and the inaccessibility of the wider context and response, six years on the vision of the *Learning is Earning 2026* video creators and the scenario-builders from IFTF and ACT stands alone. The brief and fragmented responses from the participants in the activities that justified the creation of this vision are accessible only to a determined internet sleuth. For researchers and educators, there is an important lesson here about the consequences of flows of power on narratives of the future. It highlights the need to

6 Understanding learning futures

be critical of taken-for-granted futures, but also be sensitive to how the voices of research participants, students and community members are, or are not, represented in learning futures work.

These are some of the key themes that will be discussed and developed in this book: how digital futures for learning come to be imagined and acted upon, how they might be imagined otherwise and why this matters. The book discusses the powerful role of technology-related predictions and promises in digital education and learning contexts, and how these work to open up certain futures and close down others. It explores the value of engaging with emergence, complexity and uncertainty in researching and teaching about educational technology, and introduces speculative approaches as tactics for studying and engaging with digital futures for learning. Drawing on a growing body of speculative research and education literature, and four in-depth accounts of work from the past decade, I will discuss how to design and conduct speculative research and teaching to open up digital education futures in new and generative ways.

This chapter begins with a snapshot of the context of digital education that has informed this book, highlights some of the learning futures that are in play at the time of writing and situates the book in the context of critical education futures work. It then introduces speculative methods and pedagogies and gives an overview of their role in working with learning futures. I locate this work in the context of my own position and commitments, and close by outlining how this book will unfold.

Educational technology and learning futures

This book emerges from within a context of intense interest in digital technologies and data-driven education and learning, and profound concerns and hopes about what digital learning futures might emerge. It is useful to begin by briefly setting out what I mean by "digital", and "learning", and to explain the focus of the book on higher education and informal learning spaces (particularly museums, galleries and other heritage spaces).

Defining "digital" is not straightforward, and requires attention to technologies, platforms, databases and algorithms, but also the relationships, identities, practices, mobilities, objects and materials that are produced, changed or mediated through them. Furthermore, as theorists of the post-digital are correctly arguing, there is now no part of the social, cultural, economic, political or cultural world that could be described as "non-digital", and no clear distinctions between online and offline in most adults' experiences of daily life, including in education. As a result, this book could have dropped "digital" from the title (and in the final week of writing, I was considering doing so) and it would still not have been particularly strange to find it full of apps, online and open courses, and web sites. The reason I have kept digital foregrounded is partly historical, in recognition of the influence of the field that has been called "digital education" on all of the work in Part 2, for example; and partly as a way of signalling that there are many things to say about the role of digital technologies in how learning futures are understood. We cannot disentangle them from the rest of life, but we might have choices to make about what they are, and what they do with and to futures, that benefit from considering the meanings that are attached to them. There is a third reason, too, which is that I hope the book will appeal to a range of people, including learning technologists and instructional designers, who understand their work as being about and with digital technologies and practices.

The phrase "digital learning futures" is intended to signal the emphasis in this book on examining and reimagining how futures are told, with a focus on digital technologies and their impact on learning and education. However, the term "learning" is somewhat problematic, and my discomfort with it reflects a distinction in educational research: between a focus on individual, internalised, cognitive processes of skills or knowledge acquisition or transformation (often described as learning), and a focus on the social, cultural, material and discursive construction of educational settings, tasks, spaces and relationships. However, despite my belief that "education" better captures the theoretical commitments and focus of this book than "learning", "education" also often suggests a formal setting like a school. This is a problem because although this book discusses higher education extensively, it also includes work on informal or lifelong learning settings and situations, like museums and Massive Open Online Courses. In Chapter 3, I explore the concept of learning, and how to use it in ways that account for complexity and make room for speculation, but the issue remains thorny.

Across the first decades of the 20th century, technology and education have become increasingly entwined in popular, policy and educational debates, as well as in practice. Hopes and concerns about the role of digital technologies in personalisation, massification, access and collaboration have been playing out at all levels of formal and informal learning. Increasing monitoring and datafication of engagement and attainment through the development and deployment of learning analytics are heralding an understanding of learning as quantifiable and measurable at remarkably fine-grained levels (Slade and Prinsloo, 2013; Wilson et al., 2017). The promise and threat of automation and artificial intelligence has sparked debates about assessment, accreditation and the role of education in preparing people for futures of work and living that are seen as rapidly shifting (Williamson, 2017). Planetary, economic, health and democratic futures are seen as opaque and threatening, and mastery of digital literacies (Bhatt and MacKenzie, 2019), coding and computational thinking (Luckin, 2018) and self-presentation in a fast-paced attention economy (Duffy and Chan, 2019) are understood as urgently needed skills, in both formal and informal learning settings (Meyers, Erickson and Small, 2013). Despite a long history of disappointment as e-learning and digital education in its various forms has failed to live up to the grandest claims made for it (Hedberg, 2006), promises, and investments of time and resource, continue to be made.

8 Understanding learning futures

Some education futures have received more attention than others: for example, the past few years have seen the publication of two books about possible futures for American higher education – Alexander's (2020) book on trends and scenarios for the future of higher education and Staley's (2019) exploration of speculative scenarios aimed at prompting insights and innovation in the higher education sector. Both books reflect on a range of technological dimensions (Staley does not call these "disruptions" as he considers this concept too transactional), including: scale, platforms, mobilities and embodiment (Staley); and automation, 3d printing, mixed reality and augmentation, and open education (Alexander). The range of possible futures put forward by these writers give a useful indication of the kinds of interests and concerns that are animating debate about the future of the US higher education system, and I will pick up on Staley's work further in Chapter 4.

With technological developments and predictions have come urgent questions about privacy, consent, creativity and the consequences of datafication. Social justice, equality, participation and representation are under the spotlight as potential and actual harms from surveillance and monitoring (Prinsloo, 2017; Costa et al., 2018; Gilliard and saheli singh, 2021; Beetham et al., 2022), commercialisation and unbundling of educational functions (Cottom, 2018; Selwyn et al., 2020), algorithmic bias (O'Neil, 2016) and the inscrutability of data-driven decision-making come to be better understood. Digital technologies and their role in learning futures are seen as in urgent need of reshaping at a very fundamental level, as noted in a key report from UNESCO on the future of education:

> They can do so much more to empower and connect people than the usually commercial moulds we have established for them, and now expect. Creating a more supple digital environment will require some uncoupling of its underlying infrastructures from the business models and authoritarian regulatory impulses that currently constrain positive development and the potential common good that can be created.
>
> *(International Commission on the Futures of Education, 2021, p. 37)*

Many issues demand and are receiving a critical response: the role of the teacher and shifting power dynamics in higher education (Bayne, 2015), the impact of technologies on the spaces and times of learning (Sheail, 2018), the persistence of widely divergent life and educational outcomes despite increasing access to technologies that were alleged to level the playing field for learning through life (Eynon and Malmberg, 2021), and the colonisation of the production of open education by wealthy countries and educational systems (Knox, 2013; Olakulehin and Singh, 2013; Rhoads, Berdan and Toven-Lindsey, 2013). The "digital pivot" in 2020 in response to the Covid-19 pandemic brought many of these issues further to the surface, as educators and learners encountered – some for the first time – the promise and complexity of online learning in universities (Czerniewicz et al., 2020; Veletsianos and Houlden, 2020).

The informal learning context is equally contested and complex in relation to digital technologies and futures. Beyond formal education settings, culture, politics and leisure were already becoming more digital before the Covid-19 pandemic pushed many more interactions online (Stalder, 2018). Mediated forms of communication, engagement and entertainment, and the centrality of digital social networks and social media, were spurring organisations to invest in digitising, personalising and gamifying their offerings, and in the process changing the nature of informal learning and engagement for people of all ages (Drotner et al., 2019). Defining informal learning, and distinguishing between formal, informal and lifelong learning, is a task that is becoming more difficult as the boundaries between learning activities, spaces and identities become more porous, and social networks and information spaces overlap (Boys, 2011; Greenhow and Lewin, 2016). For instance, Goodyear (2021) defines "informal lifelong learning" as: "activities that are not formally organised through engagement with educational or quasi-educational institutions. Typically, such activities connect over substantial portions of the life course (years or decades), are self-organised and accompany other personally valued activities" (p. 1596). The organisation and self-organisation of informal learning activities may take place in learning spaces of various kinds. Degner et al. (2022) suggest that museums, botanical gardens and other heritage spaces might be characterised as "institutional informal learning places" where informal learning takes place in un-coordinated ways, and discoveries are spontaneous or even random. Such discoveries may vary in how meaningful they are – for example, examining the use of virtual reality experiences in a public library, Dahya et al. (2021) observe that "the idea that virtual reality can be used to 'experience' the lives of the Other warrants further discussion" (p. 631), including where VR users might believe they can "witness or embody the emotional, physical, and economic struggles and conflict of communities already marginalized from mainstream society" (ibid). Where and how such discussion might take place, and who would be involved, is uncertain, rendering informal learning subject to the assumptions of participants, mediamakers, spatial planners and others, as social relations and practices become "naturalised" by informal learning spaces (Berman, 2020).

Not just individuals or communities but also organisations, cities and societies are increasingly seen through a lens of learning (Ra, Jagannathan and Maclean, 2021). The learning city, for example, is a site of considerable attention and international agendas for learning futures (Facer and Buchczyk, 2019). A long tradition of collective social movement learning is finding expression in and generating new digital and hybrid spaces of activism and social movements (Emejulu and McGregor, 2019; Boulianne, Lalancette and Ilkiw, 2020; Lynch, 2020;

Carlson and Berglund, 2021). Nevertheless, visions for the future of informal digital education are proving to be stubbornly individualistic.

The nature of informal learning is shifting along with other forms of education as changing policy priorities in the global North have, in recent decades, seen a move towards education and learning opportunities geared to producing "enterprising selves" (Edwards, 2002) capable of responding to social, economic or other demands through their position as "deterritorialized, individualized and flexible consumers of learning opportunities" (p. 359). An emphasis is increasingly placed on individual skills and away from broader capabilities that are critical to living in and being part of a functioning society (Bynner, 2017, p. 82). UNESCO's 2020 report on lifelong learning futures recommends a "learner-centric, demand-led approach to education that enables learners of all ages and backgrounds to co-design actively and use any learning process and its outcomes to achieve their full potential" (UNESCO and Institute for Lifelong Learning, 2020).

We can see some evidence of demand-led informal learning in creative digital spaces that serve various "fandoms" (Magnifico, Lammers and Curwood, 2020), and in the growing understanding of makerspaces and other community-led "tinkering" spaces as learning spaces (Peppler, Halverson and Kafai, 2016). However, these spaces and practices are not equally accessible to all, and inequalities in access and engagement with digital forms of informal learning present an ongoing challenge. In two papers, written ten years apart, Eynon and Helsper (2011) and Eynon and Malmberg (2021) observe that the distinction between choice and exclusion is not a simple one in the context of online informal learning (2011), and that those who were better off, had stronger education backgrounds and were less precariously employed were also those most likely to engage in lifelong learning (2021, p. 569). Others, even when they do engage in activities, benefit less from this engagement (personally and in terms of their capital).

This is the context in which the work of this book has taken place, and a grounding for what you will find in the chapters that follow. The futures that have emerged from within this context have been influential in learning organisations, educational technology companies, the media, policy spaces and in the practices of educators and learners. What is the nature of these futures, and how do they come to matter?

The future, multiple futures and critical futures

Within and beyond specific debates in the field of digital education, there is a growing body of work in educational research and policy that explicitly engages with learning futures, and research that focuses on education as an important site for futures studies work (Hicks et al., 1998). This work sometimes focuses on technology, but often in the context of other key issues such as sustainability, equality and inclusion, work, culture and participation. As a key example, when UNESCO published their *Reimagining Our Futures Together* report in late 2021, the report authors proposed a "reinvention" of education, involving a new social contract to address global risks and challenges:

> The new social contract for education must help us unite around collective endeavours and provide the knowledge and innovation needed to shape sustainable and peaceful futures for all anchored in social, economic, and environmental justice.
>
> *(International Commission on the Futures of Education, 2021, p. 11)*

This report was the culmination of a multi-year period of engagement and analysis. Its publication was an important contribution to debates about not only what education might look like in the future, but what it should be *for*. Published in midst of a global pandemic, it emphasises the interconnected nature of the problems facing the world, and the role of collective knowledge and action in addressing them.

The reference to learning "futures", rather than "the future", in much of this work, including in this book, is deliberate. It makes explicit that there is no single present, let alone a single future to which all efforts can be directed. In this book, it also reflects an interest in the future as a topic of critical examination, including how past, present and future are bound up together in particular ways to produce particular narratives, and how current narratives of the future could be otherwise. This locates the book broadly in the tradition of critical education futures research (Milojević, 2005), which involves three key "tasks": to "unmask alleged 'realistic' futures" (p. 15), discuss alternatives on an equal footing to hegemonic ones (p. 16) and recognise the ways "we daily live the many utopian and dystopian visions of the past" (p. 16). These tasks are tackled in various ways in the chapters that follow, as I argue that speculative approaches to research and teaching can unsettle expected futures and generate new ones, but also that they are enacted within complex and shifting contexts of technology and learning that require explicit engagement with the provisionality, partiality and positionality of the futures that are being made (see Chapter 3).

Not all futures work in education is in this critical tradition – indeed, much of it is not, and articulates instead three tendencies that Facer (2016) describes: for viewing education in terms of optimisation, colonisation or protection. Each of these tendencies reflects a particular understanding of the future: a knowable but unchangeable one that requires education to prepare people to participate; an open territory that can be shaped; or a space of impending disaster that requires education as a source of individual safety. Working against these tendencies, she argues, is necessary to keep open the possibility of difference and novelty in the future. This can be difficult, however, because "anticipatory regimes" in education tend to focus on identifying and eliminating possible future risks, at the expense of "collective action and forward dreaming" (Amsler and Facer, 2017, p. 10).

12 Understanding learning futures

Nevertheless, we see critical futures work emerging and flourishing in a number of places. Facer (2021), in a paper commissioned for the UNESCO report mentioned above, outlines five distinct orientations to futures work in education: predictive, preparatory, reflexive, liberatory and reparative – each of which raise particular core questions and suggest ethical directions. This book focuses on speculative work, which fits most closely into Facer's "education in the future" orientation – predictive or imaginative work that aims to understand what education might look like in the future. She suggests that critical futures work fits into this category, but also that this orientation is dominated by professional consultants and commercial actors working with trends, scenario development and other futuring methods. Digital education futures work often inhabits such tensions – with critical perspectives vying for attention amongst the many kinds of stories that are being told (and sold). As I argue in Chapter 4, there is a need to engage in these spaces in ways that offer open-ended and generative approaches to working with the future. This book offers examples of how such engagement can take place using speculative approaches.

Speculative methods and pedagogies

A few jokes from stand-up comedy sketches have made their way into the shorthand that my spouse and I have developed over the years. One such joke was told by Irish comedian Dylan Moran in the mid-2000s, and several versions are available online. In it, a deadpan Moran explains to the audience why the self-help notion of "releasing your potential" is ill-advised:

> 'Release your potential' – now that's a very very dangerous idea. You should stay away from your potential. That is something you should leave absolutely alone. Don't – you'll mess it up! It's potential, leave it!… Leave it as a locked door within yourself… that way, in your mind, the interior will always be palatial.
>
> *(Moran, 2007)*

Since we first saw this, we can reasonably often be heard to say to one another about some scheme or worry: "Leave it! It's your potential!". This is both funny and reassuring to us. The ambiguity of potential – and that approaching it changes it – is central to the work of this book.

Where and when potential actually exists is relevant, too. Wilkie, Savransky and Rosengarten (2017) have described speculation as resisting probable or plausible visions of the future, instead engaging with "the unrealised potential of the present" (p. 8). The "unfinished present" (p. 26) is what predictions of the future of learning generally fail to centre. This failure makes the field of digital education vulnerable, both to edtech imaginaries that offer technological visions of the future that may not serve learners, educators and communities (more on this in Chapter 2), and to discourses of "what works" as the most meaningful space for education to inhabit (see Chapter 3). Through this book, I aim to show that speculative methods offer a way of taking risks that allow alternative or unexpected futures to emerge – and keep emerging – in the field of digital education and learning.

For my purposes, **a speculative approach works with the future as a space of uncertainty, and uses that uncertainty creatively in the present**. Working in a critical or questioning way with digital education futures requires methods that can bring particular ideas or issues into focus by envisioning or crafting conditions which may not yet currently exist, working to trouble established imaginaries. Speculative methods in both research and teaching offer a generative approach to this work (Ross, 2017) by engaging futures as "vectors of risk and creative experimentation" (Wilkie, Savransky and Rosengarten, 2017, p. 5).

What this means in practice can vary considerably, as we will see. Speculative methods in education research use approaches including fictions, researcher-made objects, design activities for participants and speculative analysis. Speculative pedagogies, beginning to be applied in a number of disciplines, tend to centre emergence, creative experimentation and open-endedness. In both research and teaching, speculative approaches reject the articulation of best practice, and the production of predictions, in favour of an orientation to the future that plays with tensions between groundedness, unfamiliarity, responsibility and risk.

Along with their debt to critical education futures scholarship, discussed above, I consider the approaches discussed in this book to belong in the tradition of post-qualitative inquiry and what Lury (2021) refers to as "compositional methodology". This is where things get especially interesting in a methodological sense, because as St Pierre (2021) notes, post-qualitative inquiry has to be invented differently for each problem or study it addresses. Lury (2021) describes this creation in terms of "putting a problem together", and "problem space" where "the problem is not acted on in a space but emerges across a problem space, from with-in and out-with" (p. 3). In social science research, creative methods are increasingly understood as necessary to grapple with the messiness of the social world (Law, 2004) – but Lury and St Pierre are going beyond a call for creative, arts-based approaches or more interpretative methods. Instead, they are observing, like Law (2004), Barad (2007) and other philosophers of the sociomaterial (more on this theoretical perspective in Chapter 3), that realities are made by and through methods and methodologies, and asking what we are to *do* with that observation.

My answer – or the answer of this book, anyway – is that we apply such thinking to our work on digital learning futures by understanding futures as complex and provisional. Speculative work on futures does particular things, relating to its temporal, performative and epistemological qualities (see Chapter 4), but it does so in ways that are theoretically congruent with post-qualitative, inventive

14 Understanding learning futures

and compositional approaches to knowledge production. There is a balance to be struck – and I discuss this balance in different places in the book, but particularly in Chapter 9 – between how speculative work values and encourages playful, imaginative, glitchy and strange encounters, and the need to take this work seriously, and consider how to do it in ways that are responsible to the future and to those people, objects and practices that are enrolled in its various arrangements. An ethical stance towards the future is central to the speculative methods and pedagogies proposed in this book, and this is discussed particularly in Chapters 2, 9 and 10.

My commitments and position

The analysis of speculative data and outcomes in this book, and the design of the work that produced them, is informed by my interest in examining how visions of the future come to be, and could be otherwise, but also by my own commitments and experiences. Various aspects of my identity are therefore relevant to what you will find here. For instance: I am a naturalised citizen of the United Kingdom, my home for 25 years. I was born and grew up in Canada. My sense of home was uncomplicated, though I see this as partly a result of how little I knew about Canada when I lived there. Now I grapple with personal and cultural meanings and histories of belonging in a British and Scottish context of whiteness and migration. I only speak English fluently, but I have the remnants of a French language education that I daydream about someday revisiting. Or perhaps: I have a wife, a managed but chronic health condition, and a family that is spread out over several countries. How about: I have a permanent job at a research-intensive university, and have taught mostly adults, mostly online, for 15 years. I came to an academic career through a non-traditional route and finished a part-time PhD a decade ago. To summarise (?): my privileges of race, immigration status, income and employment are significant, but I also rely – for my health, my citizenship and my family life – on a society that is affluent and tolerant.

These facts may tell you something you need to know. Or they may not – there may be others, of which I am unaware or prefer not to share, that matter more. I invite you to approach this book with a critical eye to the gaps you will find here – and to consider the speculative potential in those gaps. I hope it will become clear that a central aim of this book is to suggest but not insist on what might be learned from the work in this space that has gone before, and point the way to possibilities for research and teaching that you might take up.

For instance, while this book focuses on higher education and informal learning futures, with a focus on digital technologies and practices, there has been important work in the past decade that focuses in a critical way on the schools sector, such as Facer's (2011) analysis of education and technology, and Selwyn's (2019) exploration of automation and artificial intelligence. In addition, as we

Introduction **15**

will see in Chapter 4, a range of speculative methods have been used to engage with young people about futures of different kinds, and so the focus on adults in this book is a feature of my own areas of expertise, not a limitation of the wider literature or critical futures practice.

Structure of this book

The book is structured in three parts. The first, **Understanding learning futures**, gives a broad overview of how futures thinking, theories of complexity, emergence and anticipation, and speculative and inventive approaches can be used to explore learning across a range of settings.

Chapter 2 explores how ideas of the future are produced and how they come to be accepted. It emphasises that different approaches to thinking about the future of learning generate different kinds of understandings of what is possible, probable and preferable. The politics and methodologies of future-making, the nature of anticipation and its relationship to speculation, and the importance of language and imaginaries are all discussed and explored in the context of how we might treat the future as a site of critical engagement.

In Chapter 3, the complexity of learning and of working with futures comes into focus, through lenses of non-linearity, indeterminacy and contingency. The chapter critiques deterministic forms of education research, outlining the role of complexity theory in educational research and digital education. It introduces the concept of "not-yetness" as a way of valuing emergence and the uncertainty of the future, arguing that learning futures exist as troublesome objects to think and work with, and that this trouble can be productive.

Chapter 4 focuses on speculation in design, research methodology and teaching. Situating the speculative methods and pedagogies of this book within a small but growing body of speculative research and scholarship of speculative teaching and learning, it discusses the temporal, epistemological and performative qualities of speculative methods. In speculative research, we see an attempt to attune to different sensibilities – of participants, of data, of the process of making futures. In speculative teaching methods, questions about the nature of learning, but also about the structures, spaces and processes of education, are overtly addressed.

Part 2, **Speculative objects to think with**, introduces four projects where speculative approaches were used to investigate learning in a range of contexts. Each chapter in this part explores an example in depth, showing how it was made as well as what it revealed: a teacherbot, an app for expressing engagement with art, a student-led course for learning about the future and a data storytelling tool. Together these chapters trace the trajectory of debate about education futures over a ten-year period, showing how these futures are always in the process of becoming. Each chapter shows how speculative objects can be put into conversation with theory and practice to help students, teachers, learning

16 Understanding learning futures

technologists, museum professionals and others be critical and imaginative about the futures they want to see.

Chapter 5 introduces "Teacherbot", a Twitter bot created for the E-learning and Digital Cultures Massive Open Online Course (MOOC) in 2014, and situates it in the context of developments around online teaching at scale and imaginaries of automation in education. It describes what the bot was designed to do, and what it did, offering its glitchiness as a speculative intervention and the Teacherbot as a speculative object that was able to provoke, invite, include and acknowledge MOOC participants in ways that both opened up and complicated discussions about online education futures and the role of the teacher within them.

In Chapter 6, the focus turns to speculative pedagogy in a formal learning context, with a case study of a postgraduate course on digital learning futures that was generated with and by students through the production of peer- and teacher-assessed Open Educational Resources (OERs). Exploring this course in the context of open education and the hopes pinned on it in the early 2000s, as well as the more critical perspectives emerging in the 2010s, the chapter details the development and evolution of the OER assignment. It examines the kinds of futures made through the OERs themselves and how these futures, in turn, shaped the course in each of its many iterations. The student-generated content, the peer feedback mechanisms, and the persistence and openness of the materials created a speculative, experimental space for learning and teaching that sheds some light on the nature of openness and the possibilities of speculative pedagogies in higher education.

Chapter 7 explores informal learning spaces of museums and galleries, and how speculative objects can help produce new and different futures for supporting and evaluating engagement with cultural heritage. The Artcasting research project in 2015–6 took place at a time of significant debate about how digital technologies should intersect with heritage spaces and visitors, and concerns about the practices of evaluation that might measure engagement. The production and use of a speculative object, the Artcasting app, and the methods of analysis that accompanied it, unsettled assumptions and showed how evaluation of engagement might have different and unexpected futures in museums and galleries.

Data futures of higher education are the focus of Chapter 8, which takes as a starting point contemporary surveillance cultures in universities in the late 2010s, and the difficulties and power relations involved in discussing and critiquing these. The chapter introduces the "Data Stories" project, a short research project that developed a speculative participatory storytelling tool and scaffolded process to support the creation of stories about forms, processes and purposes of scrutiny. With an analysis of some of the stories produced with the tool, and a discussion of how and why it was produced, the chapter argues that stories can be productive objects-to-think-with and that working even with dystopian futures can function to counter resignation and a sense of inevitability.

The final part, **Keeping learning futures moving**, offers critical observations for approaching educational research (Chapter 9) and teaching

(Chapter 10) speculatively, highlighting key issues that will help researchers and educators develop their own methods and pedagogies.

Chapter 9 outlines four elements of a speculative research engagement: a futures question, an "object-to-think-with", an audience to engage with and a way to capture responses and other materials generated through the research, before discussing ethical considerations and the matter of truth claims. It offers a "speculative deep dive" into some converging issues around representation, identity and learning to identify and begin to scope out a possible new speculative project.

Chapter 10 turns to the use of speculative approaches in formal and informal learning settings, and looks at issues of participation, design and supporting futures work from an educator's point of view. Matters of assessment, responsibility, hybridity and co-creation are discussed, and I share insights from the development of a new course on the topic of "culture, heritage and learning futures" to show how these matters can be operationalised in practice.

To close, Chapter 11 serves as a call to researchers, teachers, facilitators, students, policymakers and leaders to maintain a speculative stance to counter uncritical visions of digital futures for learning. It reiterates and interweaves key messages from the book: that the interplay of past, present and future produces speculative approaches; that the futures made by speculative approaches are creative and imaginative, and that speculative approaches produce realities in sociomaterial worlds. It closes by reflecting on some implications for the time and space needed, the provisionality and relationality of learning and of understanding learning futures, the value of good questions and taking risks, and, finally, for working with digital futures for learning in hopeful ways.

Notes

1 https://en.wikipedia.org/wiki/ACT(test), accessed 14 May 2021.
2 A call for papers arrived in my inbox as I was writing an early draft of this section (in May 2021), for a special issue of the journal *Blockchain: Research and Applications*, on the topic of "Blockchain-Based Decentralised Solutions for Learner Empowerment, Education Reengineering and Public Sector Transformation". The issue editors proposed that blockchain "holds the potential to revolutionise several aspects of education and employment, most notably the award, management and verification of qualifications". https://www.journals.elsevier.com/blockchain-research-and-applications/call-for-papers/blockchain-based-decentralised
3 https://web.archive.org/web/20170615022956/http://www.learningisearning2026.org/

References

Alexander, B. (2020) *Academia Next: The Futures of Higher Education*. Baltimore: JHU Press.

Amsler, S. and Facer, K. (2017) 'Contesting anticipatory regimes in education: exploring alternative educational orientations to the future', *Futures*, 94, pp. 6–14. doi:10.1016/j.futures.2017.01.001.

18 Understanding learning futures

Barad, K. (2007) *Meeting the Universe Halfway: Quantum Physics and the Entanglement of Matter and Meaning*. Durham: Duke University Press.

Bayne, S. (2015) 'Teacherbot: Interventions in automated teaching', *Teaching in Higher Education*, 20(4), pp. 455–467. doi:10.1080/13562517.2015.1020783.

Beetham, H. et al. (2022) 'Surveillance practices, risks and responses in the post pandemic university', *Digital Culture & Education*, 14(1). Available at: https://www.digitalcultureandeducation.com/volume-14-1

Berman, N. (2020) 'A critical examination of informal learning spaces', *Higher Education Research & Development*, 39(1), pp. 127–140. doi:10.1080/07294360.2019.1670147.

Bhatt, I. and MacKenzie, A. (2019) 'Just Google it! Digital literacy and the epistemology of ignorance', *Teaching in Higher Education*, 24(3), pp. 302–317. doi:10.1080/135625 17.2018.1547276.

Boulianne, S., Lalancette, M. and Ilkiw, D. (2020) '"School Strike 4 Climate": Social media and the international youth protest on climate change', *Media and Communication*, 8(2), pp. 208–218. doi:10.17645/mac.v8i2.2768.

Boys, J. (2011) *Towards Creative Learning Spaces: Re-Thinking the Architecture of Post-Compulsory Education*. London, United Kingdom: Taylor & Francis Group.

Bynner, J. (2017) 'Whatever happened to lifelong learning? And does it matter?', *Journal of the British Academy*, 5, pp. 61–89. doi:10.5871/jba/005.061.

Carlson, B. and Berglund, J. (2021) *Indigenous Peoples Rise Up: The Global Ascendency of Social Media Activism*. New Brunswick: Rutgers University Press.

Costa, C. et al. (2018) 'Higher education students' experiences of digital learning and (dis)empowerment', *Australasian Journal of Educational Technology*, 34(3), pp. 140–152.

Cottom, T.M. (2018) *Lower Ed: The Troubling Rise of For-Profit Colleges in the New Economy*. New York: The New Press.

Czerniewicz, L. et al. (2020) 'A wake-up call: Equity, inequality and covid-19 emergency remote teaching and learning', *Postdigital Science and Education*, 2(3), pp. 946–967. doi:10.1007/s42438-020-00187-4.

Dahya, N. et al. (2021) 'Perceptions and experiences of virtual reality in public libraries', *Journal of Documentation*, 77(3), pp. 617–637. doi:10.1108/JD-04-2020-0051.

Degner, M., Moser, S. and Lewalter, D. (2022) 'Digital media in institutional informal learning places: A systematic literature review', *Computers and Education Open*, 3, p. 100068. doi:10.1016/j.caeo.2021.100068.

Drotner, K. et al. (Eds) (2019) *The Routledge Handbook of Museums, Media and Communication*. Abingdon: Routledge. doi:10.4324/9781315560168.

Duffy, B.E. and Chan, N.K. (2019) '"You never really know who's looking": Imagined surveillance across social media platforms', *New Media & Society*, 21(1), pp. 119–138. doi:10.1177/1461444818791318.

Edwards, R. (2002) 'Mobilizing lifelong learning: Governmentality in educational practices', *Journal of Education Policy*, 17(3), pp. 353–365. doi:10.1080/02680930210127603.

Emejulu, A. and McGregor, C. (2019) 'Towards a radical digital citizenship in digital education', *Critical Studies in Education*, 60(1), pp. 131–147. doi:10.1080/17508487. 2016.1234494.

Eynon, R. and Helsper, E. (2011) 'Adults learning online: Digital choice and/or digital exclusion?', *New Media & Society*, 13(4), pp. 534–551. doi:10.1177/1461444810374789.

Eynon, R. and Malmberg, L.-E. (2021) 'Lifelong learning and the internet: Who benefits most from learning online?', *British Journal of Educational Technology*, 52(2), pp. 569–583. doi:10.1111/bjet.13041.

Facer, K. (2011) *Learning Futures: Education, Technology and Social Change*. 1st edn. Abingdon: Routledge. doi:10.4324/9780203817308.

Facer, K. (2016) 'Using the future in education: Creating space for openness, hope and novelty', in Lees, H.E. and Noddings, N. (Eds) *The Palgrave International Handbook of Alternative Education*. London: Palgrave Macmillan UK, pp. 63–78. doi:10.1057/978-1-137-41291-1_5.

Facer, K. (2021) *Futures in Education: Towards an Ethical Practice*. UNESCO. Available at: https://unesdoc.unesco.org/ark:/48223/pf0000375792 (Accessed: 12 May 2021).

Facer, K. and Buchczyk, M. (2019) 'Towards a research agenda for the "actually existing" learning city', *Oxford Review of Education*, 45(2), pp. 151–167. doi:10.1080/0305498 5.2018.1551990.

Gilliard, C. and saheli singh, sava (2021) 'Introduction, themed issue: Surveillance and educational technology', *The Journal of Interactive Technology and Pedagogy*, 20. Available at: https://jitp.commons.gc.cuny.edu/?p (Accessed: 7 January 2022).

Goodyear, P. (2021) 'Navigating difficult waters in a digital era: Technology, uncertainty and the objects of informal lifelong learning', *British Journal of Educational Technology*, 52(4), pp. 1594–1611. doi:10.1111/bjet.13107.

Greenhow, C. and Lewin, C. (2016) 'Social media and education: Reconceptualizing the boundaries of formal and informal learning', *Learning, Media and Technology*, 41(1), pp. 6–30. doi:10.1080/17439884.2015.1064954.

Hedberg, J.G. (2006) 'E-learning futures? Speculations for a time yet to come', *Studies in Continuing Education*, 28(2), pp. 171–183. doi:10.1080/01580370600751187.

Hicks, D. et al. (1998) *World Yearbook of Education 1998: Futures Education/Edited by David Hicks and Richard Slaughter*. London: Kogan Page (World Yearbook of Education, 1998).

IFTF (2019) *Learning is Earning 2026*. Available at: https://web.archive.org/ web/20190730163724/http://www.learningisearning2026.org/ (Accessed: 14 May 2021).

Institute for the Future (n.d.) *IFTF: Learning is Earning, Institute for the Future*. Available at: https://www.iftf.org/learningisearning/ (Accessed: 14 May 2021).

Institute for the Future (IFTF) (2016) *Learning is Earning 2026 – A Partnership between ACT Foundation & IFTF*. Available at: https://www.youtube.com/watch?v=Zssd6eBVfwc (Accessed: 14 May 2021).

International Commission on the Futures of Education (2021) *Reimagining Our Futures Together: A New Social Contract for Education*. Paris: UNESCO.

Knox, J. (2013) 'Five critiques of the open educational resources movement', *Teaching in Higher Education*, 18(8), pp. 821–832. doi:10.1080/13562517.2013.774354.

Law, J. (2004) *After Method: Mess in Social Science Research*. Abingdon: Routledge.

Luckin, R. (2018) *Machine Learning and Human Intelligence: The Future of Education for the 21st Century*. London: UCL Institute of Education Press.

Lury, C. (2021) *Problem Spaces: How and Why Methodology Matters*. Newark, United Kingdom: Polity Press.

Lynch, C.R. (2020) 'Unruly digital subjects: Social entanglements, identity, and the politics of technological expertise', *Digital Geography and Society*, 1, p. 100001. doi:10.1016/j.diggeo.2020.100001.

Magnifico, A.M., Lammers, J.C. and Curwood, J.S. (2020) 'Developing methods to trace participation patterns across online writing', *Learning, Culture and Social Interaction*, 24, p. 100288. doi:10.1016/j.lcsi.2019.02.013.

20 Understanding learning futures

Means, A.J. (2018) 'Platform learning and on-demand labor: Sociotechnical projections on the future of education and work', *Learning, Media and Technology*, 43(3), pp. 326–338. doi:10.1080/17439884.2018.1504792.

Meyers, E.M., Erickson, I. and Small, R.V. (2013) 'Digital literacy and informal learning environments: An introduction', *Learning, Media and Technology*, 38(4), pp. 355–367. doi:10.1080/17439884.2013.783597.

Milojević, I. (2005) *Educational Futures: Dominant and Contesting Visions*. Abingdon: Taylor & Francis Group.

Moran, D. (2007) *Potential (Monster)*. Available at: https://www.youtube.com/watch?v=yNKoH84ioz0 (Accessed: 6 July 2021).

O'Neil, C. (2016) *Weapons of Math Destruction: How Big Data Increases Inequality and Threatens Democracy*. 1st edn. New York: Crown.

Olakulehin, F.K. and Singh, G. (2013) 'Widening access through openness in higher education in the developing world: A Bourdieusian field analysis of experiences from the National Open University of Nigeria', *Open Praxis*, 5(1), pp. 31–40. doi:10.5944/openpraxis.5.1.40.

Peppler, K., Halverson, E. and Kafai, Y.B. (2016) *Makeology: Makerspaces as Learning Environments*. New York: Routledge.

Prinsloo, P. (2017) 'Fleeing from Frankenstein's monster and meeting Kafka on the way: Algorithmic decision-making in higher education', *E-Learning and Digital Media*, 14(3), pp. 138–163. doi:10.1177/2042753017731355.

Ra, S., Jagannathan, S. and Maclean, R. (2021) *Powering a Learning Society During an Age of Disruption*. Singapore: Springer.

Rhoads, R.A., Berdan, J. and Toven-Lindsey, B. (2013) 'The open courseware movement in higher education: Unmasking power and raising questions about the movement's democratic potential', *Educational Theory*, 63(1), pp. 87–110. doi:10.1111/edth.12011.

Ross, J. (2017) 'Speculative method in digital education research', *Learning, Media and Technology*, 42(2), pp. 214–229. doi:10.1080/17439884.2016.1160927.

Selwyn, N. (2019) *Should Robots Replace Teachers? AI and the Future of Education*. Hoboken: John Wiley & Sons, Inc.

Selwyn, N. et al. (2020) 'What's next for Ed-Tech? Critical hopes and concerns for the 2020s', *Learning, Media and Technology*, 45(1), pp. 1–6. doi:10.1080/17439884.2020.1694945.

Sheail, P. (2018) 'Temporal flexibility in the digital university: Full-time, part-time, flexi-time', *Distance Education*, 39(4), pp. 462–479. doi:10.1080/01587919.2018.1520039.

Slade, S. and Prinsloo, P. (2013) 'Learning analytics: Ethical issues and dilemmas', *American Behavioral Scientist*, 57(10), pp. 1510–1529. doi:10.1177/0002764213479366.

St. Pierre, E.A. (2021) 'Post qualitative inquiry, the refusal of method, and the risk of the new', *Qualitative Inquiry*, 27(1), pp. 3–9. doi:10.1177/1077800419863005.

Stalder, F. (2018) *The Digital Condition*. Cambridge: Polity Press.

Staley, D.J. (2019) *Alternative Universities: Speculative Design for Innovation in Higher Education*. Baltimore: JHU Press.

Tapscott, D. and Kaplan, A. (2019) *Blockchain Revolution in Education and LifeLong Learning: Preparing for Disruption, Leading the Transformation*. Blockchain Research Institute, (p. 46).

UNESCO and Institute for Lifelong Learning (2020) *Embracing a culture of lifelong learning contribution to the futures of education initiative: Report: A transdisciplinary expert consultation.*

Veletsianos, G. and Houlden, S. (2020) 'Radical flexibility and relationality as responses to education in times of crisis', *Postdigital Science and Education*, 2(3), pp. 849–862. doi:10.1007/s42438-020-00196-3.

Wilkie, A., Savransky, M. and Rosengarten, M. (2017) *Speculative Research: The Lure of Possible Futures*. Abingdon: Routledge. doi:10.4324/9781315541860.

Williamson, B. (2017) *Big Data in Education: The Digital Future of Learning, Policy and Practice*. London: SAGE.

Wilson, A. et al. (2017) 'Learning analytics: Challenges and limitations', *Teaching in Higher Education*, 22(8), pp. 991–1007. doi:10.1080/13562517.2017.1332026.

2
HOW LEARNING FUTURES ARE MADE

Introduction

In current policy, media and academic spheres, when there is talk about the future of learning, there is often talk of digital and data technologies. Learning futures and technology futures are seen to intersect at the level of the system, the organisation, the community, the teacher and the individual, with implications for sustainability, attainment, human relationships and access to knowledge and culture. Themes of automation, efficiency, openness, engagement, visibility and ubiquity are the focus of attention, discussion and often heated debate.

These and other aspects of digital futures for learning will be examined in more detail in the case studies in Part 2. The aim of this chapter is to look at *how* ideas of the future are produced and how they come to be accepted. This is a methodological matter, but also a philosophical and a political one, because predictions and other accounts of the future are not neutral. Who sees, communicates, interprets and receives ideas of the future? Many predictions are made, but which predictions take hold, and how? How do some futures become probable while others are seen as impossible? What makes a future durable and able to become common sense? All of these questions are, at their heart, about flows of power and information, and about the interplay of expectation and disruption. In other words, they are about the past and present, as well as the future.

This chapter explores a range of future-making tactics, including their limitations and issues in the context of digital futures for learning. It opens by exploring two key aspects of understanding how futures act in the present: the role of language and discourse in producing persuasive futures, and theories of anticipation. Moving on, I identify some of the specific ways that ideas about digital learning futures come into being through promissory organisations

DOI: 10.4324/9781003202134-3

and data-driven future-making. The chapter closes with a look at some of the research and thinking that has helped open up futures work as a site of critical engagement and learning.

Sociotechnical and edtech imaginaries

Language and discourse are at the heart of how futures are made, because visions of the future have to be told or brought into being in ways that can be shared, circulated, worked with and materialised (or not). So, examining how discursive constructions of the future work in the present, and what they can do, is a valuable starting point for considering learning futures.[1] Discourse describes the system of knowledge that shapes and bounds what can be said and thought. Foucault (1980) defined discursive practices as:

> characterized by the delimitation of a field of objects, the definition of a legitimate perspective for the agent of knowledge, and the fixing of norms for the elaboration of concepts and theories. Thus, each discursive practice implies a play of prescriptions that designate its exclusions and choices.
>
> *(p. 199)*

Delimitation, definition and fixing have the effect of settling (in some particular context) what counts, and what does not count, as knowledge. Context matters, because we are always in a historical moment with regard to power-knowledge configurations – and this includes configurations of the future.

Discourse analysis methods for examining "anticipatory discourse" (Saint-Georges, 2012) can help identify and follow the language of learning futures. Building on Scollon and Scollon (2000), Saint-Georges highlights the worth of focusing on "discursive strategies which open or shut down particular lines of action at particular moments for particular individuals or social groups"; and how knowledge and agency are asserted in these strategies (p. 2). Specific conversational and material markers can be analysed, as well as the overall shaping of specific possibilities for the future that are set forth in various domains – the attitudes and choices shaped by one domain will be different from another, and affect how people understand and are positioned in relation to the future. Discussing education, Saint-Georges observes that representations of trajectories of success and of inclusion and exclusion are particularly common. As an example of what this can look like, Erstad and Silseth (2019)'s research about "futuremaking" through digital participation describes "how young people take advantage of digital technologies in pursuing learning futures for themselves based on interests developed outside of school". The authors examine this by tracking "individual learning trajectories" (p. 309). Here knowledge (interests developed outside of school) and agency (taking advantage of technology, pursuing learning futures) are situated in the context of the individual, and their study focuses on how

24 Understanding learning futures

young people learn over time. Schools are part of these trajectories, but futures are made by individuals through the networking of resources available to them through multiple spaces and over time. Their article offers a vision of individuals as agentic and able to make choices, and digital tools as existing to be mobilised and taken advantage of, as instruments rather than actors in future-making. This indicates a particular configuration or *imaginary* of learning and technology.

The imaginary is a particular type of discursive framing that is central to futures work. Taylor (2002) defines the *social* imaginary as "the ways in which people imagine their social existence, how they fit together with others, how things go on between them and their fellows, the expectations that are normally met, and the deeper normative notions and images that underlie these expectations" (p. 106). Taylor's emphasis on learning and normativity has informed other versions of the imaginary.[2] In the context of digital education futures, the idea of the *sociotechnical* imaginary and how it is represented in various kinds of discourse is significant. Sociotechnical imaginaries are:

> collectively held, institutionally stabilized, and publicly performed visions of desirable futures, animated by shared understandings of forms of social life and social order attainable through, and supportive of, advances in science and technology.
>
> *(Jasanoff, 2016, p. 4)*

Jasanoff notes the tendency of sociotechnical imaginaries to present a positive vision of the future in interplay with fears of harms from technological innovation (or lack of innovation). This is confirmed by work in various domains – for example, in Dourish and Bell's (2011) work on ubiquitous computing, where they explore in depth the "mythologies" that motivate, produce and shape it: "what technology can do for people, the places it will go, and the needs it will address" (p. 4). Jasanoff highlights the moral and ethical dimensions of imaginaries (2016, p. 7), and the organised work and practices that constitute imagination and the production of imaginaries (ibid). Both particular and durable, sociotechnical imaginaries are enacted, performed and materialised, in part through practices of anticipation discussed in the next section. Jasanoff argues that this distinguishes the "imaginary" from "discourse", but I suggest that it situates the imaginary within what Maclure (2013) describes as the materiality of language.

The extent to which researchers are seeking to bring *educational* imaginaries into focus reflects an interest in discursive constructions of education. Barone and Lash's (2006) definition of the educational imaginary captures its use in educational research more generally: "a set of broadly disseminated images about what schools and school people ... are supposedly like... [eluding] the fate of objectification, its contents placed beyond the range of easy study, surveillance, and interrogation" (p. 22–3). Identifying and tracing imaginaries of education and technology as they are expressed in reports, marketing, media and other communications can be extremely fruitful. For writers about education and technology, the phrase "*edtech* imaginary" is becoming useful for explaining the power of "the stories we invent to explain the necessity of technology, the promises of technology; the stories we use to describe how we got here and where we are headed" (Watters, 2020). In a chapter on imaginaries of personalised learning, Friesen (2020) notes the tendency of the educational imaginary to appear in the form of "idealized images, metaphors or 'primal' scenes" of what education should be like (p. 144). In edtech contexts, educational failings are cast as "*engineering* problems to be *solved* 'at scale'" (ibid), for instance in repeated attempts to provide personalised learning through computers that simulate "the primal educational power of dialogue" (p. 152), and edtech practices are significantly shaped by the imaginary of tutorial dialogue (p. 153). Watters (2020) observes the persistence of pop-culture reference points – particularly the model of learning found in the film *The Matrix*, where required knowledge and skills are instantly "downloaded" into the brains and bodies of the film's characters, to be used within the virtual world of the Matrix. She also argues that the implications of edtech imaginaries tend to be exclusionary, profit-driven and objectionable in terms of labour practices. Kerr (2020) concurs, critiquing edtech imaginaries of the benefits of technological innovation and privatisation that have become influential in the field of English language teaching. The edtech imaginary is a specific genre of sociotechnical imaginary that expresses ideals of education in terms of scale, personalisation, commercialisation and innovation, and proposes learning futures that, as Selwyn (2021b) notes, are orientated towards technological abundance and endless growth. These are powerful imaginaries, and they underpin policy and practice in both overt and subtle ways.

Urry (2016) identifies the production of utopias and dystopias as two of six main methods for making futures (along with learning from past visions of the future, studying failed futures, extrapolating and scenario-building). In sociotechnical imaginaries in general, and edtech imaginaries in particular, the interplay of utopian and dystopian visions is notable. In 2018, Martin Weller observed a shift from a naïve utopianism in edtech discussions to increasing sensitivity to "the dangers of overreliance on and trust in edtech" (2018, p. 46) mirroring social problems with abuse, surveillance and privacy breaches online. These swings between hope and despair align with shifts in understanding technology either in terms of its instrumental or enhancement value (Bayne, 2015), or in terms of its failure to mitigate against social, political or economic crises impacting on education. Because of the constant development of new technologies, and new articulations of their use, such "failures" need never be confronted, so the cycle can always begin anew (Goodchild and Speed, 2019).

Goodchild and Speed (2019), drawing on Glynos and Howarth's (2007) "critical logics approach" (p. 949), identify beatific and horrific "fantasmatic logics" of educational technology which echo utopian and dystopian categories. For instance, examining strategy documents from higher education institutions,

26 Understanding learning futures

Matthews (2021) directly links discourses in education technology to a binary of utopian and dystopian accounts, and describes this as limiting the imagination and creation of new possibilities for technology. We can frame these, too, as "narratives of promise and threat" (Hand, 2008) playing out in public understanding of digital cultures. These narratives, Hand argues, continue to hold sway in accounts of access, interactivity and authenticity. Tensions between fluidity and territorialisation, ownership and circulation, democratisation and authority generate visions of digital culture. The way these ideals, artefacts, identities and models shape futures, and how futures in turn are mobilised in the present, can usefully be theorised in terms of anticipation.

Anticipation and mobilising the future in the present

The nature of human relations with the future has been taken up in a number of philosophical and sociological domains. One of the most useful for our purposes is the field of anticipation studies, which explores the "distinctive temporal phenomenon" of the future (Facer, 2019, p. 6), and anticipatory behaviours in different aspects of decision-making and interaction:

> An anticipatory behavior is a behavior that 'uses' the future in its actual decision process. Anticipation as here understood includes two mandatory components: a forward-looking attitude, and the use of the former's result for action.
>
> *(Poli, 2017, p. 1)*

In other words, thinking about or being positioned towards the future is just one part of the equation of what anticipation does – it also acts in the present on the basis of that thinking. The implications of how anticipation functions are far-reaching, and Adams, Murphy and Clarke (2009) trace "the palpable effect of the speculative future on the present" (p. 247) in politics, technoscience, medicine and other fields. They describe the impacts of living in an "emergent 'almost'", where people are in a perpetual state of "imperfect knowing that must always be attended to, modified, updated" (p. 254) – a good, moral citizen stays informed, alert and vigilant at all times.

As Poli (2017) puts it, "at least some futures are definitely more than imaginings, in the sense that they are real processes in a state of latency" (p. 64). For example, individuals' data practices have been described in terms of anticipation: Kazansky (2021) discusses how technologists, educators and communities targeted with digital surveillance engage with sensemaking in a future-oriented mode, rendering unpredictability and uncertainly manageable. In this way, anticipatory knowledge practices are reductive: of social complexity, which can enable decisions to be made, but also of the openness of the future (Aykut, Demortain and Benbouzid, 2019). Many formal educational settings are framed by "anticipatory regimes", which work to foreclose "imagination of and experimentation with social futures" (Amsler and Facer, 2017, p. 11). Imaginative futures work can also be compromised by the tendency of educational policymakers, for example, to see the future as basically the same as the present – a tendency which means the status quo will always be maintained and utopian potential denied (Liveley and Wardrop, 2020). Lively and Wardrop suggest "futures literacy" as a potential solution to these tendencies, and indeed this notion of futures literacy or "anticipatory competence" (Ojala, 2017) has taken hold, as Poli (2017) observes that many scholars do not know how to raise or address "future-generating questions" (p. 70). In addition, I suggest, there is a lack of knowledge of how to work with predictions as a form of "currency" that is mobilised in social settings to influence problems and issues (Aykut, Demortain and Benbouzid, 2019, p. 5).

The relationship between anticipation and the focus of this book, speculation, has been articulated in a number of ways. Adams et al. (2009) describe anticipation as giving speculation "the authority to act in the present" (p. 249) – whatever the substance of a speculative idea, imagining or possibility, anticipation is what makes things happen in relation to it. Indeed, anticipatory regimes work through "logics of expansion", which means that "territories for speculation must be continually found to keep the anticipatory logic moving" (pp. 250–1). Elsewhere, speculation is framed in terms of uncertainty. Drawing on forms of future-making observed during the early stages of the Covid-19 pandemic, Kendig and Bauchspies (2021) describe a phase of global, local and projective "speculative anticipation" (p. 230) – action that takes place in a context of insufficient or conflicting information. Conversely, in her discussion of collaborative speculation, Light (2021) suggests anticipation as a form of *failed* speculation in design practice, speculation that does not produce engagement or impact. These matters of speculative uncertainty, temporality and engagement will be discussed in Chapter 4, but for now, it is enough to say that anticipatory behaviours, regimes and logics rely on the continual production of speculative visions of various kinds to orientate their actions in the present. Speculative approaches, such as those discussed in this book, can do more than feed anticipatory machines, but it is not automatic that they will do so. Part of the purpose of this book is to support critical approaches to futures-making that are knowing, possibly "disobedient" (Amsler and Facer, 2017, p. 13), and that do not pre-empt the future. Despite the foreclosures that anticipation entails, Adams et al. (2009) consider whether accountability to anticipation is a more productive stance than an outright refusal – a stance that might foster "kinships with the future" (p. 260). This book looks to forms of speculative accountability that are appropriate and generative in the context of digital futures for learning. The matter of responsibility to the future is discussed later in this chapter, and Chapters 9 and 10 discuss in more detail the nature of responsibility to the present in research and teaching contexts.

28 Understanding learning futures

First, we move on to discuss the kinds of influential futures that are produced through the work of promissory organisations, and the role of data-driven and analytic processes in producing and enacting predictions in education.

Futures that count: promissory organisations and data-driven future-making

The question of where accounts of digital learning futures come from is partially answered by describing entanglements of technology, learning spaces, people and social and cultural values. Some imaginaries do emerge organically over time, or fairly abruptly in response to a new reality. This happened at the start of the Covid-19 pandemic, when earlier debates about accountability and authenticity in digital assessment quickly coalesced around an edtech imaginary of technologically driven visibility and led to widespread adoption of solutions like remote invigilation – see Chapter 8 for more on this. However, the power and influence of some imaginaries, and not others, needs further explanation. It is not always obvious how futures *become* stabilised, accepted and durable. When futures come into being and then become "collectively held" as sociotechnical imaginaries, or incorporated into anticipatory regimes, something is happening. The strategic work and influence of promissory organisations offer some insight into this happening; as does the way that facts about the future are produced by data-driven predictive analytics.

Promissory organisations

Some futures and imaginaries emerge from within what Pollock and Williams (2010) call "promissory organisations". These are intermediaries that specialise in predictions – Pollock and Williams use the example of the research and advisory firm Gartner, and show how its pronouncements about the future serve as promises which enable confidence and investment in particular innovations and technologies. Promissory organisations provide analysis of trends and classifications of new technologies based on the expertise, information sources and networks of industry analysts. As Pollock and Williams note, the success of the promises made depend on their ability to "create some form of 'material reality' or 'obligatory point of passage' that others are then forced to take into account" (2010, p. 530). Successful promissory organisations are able to shape the direction of technological expectation and categorisation, which in turn shapes investment, research and decision-making in a range of other organisations. Williamson (2021) identifies the intermediary EdTech firm HolonIQ as such an organisation, and notes the complex "technoeconomic work" it performs to calculate markets and produce investable futures (p. 3).[3]

We can consider the role of promissory organisations by looking at an example of how their predictions function within educational settings. In 2020, a report titled "The future of higher education in a disruptive world" was published by KPMG International, a global professional services and accounting firm. Its author, and KPMG Australia's Special Adviser on Education, Stephen Parker, is a former university head with a background in law. Drawing on a survey of 410 institutional leaders in higher education in the US, Canada, the UK, Germany, Australia and India, the report describes the end of a "golden age" for universities globally as a result of the Covid-19 pandemic, climate change, saturation of participation due to a shrinking middle class in many countries, spiralling student debt and reducing value of a degree in terms of future earnings. As a result, traditional modes and institutions of teaching are described as facing competition from more agile organisations. The report proposes four building blocks for optimisation or transformation of HE institutions towards "customer centricity" (customers in this vision being students), the fourth of which focuses on technology. Technology is important because, as Parker explains:

> The university that expects students to battle with traffic, find a parking place, go to a lecture, write examinations by hand, get a seat in a crowded library and then go home again will be riding its luck.
>
> *(Parker, 2020, p. 11)*

In this report, the language of customer satisfaction, outcome measurement, capability development and continuous improvement is not interrogated for its possible deficiencies. Instead, it is the university sector that is framed as deficient for failing to grasp the changes going on around it and their implications. The predictions made are presented as definitive, built on "trends and the experience of sectors which were exposed earlier to the same drivers of change" (p. 2). The only choice for institutions, therefore, is to transform to achieve the required "quality of *personalized* student learning" (ibid) within a framework of maximum efficiency.

The report uses the data it has generated to position itself and its expertise. Because of the nature of the organisation and its work, its calls for unbundling of teaching and learning for reasons of scale, efficiency, affordability and competition have impacts in the present, and implications for the futures that can be imagined within and beyond higher education. Promissory organisations offer a path forward for institutions that may be struggling to read or act on the signs of the future: the report offers KPMG International's services to help higher education institutions cope with these "profound questions concerning student experience, staffing, costs, value enhancement and more" (p. 23). Readers are invited to "contact us today to get a maturity assessment of your organization's consumer-centric capabilities and insights into how your university can become more connected" (p. 24). Here we see one way that "expectations-based products and services" (Pollock and Williams, 2010, p. 542) are framed, marketed and sold, and how certain imaginaries of the future become increasingly stable and shared.

Data-driven future-making

Big data has, in recent years, become a key source of future-making, particularly in relation to education policy (Hartong, 2018). As datasets become larger and methods of analysis (including machine-learning-based methods) become more complex, the insights generated through big data in education usher in a world where "'probabilistic outcomes' and predictions about the future now prevail" (Williamson, 2017, p. 34). Probabilistic methods to generate futures are seen in the use of everything from standardised test results to learning analytics to understand what is possible in educational settings and for learners, individually and collectively.

The use of probabilities as predictive tools emerged as part of the rise of "scientific prophecy" (Adam and Groves, 2007, p. 5), which marked a major transition in thinking about the future. Its focus on knowledge of past facts (p. 27) is reflected in the use of data-driven decision-making in education today. The reliance on past facts to produce data-driven futures means that "in cases where there are no past records, no relevant causal chains or no data, the future cannot be calculated" (ibid). This partly explains the massive investments in edtech in recent years: the large-scale datafication of learning, teaching and assessment through learning analytics, routinised collection and storage of student work through plagiarism detection software, biometric data tracking activity in public and educational spaces, and the other forms of data capture now central to educational organisations, has made learning futures appear calculable. With this belief has come promises of "new degrees of control over the future and the on-going production of social worlds... based on calculations in the present" (Gulson and Webb, 2017, p. 21).

An orientation towards data is, in turn, shaping the virtual and physical spaces of learning and the labour of those who work in them (Selwyn, 2021a; Lewis and Hartong, 2021). Prinsloo (2019) describes the role of learning analytics in "truth making" and the enactment of "resource allocation, student support and learning pathways" (p. 2820). Smithers (2020) draws on Massumi's distinction between logics of prevention (which rearrange the world to optimise it against threats) and logics of preemption (which seek to "create the world otherwise" (p. 3)) to theorise the use of predictive analytics to preempt student failure and to produce students as "dividuals" – "bits of exchangeable data" (p. 7) – who succeed. Witzenberger and Gulson (2021) explore how preemption works by "replacing causal explanations for a turn towards pattern prediction through advanced computing machinery and 'frameless' data capture" (p. 3). We see similar trends emerging in other kinds of learning spaces, such as museums, where visitor experience is being recast through the use of eye-tracking and other biometric data approaches, "transforming the body of visitors into data streams and thereby changing the relationship between visitors, artefacts and museums" (Wilson-Barnao, 2020, p. 218).

How learning futures are made **31**

However, no matter how incontrovertible they may appear, futures being produced under the banner of predictive analytics also have, as Mackenzie (2015) notes, the potential to create slippages, frictions or blockages, and through these to gesture at possibilities for different kinds of action. Based on approximations, the "black boxing" of predictive analytics can make them appear more definitive than they are (Gulson and Webb, 2017). These appearances can matter a great deal, and have material impacts, but they are not a reflection of an inevitable future. This is the reason why imaginaries of the future, and the anticipatory practices they underpin, are so important to engage with critically. We can ask, for example, what it would mean to engage in "becoming-incomputable or becoming-imperceptible" (Webb, Sellar and Gulson, 2020, p. 294), or to "advocate for open student futures" (Smithers, 2020, p. 8) – but only if we first acknowledge the work that imaginaries, predictions and promises do, and how it might be done otherwise. The discussion that follows explores critical engagement with the future, and how this relates to the speculative pedagogies and methods that are at the heart of this book.

Futures work as a site of critical engagement

Technology has been the source of significant and highly contested forms of future-making in many domains, and the role of technology in learning has been one of the most visible sites of educational futures exploration in recent decades. However, as has been increasingly recognised in futures work (see, for example, Curry and Schultz (2009)), different methods produce different futures. This is also why the title of this book refers to "futures" rather than "future".

The proliferation of futures does not mean that methods to produce them are useless. Instead, it should help us tune into a different understanding of the future: something different from a singular, unchanging, knowable idea of what is to come. Rather than giving unproblematic access to the future, the ways data, expertise and language are mobilised through the methods used to engage with them produce different and not necessarily complementary or coherent sets of predictions and ideas. Evaluating these requires critical engagement with the work different methods are capable of doing, and the assumptions informing them.

Along with the ability to interrogate the production and circulation of futures, understanding how futures are made also means we are better able to engage with future-making ourselves. People in learning organisations like universities and museums, as well as in networks and community learning settings, need the capability to critically enact future-making. One way this has been done is using the structures and processes developed through the academic and professional field of "futures studies". This field spans disciplines including sociology, business, economics, design and education and tends to involve participatory, open-ended methods for examining possible futures. Sohail Inayatullah, one of the major voices in the field, makes the distinction between *futures studies* and

32 Understanding learning futures

planning, with the latter being more focused on expert voices, the short term, singular future and finding viable solutions to well-defined problems (2013, pp. 40–1). He argues that futures studies methods should not be seen in isolation, but as part of a framework for understanding the future. His "Six Pillars" framework involves mapping, scenario planning and visioning, amongst other approaches (Inayatullah, 2008). Through workshops and other structured activities with organisations, communities and groups of stakeholders, futures studies methods produce context-specific scenarios of the future for particular issues, places, people and situations. These visions, in turn, can inform organisations', communities' and even sectors' strategies and plans.

Such activities are usually taken to be agnostic about the problem or question they address – the focus is on getting the method right, from which will follow generative discussions and useful implications for practice. Inayatullah has identified four theoretical frameworks that can inform futures work: predictive, interpretive, critical and participatory (2013, p. 38). Futures studies in its critical and participatory forms involves contestation, uncertainty, polyvocality and disruption, and engages with values, ethics and power. As Facer (2021) notes, this work generates "seeds of possibility" (p. 6) because it is not predictive but aims to imagine and enact plausible and hopeful alternatives. Critical engagement with hopeful futures is generated, too, through the tradition of utopian methods that Levitas (2013) describes as "architectural": "the imagination of potential alternative scenarios for the future, acknowledging the assumptions about and consequences for the people who might inhabit them" (p. 154). Accusations of technological utopianism are often levelled at the sorts of digital futures we see in learning and education predictions, and such utopian imaginings are indeed often highly problematic. Utopias, however, have a long history and an important position in contemporary philosophy and social science, and the influence of utopian proposals for alternative worlds is worth reflecting on as an important aspect of how learning futures are made and critically revisited. Utopias (like futures studies methods) are not necessarily critical – Bloch, for instance, theorised the "utopian impulse" as an inherent part of human nature to "long for and imagine life otherwise" (Levitas, 2013, p. 5). They have also been critiqued for lack of specificity about how they can or should be reached from the standpoint of existing society (Urry, 2016). However, utopian methods that are "provisional, reflexive and dialogic" can create space for preferred futures to take on a causal role in what emerges (Levitas, 2013, p. 218). This is a matter of responsibility.

Adam and Groves (2007) focus considerable attention on the issue of responsibility towards the future. Tracing the history of how the future has been engaged with – from divination and prophecy to prediction to imagination – they highlight shifts from an idea of the future as fixed and pre-existing, to one that is "empty" and available to be filled with anything at all, including:

How learning futures are made **33**

unlimited interests, desires, projections, values, beliefs, ethical concerns, business ventures, political ambitions… the empty future of contemporary economic and political exchange is fundamentally uncertain and unknowable. At the same time, however, it appears wide open to colonisation and traversal.

(pp. 12–3)

They emphasise the many problems with such a vision, not least that it cannot account in any meaningful way for the effects of actions taken in the present. In other words, it is not able to take responsibility for the futures it sets in motion or refuses to intervene in. They argue that we must see ourselves as responsible future-makers. The future is not merely a space of experimentation for the present, and working with futures requires a balance of openness, curiosity, responsibility and care. This balance, and how researchers and educators work to achieve it, has huge implications for learning futures of all kinds. And, as they explain, "it is of practical significance whether the future is conceived as pre-given and actual, as empty possibility or as virtual realm of latent futures in the making" (p. 17). Learning to see and sort between these is one of the tasks of educational researchers and educators with an interest in futures work, and the matter of responsibility is crucial for designing speculative approaches.

Facer (2016) proposes that we need "pedagogies of the present" to allow educational spaces to be both open and hopeful for those whose futures we might otherwise be optimising, colonising or attempting to protect against. She argues that an ethical orientation to education futures (Facer, 2021) requires a range of sensitivities and commitments, and her recommendations about multiplicity and emergence will be explored further in the next chapter. Of the nine key questions she poses, the following are especially relevant for this book and the practices it proposes:

- What and whose knowledges are being used to create these ideas of the future and where are the absences? (p. 19)
- What processes were used to make these ideas of the future, and why? (p. 20)
- Who will attend to the consequence of these ideas of the future being put into the world and how? (p. 20)
- What is the role of these futures in creating hopeful politics and practices in the present? (p. 21)

The speculative approaches proposed in this book sit within the broad umbrella of futuring methods and critical futures studies. They have several important features that, together, characterise them as speculative. First, they are self-conscious about the creative, imaginative nature of the futures they make. Second, they are attuned to the way that methods produce realities. Third, they recognise the

34 Understanding learning futures

interplay of past, present and future. These orientations to the future will be discussed throughout the book, but particularly in Chapters 4 and 11.

Educators and educational researchers require sensitivity to how accounts of the future come to produce effects in the present, and this chapter has offered some insights into imaginaries and discourses of the future, anticipatory practices, and various kinds of truth claims generated through the use of data, by the work of promissory organisations, and by critical futures work. They also need critical engagement with the unstable nature of learning and education futures, and the next chapter examines this in context of complexity theory. It positions speculative learning futures within a tradition of research and teaching that works with complexity, uncertainty, emergence and wicked problems.

Notes

1 This may sound rather post-structuralist, and even though I argue throughout the book for a sociomaterial perspective on education, I am okay with this. I follow St Pierre's (2013) analysis on this issue, as she notes the post-structuralist rejection of the distinction between thinking and living (or discourse and matter): "both Foucault and Derrida critiqued ...representational logic that separates language from materiality." (p. 652)
2 Other theories of the imaginary, principally Castoriadis' (1997), have focused more on creative and undetermined dimensions of the imaginary: "for Castoriadis, the imaginary is a culture's ethos;... [for] Taylor, it is a [learned] cultural model" (Strauss, 2006, p. 323). For more on this, see Ross, J., & Sheail, P. (2017). The "campus imaginary": online students' experience of the masters dissertation at a distance. *Teaching in Higher Education*, 22, 1–16.
3 See Komljenovic (2021) for a fascinating discussion of how these investments take shape.

References

Adam, B. and Groves, C. (2007) *Future Matters: Action, Knowledge, Ethics*. Boston, the Netherlands: Brill.

Adams, V., Murphy, M. and Clarke, A.E. (2009) 'Anticipation: Technoscience, life, affect, temporality', *Subjectivity*, 28(1), pp. 246–265. doi:10.1057/sub.2009.18.

Amsler, S. and Facer, K. (2017) 'Contesting anticipatory regimes in education: Exploring alternative educational orientations to the future', *Futures*, 94, pp. 6–14. doi:10.1016/j. futures.2017.01.001.

Aykut, S.C., Demortain, D. and Benbouzid, B. (2019) 'The politics of anticipatory expertise: Plurality and contestation of futures knowledge in governance', *Science & Technology Studies*, 32(4), p. 2. doi:10.23987/sts.87369.

Barone, T. and Lash, M. (2006) 'What's behind the spotlight?: Educational imaginaries from around the world', *Journal of Curriculum and Pedagogy*, 3(2), pp. 22–29. doi:10.10 80/15505170.2006.10411593.

Bayne, S. (2015) 'What's the matter with "technology-enhanced learning"?', *Learning, Media and Technology*, 40(1), pp. 5–20. doi:10.1080/17439884.2014.915851.

Castoriadis, C. (1997) *The Imaginary Institution of Society*. Cambridge: MIT Press.

Curry, A. and Schultz, W. (2009) 'Roads less travelled: Different methods, different futures', *Journal of Futures Studies*, 13/4, pp. 35–60.

Dourish, P. and Bell, G. (2011) *Divining a Digital Future: Mess and Mythology in Ubiquitous Computing*. Cambridge: MIT Press.

Erstad, O. and Silseth, K. (2019) 'Futuremaking and digital engagement: From everyday interests to educational trajectories', *Mind, Culture, and Activity*, 26(4), pp. 309–322. doi:10.1080/10749039.2019.1646290.

Facer, K. (2016) 'Using the future in education: Creating space for openness, hope and novelty', in Lees, H.E. and Noddings, N. (Eds) *The Palgrave International Handbook of Alternative Education*. London: Palgrave Macmillan UK, pp. 63–78. doi:10.1057/978-1-137-41291-1_5.

Facer, K. (2019) 'Storytelling in troubled times: What is the role for educators in the deep crises of the 21st century?', *Literacy*, 53(1), pp. 3–13. doi:10.1111/lit.12176.

Facer, K. (2021) *Futures in education: Towards an ethical practice*. UNESCO. Available at: https://unesdoc.unesco.org/ark:/48223/pf0000375792 (Accessed: 12 May 2021).

Foucault, M. (1980) 'History of systems of thought', in Bouchard, Donald F. (Ed) *Language, Counter-Memory, Practice*. Ithaca: Cornell University Press, pp. 199–204.

Friesen, N. (2020) 'The technological imaginary in education: Myth and enlightenment in "personalized learning"', in Stocchetti, M. (Ed) *The Digital Age and Its Discontents*. Helsinki: Helsinki University Press (Critical Reflections in Education), pp. 141–160. doi:10.2307/j.ctv16c9hdw.12.

Glynos, J. and Howarth, D. (2007) *Logics of Critical Explanation in Social and Political Theory*. London: Routledge.

Goodchild, T. and Speed, E. (2019) 'Technology enhanced learning as transformative innovation: A note on the enduring myth of TEL', *Teaching in Higher Education*, 24(8), pp. 948–963. doi:10.1080/13562517.2018.1518900.

Gulson, K.N. and Webb, P.T. (2017) 'Mapping an emergent field of "computational education policy": Policy rationalities, prediction and data in the age of Artificial Intelligence', *Research in Education*, 98(1), pp. 14–26. doi:10.1177/0034523717723385.

Hand, M. (2008) *Making Digital Cultures: Access, Interactivity and Authenticity*. Aldershot: Ashgate.

Hartong, S. (2018) 'Towards a topological re-assemblage of education policy? Observing the implementation of performance data infrastructures and "centers of calculation" in Germany', *Globalisation, Societies and Education*, 16(1), pp. 134–150. doi:10.1080/14767724.2017.1390665.

Inayatullah, S. (2008) 'Six pillars: Futures thinking for transforming', *Foresight*, 10(1), pp. 4–21. doi:10.1108/14636680810855991.

Inayatullah, S. (2013) 'Futures studies: Theories and methods', in Al-Fodhan, Nayef (Ed) *There's a Future: Visions for a Better World*. BBVA.

Jasanoff, S. (2016) 'Future imperfect: Science, technology, and the imaginations of modernity', in Jasanoff, S. and Kim, S.-H. (Eds) *Dreamscapes of Modernity: Sociotechnical Imaginaries and the Fabrication of Power*. Chicago: University of Chicago Press.

Kazansky, B. (2021) '"It depends on your threat model": The anticipatory dimensions of resistance to data-driven surveillance', *Big Data & Society*, 8(1), p. 2053951720985557. doi:10.1177/2053951720985557.

Kendig, C. and Bauchspies, W.K. (2021) 'The ethics of speculative anticipation and the Covid-19 pandemic', *Hypatia*, 36(1), pp. 228–236. doi:10.1017/hyp.2020.56.

Kerr, P. (2020) *The EdTech imaginary in ELT*. Adaptive Learning in ELT, 13 January. Available at: https://adaptivelearninginelt.wordpress.com/2020/01/13/the-edtech-imaginary-in-elt/ (Accessed: 14 May 2021).

36 Understanding learning futures

Komljenovic, J. (2021) 'The rise of education rentiers: Digital platforms, digital data and rents', *Learning, Media and Technology*, 46(3), pp. 320–332. doi:10.1080/174398 84.2021.1891422.

Levitas, R. (2013) *Utopia as Method*. London: Palgrave Macmillan UK.

Lewis, S. and Hartong, S. (2021) 'New shadow professionals and infrastructures around the datafied school: Topological thinking as an analytical device', *European Educational Research Journal*. doi:10.1177/14749041211007496.

Light, A. (2021) 'Collaborative speculation: Anticipation, inclusion and designing counterfactual futures for appropriation', *Futures*, 134, pp. 1–15. doi:10.1016/j. futures.2021.102855.

Liveley, G. and Wardrop, A. (2020) 'Challenging chronocentrism: New approaches to futures thinking in the policy and praxis of widening participation in higher education', *Teaching in Higher Education*, 25(6), pp. 683–697. doi:10.1080/13562517.2020. 1733957.

Mackenzie, A. (2015) 'The production of prediction: What does machine learning want?', *European Journal of Cultural Studies*, 18(4–5), pp. 429–445. doi:10.1177/1367549415577384.

MacLure, M. (2013) 'Researching without representation? Language and materiality in post-qualitative methodology', *International Journal of Qualitative Studies in Education*, 26(6), pp. 658–667. doi:10.1080/09518398.2013.788755.

Matthews, A. (2021) 'Sociotechnical imaginaries in the present and future university: A corpus-assisted discourse analysis of UK higher education texts', *Learning, Media and Technology*, 46(2), pp. 204–217. doi:10.1080/17439884.2021.1864398.

Ojala, M. (2017) 'Hope and anticipation in education for a sustainable future', *Futures*, 94, pp. 76–84. doi:10.1016/j.futures.2016.10.004.

Parker, S. (2020) *The Future of Higher Education in a Disruptive World*. Melbourne: KPMG International.

Poli, R. (2017) *Introduction to Anticipation Studies*. Cham: Springer International Publishing (Anticipation Science). doi:10.1007/978-3-319-63023-6.

Pollock, N. and Williams, R. (2010) 'The business of expectations: How promissory organizations shape technology and innovation', *Social Studies of Science*, 40(4), pp. 525–548. doi:10.1177/0306312710362275.

Prinsloo, P. (2019) 'A social cartography of analytics in education as performative politics', *British Journal of Educational Technology*, 50(6), pp. 2810–2823. doi:10.1111/bjet.12872.

Saint-Georges, I.D. (2012) 'Anticipatory discourse', in Chapelle, Carole A (Eds) *The Encyclopedia of Applied Linguistics*. Blackwell Publishing Ltd. doi:10.1002/9781405198431.wbeal0032.

Scollon, S. and Scollon, R. (2000) 'The construction of agency and action in anticipatory discourse: Positioning ourselves against neo-liberalism', in *Third Conference for Sociocultural Research UNICAMP*, Campinas, São Paulo, Brazil, July, pp. 16–20.

Selwyn, N. (2021a) 'The human labour of school data: Exploring the production of digital data in schools', *Oxford Review of Education*, 47(3), pp. 353–368. doi:10.1080/03054985.2020.1835628.

Selwyn, N. (2021b) 'Ed-Tech within limits: Anticipating educational technology in times of environmental crisis', *E-Learning and Digital Media*, 18(5), pp. 496–510. doi:10.1177/20427530211022951.

Smithers, L. (2020) 'Student success as preemption: Predictive constructions of futures-to-never-come', *Futures*, 124, pp. 1–10. doi:10.1016/j.futures.2020.102639.

St. Pierre, E.A. (2013) 'The posts continue: Becoming', *International Journal of Qualitative Studies in Education*, 26(6), pp. 646–657. doi:10.1080/09518398.2013.788754.

Strauss, C. (2006) 'The imaginary', *Anthropological Theory*, 6(3), pp. 322–344. doi:10.1177/1463499606066891.

Taylor, C. (2002) 'Modern social imaginaries', *Public Culture*, 14(1), pp. 91–124.

Urry, J. (2016) *What is the future?* John Wiley & Sons.

Watters, A. (2020) *The Ed-Tech Imaginary*. Hack Education, 21 June. Available at: http://hackeducation.com/2020/06/21/imaginary (Accessed: 14 May 2021).

Webb, P.T., Sellar, S. and Gulson, K.N. (2020) 'Anticipating education: Governing habits, memories and policy-futures', *Learning, Media and Technology*, 45(3), pp. 284–297. doi:10.1080/17439884.2020.1686015.

Weller, M. (2018) 'Twenty years of Edtech', *Educause Review Online*, 53(4), pp. 34–48.

Williamson, B. (2017) *Big Data in Education: The Digital Future of Learning, Policy and Practice*. Los Angeles, London: SAGE.

Williamson, B. (2021) 'Meta-Edtech', *Learning, Media and Technology*, 46(1), pp. 1–5. doi:10.1080/17439884.2021.1876089.

Wilson-Barnao, C. (2020) 'The quantified and customised museum: Measuring, matching, and aggregating audiences', *PUBLIC*, 30(60), pp. 208–219. doi:10.1386/public_00016_7.

Witzenberger, K. and Gulson, K.N. (2021) 'Why EdTech is always right: Students, data and machines in pre-emptive configurations', *Learning, Media and Technology*, 46(4), pp. 420–434. doi:10.1080/17439884.2021.1913181.

3
COMPLEXITY, EMERGENCE AND LEARNING FUTURES

Introduction

Different approaches to thinking about the future of learning generate different kinds of understandings of what is possible, probable and preferable. As we have seen, some approaches focus on trends or predictions, while others emphasise the uncertainty and complexity of future-making. In futures work, a complexity lens can counter an understanding of causality as "linear, sequential, reductive and past-based" (Adam and Groves, 2007, p. 179) – an understanding which can undermine engagement with "living futures" (ibid). Adam and Groves note instead the need for "reflexive, autopoietic, non-sequential, non-linear" understanding (ibid) that can go beyond mechanistic perspectives on causality. In higher education and lifelong learning literature, an analysis of complexity offers a counterpoint to instrumental accounts of the economic benefits of education for individuals and societies, and contributes to a rich understanding of what Edwards (2010a) calls "incalculability to the future" (p. 148). This chapter examines the role of complexity in learning, in digital education and in digital learning futures.

I begin this chapter by setting out some lenses through which the complexity of learning and education can be viewed: relationality, indeterminacy and contingency. I go on to explore the current educational context and the role that complexity theory has played in shaping the research and pedagogical landscape of digital education. I discuss how complexity thinking troubles and challenges predictive and linear accounts of the future, especially digital technologies and learning futures, and introduce the concept of "not-yetness" as a way of engaging with this challenge. In making the case for the place of uncertainty in educational technology research, the chapter closes by discussing the relationship

DOI: 10.4324/9781003202134-4

of emergence and speculation, setting the scene for the detailed examination of speculative methods and pedagogies in Chapter 4.

Understanding the world as complex

Complexity theory emerged from work in the natural sciences, and observations of systems that are:

- non-linear in terms of cause and effect (like weather systems)
- emergent, because "interactions among components both with each other and with the whole of which they are part are constitutive of properties of systems"
- far from equilibric, meaning they have the potential for radical change.
  (Byrne and Callaghan, 2014, pp. 18–25)

Complexity theory builds on these features and on concepts including phase space (in which all possible states of a system are represented), autopoiesis (self-producing), topology and assemblage to provide a framework for analysing the world and its sociomateriality. Sociomateriality describes the way that knowledge, space, actions and objects are produced through the entanglement and interconnection of human, non-human and more-than-human actors. Such entangled systems are also complex systems, requiring methods that can engage with, rather than only reduce, complexity. This is because complex systems are made up not just of a range of components, but of relationships between each of those components (Cilliers, 1998).

Handling intricate, non-linear and emergent relationships requires methods and methodologies that are sensitive to them. These are what Byrne and Callaghan refer to as "complexity congruent" approaches (2014, p. 192). For them, these include data-based simulation, systematic comparison, process tracing and co-production through dialogue. These methods can work with data sources including text-based narratives, social surveys and administrative data, social network analysis and ongoing observational data. Byrne and Callaghan do not explicitly discuss methods for exploring futures, but they do note that complexity-informed approaches can help to determine what kinds of actions might generate particular futures. A distinction between research that aims to predict and that which, as in this book, aims to engage with futures in more exploratory ways is an important one for understanding the role of complexity in futures work, and it also directly correlates with the categories of "firmative" and "affirmative" speculation, which are introduced in Chapter 4.

Ovens (2017) identifies ontological, conceptual and reflexive dimensions of complexity in the domain of education. He explains that the ontological

40 Understanding learning futures

dimension means understanding education as **relational**, with a focus on becoming and emergence rather than essence and being. The conceptual domain involves questioning assumptions behind educational practice, viewing it instead as **indeterminate**. The reflexive domain requires researchers and teachers to be aware of the **contingent** nature of education. These three factors – relationality, indeterminacy and contingency – provide a helpful framework for explaining the relevance of complexity theory for the work of this book.

The matter of **relationality** is central to examining the sociomaterial world using a complexity lens. It describes how sociomaterial entanglements and interconnections function to bring the world into being. This function is complex because it is non-linear: cause and effect relate in ways that are not deterministic or static. Non-linearity poses an important challenge to thinking about the future, as relations between past, present and future are unstable, leading to a situation where new rules and responses, with uncertain outcomes, have to be created on the fly (Bastrup-Birk and Wildemeersch, 2013). A requirement to invent new responses explains the need for the speculative approaches proposed in this book. This is because, contrary to the possible charge that "anything goes" in studying such a world, it is very difficult to build realities (Law, 2004, p. 13). Following Deleuze and Guattari's (1988) concept of assemblage, Law describes the work of reality-building as a "method assemblage" (p. 13), where realities are made by working with some patterns and ignoring others, generating signals and silences in the process. Ultimately, Law concludes that signals and silences are produced in a *mediated relation* to one another (p. 146), not as binaries. In an educational context, this relationality might also be understood in terms of dialogical thinking, which also challenges binaries and disciplinary boundaries (Alhadeff-Jones, 2019).

A second core aspect of complexity, **indeterminacy**, deals with matters of liminality, uncertainty and unpredictability (Campbell, 2020), and is defined by its open-endedness. The implications for indeterminacy in attempting to understand the sociomaterial world have been explored in depth by Karen Barad (2007) in their influential work bringing together philosophy and quantum physics. Barad, building on insights from quantum physicists Bohr and Heisenberg, refuses a distinction between apparatuses and the phenomena being observed, and proposes instead that apparatuses are open-ended practices and intra-actions (Barad, 2003). As such, phenomena (including words and things) come into being in specific ways by being observed in specific ways, and their indeterminacy can only be temporarily or locally resolved. Barad argues that causality and indeterminacy are related in a complex and ambiguous way in a "space of agency" (Barad, 2007, p. 225). This space of agency is critical to a complexity-informed view of education. It offers a justification for these efforts, where otherwise there might be a tendency to throw up our hands and assume that, as nothing can be planned or predicted, there is little point to the endeavour

Complexity, emergence and learning futures **41**

(Morrison, 2008). However, to offer a space of agency does not guarantee success, and failure is always an option – and not necessarily a negative one. For instance, Alhadeff-Jones (2012), writing about complexity in education, highlights the role of "disorder" and how it can be useful in working with uncertainty and considering limitations and otherness in playful ways.

The relationship of failure, indeterminacy and speculation is one that interests me (Bodden and Ross, 2021), especially the engaging ways it has been explored in queer theory. As Haber (2016) notes, queer theory is generally understood to be a tool for deconstructing disciplines, practices and methods. However, he argues that it can also offer insights on an ontological level: "a queer politics of ontological interconnection and indeterminacy" (p. 151), and he sketches an approach that involves experimentation with sensor technologies. In work that explores the queer meanings of failure, Halberstam (2011) notes that critique and refusal are negative realms that nevertheless reveal alternatives, including the dismantling of logics of success. There is more on the generative dimensions of failure in the next chapter, and in Chapter 5's discussion of the glitching Teacherbot.

Finally, working with indeterminacy requires a stance that is attuned to the **contingency** of knowledge claims and the contextual nature of learning. In settings where the identification of "best practice" is seen as a laudable end goal, this is not a trivial challenge. It matters, though, because constructions of knowledge and the way these are engaged with are inevitably provisional. Museum ethics, for example, have been described as contingent because they change over time depending on social, political, technological and economic factors (Marstine, 2011). In museum learning, too, the contingency of knowledge must be grappled with – with museum educators often mediating between curatorial agendas and learners' knowledge (Bell, 2017). In work on the future of museum design, Gurian (2018) links the potential for peace with societal tolerance for messiness and complexity, and observes that museum exhibitions need to be designed differently to support this. In her future exhibition, technology will support more relational and indeterminate possibilities for engagement:

> The audience will be encouraged to do something else if they wish. There will be a glossary of possibilities embedded in the orientation. The director, as a matter of policy, will demand that multiple modalities with differing points of view or simply raw data be overlaid on the exhibitions in forms (probably technical) that do not interfere with the frame but are just as easy and comfortable to use. The audience, rather than chastising themselves for not following the intended plot, will be encouraged to follow a personal quest or to dig deeper in some parts because of the availability of both visual storage and access to the internet for further exploration. Access to conflicting points of view will be expected.
>
> *(p. 40)*

42 Understanding learning futures

This relationship of digital information space to multiplicity and complexity is one that was established in the early days of the world-wide web, when hypertext was celebrated for its non-linearity. The multimodal, layered, exploratory and open-ended vision presented here suggests that such a relationship may still have more to offer, including in troubled political times (in Gurian's case, in the aftermath of the 2016 elections in the US). It has further implications, too, as Cameron and Mengler (2009) have argued in their framing of digital spaces as "hyper-complex", where networked objects mediate as they circulate online, creating new forms of public interaction with and between objects and museums.

Engaging with complexity in education and learning, in both formal and informal contexts, and especially where technology is involved, requires attention to their relationality, indeterminacy and contingency. These factors also help us explore what is meant by learning itself.

Learning as relational, indeterminate and contingent

Learning encompasses a huge diversity of practices, experiences and outcomes, within but also well beyond formal educational spaces. Examples might include participating in a museum tour, a workplace mentoring relationship, community activism, apprenticeship, fan fiction writing or taking part in activities in a Massive Open Online Course or makerspace. Open learning departments run by universities or local governments, online videos or curated playlists that demonstrate a creative or practical skill, for-profit language learning apps, art groups set up by a gallery, and companies: all are potential sources of engagement beyond formal educational settings that may lead to learning. Discourses and imaginaries of lifelong learning sometimes recognise this multiplicity, but equally they often seek to mobilise lifelong learning as a particular kind of response to complexity, one that can master and mandate the future (Edwards, 2010a).

More challenging still, and often glossed over in discussions of both formal and informal education, is that learning itself is an emergent phenomenon, not one that proceeds predictably or describes a single type of interaction or acquisition. Fenwick (2010) highlights, in relation to workplace learning research, how rarely learning is actually defined. She observes, through a meta-review of six years of workplace learning literature, eight different enactments of learning, from individual acquisition of knowledge to development within communities of practice and networks. In analysing these enactments, she identifies differences that go beyond the definitional to the ontological. She proposes to navigate this by working with questions of the purposes of learning, but also to value difference, incoherence and messiness instead of always seeking "seamless continuity" (p. 92).

Attempts to define learning frequently provide normative statements of what is good or desirable for learners. Biesta (2018) describes this as a "slippage from 'is' to 'ought'" (p. 31), and argues that this normative judgement inevitably points to educational questions. These, he maintains, can only be answered contingently,

Complexity, emergence and learning futures **43**

for some specific context or setting. They are questions about exactly what is to be learned, how and by whom.

Terms like lifelong learning, then, face the problem of definition – if the scope is wide enough to capture what might be implied by "lifelong", then the understanding of learning becomes increasingly vague. Defining the nature of learning more tightly or framing it in terms of its specific educational context risks losing a sense of the richness and diversity of contexts and relationships evoked by the idea of a process that is "lifelong".

So, how are we to proceed in thinking about and working with futures of learning? Biesta offers a definition of learning that indicates the complexity of the terrain this book is also navigating. Learning, he proposes, is:

> a reaction to a disturbance... an attempt to reorganise or reintegrate as a result of disintegration... responding to what is other or different, to what challenges, irritates and disturbs us, rather than as the acquisition of something that we want to possess.
>
> *(Biesta, 2005, p. 62)*

This aligns well with Hager and Beckett's (2019) description of learning as a "complex relational web" (p. 117). These key matters – disturbance, difference, irritation and dis- and re-integration – will return again the next chapter when I discuss how speculative methods have been used to tackle some fundamental tensions in research. They offer a bridge between methods and pedagogies, suggesting how we might consider both as tools for navigating relationality. And they give a helpful reminder that working with futures requires curiosity, tolerance of ambiguity and a commitment to responsible experimentation (Edwards, 2010b).

We can see something of how defining learning as "reaction to disturbance" is currently playing out in the turn to framing education in terms of "wicked problems". For instance, McCune et al. (2021) argue that university teachers need to attend to curriculum design in order to better support students to work and live with wicked problems. This requires developing students' ability to work dynamically within and beyond disciplines, negotiate epistemological positions and build consensus, as well as to come to terms with the complexity of wicked problems. This complexity comes about, they explain, because of their many interacting elements, the lack of clear boundaries between problems, the co-existence of different dimensions of effects (local, global, national and so on), the uncertainty about impacts of interventions, and imperfect framings.

Tackling wicked problems in educational settings is an excellent example of the role of pedagogical experimentation in engaging with complexity. Methodological inventiveness, too, has role to play here, and researchers can use it to work against assumptions and practices in educational research that are not complexity-congruent.

44 Understanding learning futures

From causality to complexity: digital education research[1]

The relationship of educators, institutions and educational researchers to technology is one that has often been characterised by attempts at control, efficiency and enhancement (Bayne, 2014), underplaying more "disruptive, disturbing and generative dimensions" (p. 3). Educational researchers are frequently asked, including by funders and policymakers, for research to support evidence-based practice, and what counts as "evidence-based" is increasingly circumscribed. For example, in the UK, randomised controlled trials, where research participants are randomly allocated to either a baseline "control" group or one or more "intervention" groups, have been recommended by the Department for Education in England as the "gold standard" for educational research (Goldacre and Plant, 2013). MacLure (2006) describes these kinds of policy moves as being "animated by the desire for certainty, willing to sacrifice complexity and diversity for 'harder' evidence and the global tournament of standards" (p. 730).

In digital education contexts, one of the most influential strands of evidence-based practice has come in the form of design-based research. Design-based research emerged as a response to claims that educational research was too divorced from practice and needed to be made more valuable by having more direct impacts. It is explicitly about generating generalised claims about learning (Barab and Squire, 2004). Anderson and Shattuck (2012) characterise it as aiming to increase impact of education research by translating it to improved practice. In their review of the literature on design-based research, they found that more than half the research interventions focused on or involved online and mobile technologies. More recent studies have used design-based research to examine blended synchronous learning (Zydney, Warner and Angelone, 2020), culturally responsive MOOCs (Chen and Oakley, 2020), and mixed-reality skills development (Cowling and Birt, 2018). Hoadley (2007) describes design-based research as particularly suitable for digital education research. However, Walker (2011) points out that this method achieves some of its reputation for utility at the expense of meaningful engagement with epistemological issues.

Biesta's work on evidence-based practice (see for example Biesta, 2007, 2010) highlights some difficulties inherent in making claims of generalisability ("what works") for educational research. In practice, the question of "what works" in learning settings is typically answered with large-scale experimental or quasi-experimental studies designed to be replicable and generalisable and to focus on identifying whether interventions, necessarily incrementally and narrowly defined, produce measurable increases in student achievement or other pre-defined outcomes. Biesta identifies three areas of deficit in evidence-based practice – in knowledge, efficacy and application – and argues that these ought to lead us to a much more critical position in relation to evidence than is usually seen (Biesta, 2010). The "knowledge deficit" refers to the inability of experiment-based evidence to provide "rules for action", because interventions

Complexity, emergence and learning futures **45**

inevitably change the world they are trying to engage with. An "efficacy deficit" comes about because education is an "open recursive semiotic system" (p. 500) – interactions within the system are probabilistic, feed back into themselves, and are based on meaning-making between actors. The relationships between interventions and results or effects are therefore non-linear, so making sense of educational realities involves making choices about what to pay attention to, which is inevitably a political act. Finally, the "application deficit" addresses the extent to which experiment-based methods produce a special kind of knowledge in the "lab" which allows for effective interventions in the world. Biesta, drawing on Latour, argues that the world is *changed* to accommodate or incorporate this scientific knowledge. As with the efficacy deficit, the work taken to bridge the application deficit is political, and therefore can never leave aside questions of values and priorities. As a result, research can only give an "understanding of possibilities" and of "what the problem might be" (2007, p. 16), not tell us what to do. Asking "what works", or what educational techniques are effective, is a problem because the question obscures its own contestability. He invites us to think about research of all kinds as a support for the "intelligent selection of possible lines of action" (ibid).

Experimental and quasi-experimental research requires well-established methodological techniques, but it also requires questions and hypotheses to be framed in particular, limited ways. This can be a strength, but to believe that this, or any, research method will deliver simple answers or clear guides for action in education is to misunderstand what research does. This means that the door is open for many more kinds of research, and research questions, to help us solve problems intelligently.

Lather (2006) calls multiplicity in educational research "paradigm proliferation". Her work on educating educational researchers has drawn attention to the problem of privileging positivism as the gold standard in educational policy and practice. Instead, the strength of educational research is in its paradigm proliferation, which rejects the possibility of identifying best practice and instead acknowledges the importance of incompatibilities between paradigms. Proliferation, in other words, is not about determining which approaches are most legitimate, or arriving at a middle ground, but of fostering our ability to value and work with a whole range of methodologies, including those which challenge the "limits of intelligibility" (p. 41) and work with complexity, relationality, indeterminacy and contingency.

Digital education researchers, educators and technologists within education communities have a particular responsibility to be ready and able to engage productively as research users and creators with varied epistemological and methodological approaches. Digital education research works with ideas and methods from fields as varied as cultural studies, informatics and design, as well as from more established educational research disciplines such as psychology and sociology, and such a variety of influences and sources of knowledge inevitably will

46 Understanding learning futures

lead to the sorts of fractures and tensions that the question of "what works" attempts to write out. To write them back in to enable working in interdisciplinary teams, or to refuse such erasure to try to address new questions, requires allowing complex and wicked problems to remain unresolvable. The concept of "best practice" assumes linear progress and predictable outcomes, ignoring the volatility that comes with working with emerging technologies in education (Bayne et al., 2020). Education and learning settings and contexts always interact in complex ways with technologies, and this is particularly the case where uses of newer technologies are still not settled or fixed into particular configurations of practice.

As we saw in the previous chapter, digital education as a field is strongly influenced by edtech imaginaries and visions of the future put forward by a range of stakeholders, including political, commercial and media interests. For this reason, it needs researchers who can offer accounts which address, for example, issues of equality, diversity and social justice. Maintaining a creatively critical stance towards digital futures for education involves navigating multiple and often competing visions *without* succumbing to cynicism, a narrowing of perspective, or a turn away from indeterminacy. As Barnett (2013) says of the university, the field of digital education needs "a *proliferation* of ideas… if only to begin to demonstrate that things could be other than they are" (p. 5). Digital education research also needs "political teeth", and one way to accomplish this is through an approach that tries to see things in terms of what they might become, not just what they currently are (Martin and Kamberelis, 2013). In the next section, the idea of "what might become" is explored in the context of the concept of "not-yetness". Then, in the final section of this chapter, I will explore the relationship of becoming, complexity and the future that underpins speculative approaches.

Not-yetness

The concept of "not-yetness" as it is used in this book was sparked by a collaboration with Amy Collier on a chapter about emerging technologies (Ross and Collier, 2016). It came about through our discussions as we engaged with the writing of our colleague George Veletsianos (2010), who defined emerging technologies "not yet fully understood and not yet fully researched, or researched in a mature way" (p. 15). Not-yetness is a concept that we have used generatively – together and separately – in a number of contexts since then.

We have argued that it is not only technologies, but also practices, subjectivities and pedagogies involved with them which are marked by this "not-yetness" (Ross and Collier, 2016). Working with the not-yetness of digital education means engaging with complexity, uncertainty and risk, not as factors to be minimised or resolved, but as necessary dimensions of technologies and practices which are unknown and in flux. Not-yetness – that which is perpetually incomplete, always uncertain, not fully understood, but still expected – provides a

Complexity, emergence and learning futures **47**

meaningful way to push back against the conviction with which education and its futures are often presented.

Not-yetness has also been used in a range of other scholarly contexts, not all connected to one another but evoking the same tension between expectation and uncertainty about the future, and this section outlines some of these uses as they have emerged from philosophical traditions of existentialism and Marxism, science and technology studies and innovation studies, queer theory and political and social sciences and research methods. As a concept, not-yetness carries a sense of both inevitability and unpredictability – it pops up again and again in unconnected settings, across contexts and disciplines, shifting in tone and significance and used to explain or problematise engagements with knowledge, consensus and potential.

In philosophy, not-yetness is one translation offered for Heidegger's existential hermeneutics, where "not-whole-ness, not-yet-ness (etwas noch nicht sein) – functions as a shattering of sameness and unity" (Lurcza, 2014, p. 72). Drawing on Heidegger, in the cultural domain, Fadda (2006) wrote a chapter titled "Not-yet-ness"[2] for a book about Palestine as a liminal space. She defines not-yetness as "that which is, and which is not. Or that with the potential to be, but is not." (p. 227). She goes on to explore the ambiguity of not-yetness, which comes through an interplay of force, assertion and negation:

> Not-yet, in its capacity to incorporate all tenses leading to futurity, is still a phrase with a negation. This status of negation or not, however, somehow manages to introduce an assertion, alluding to a somewhat prophetic force or voice of that which is about to happen. Free will and agency are conjured to assert the future implicit in the not-yet.
>
> *(p. 229)*

Less ambiguous and more utopian is Barnett and Bengtsen's (2017) use of Heidegger to frame the not-yetness of the future university. They offer the concept of the "optimistic university", which is generated from the known world and the "not-yet-ness of the world" (p. 8). Innovation literature in the higher education context, too, has touched on not-yetness, this time in the concept of "alien entrepreneurship" that creates values for "what is to come": "an Entrepreneurship of the not-yet-ness, an entrepreneurship of fecundity, where value creation becomes the terroir of possible futures, for societies and generations yet to come" (Shumar and Bengtsen, 2021).

The relationship between invention, novelty and the idea of "waiting" is a key aspect of not-yetness beyond the educational literature, too. Peschl (2020) draws on Marxist theorist Ernst Bloch's (1986) conception of the Not Yet,[3] and describes innovation artefacts that "are not-yet, that want to emerge" (p. 67). He argues that novel objects, qualities and so on exist, but have not yet been seen or enacted – something must trigger them to become. Put another way, they

48 Understanding learning futures

have not become objects of knowledge (such as gadgets, machines or selves) (Mackenzie, 2005), but are "not-yet structured potentials" (p. 393). The possibility of invention is located in this not-yetness, because: "only to the extent that individuals, things, or systems are not yet actors, only to the extent they embody unresolved contradictions, incompatibilities and tensions can they participate in invention and can collectives eventuate" (p. 395).

Not all visions of not-yetness are utopian or hopeful ones. In her critical account, Stengers (2000) discusses how science is historicised to frame past ignorance as a time when "we did not yet know" (p. 125), smoothing over transformations that occurred and continue to occur. She describes the "mobilized scientists" who see anything that cannot be accounted for in their laboratories as obstacles that have "'not yet' been reduced" (p. 128). These obstacles are mistrusted and framed as "negligible, irrational, or destined to sort themselves out" (ibid). She critiques this use of the "not yet", and argues that it blocks a crucial question: "What risks does this situation make our judgments run to, what becoming and what sensibilities does it impose on us?" (p. 157).

Some objects can embody not-yetness, for example, the human embryonic stem cell (hESC) – a cell which can differentiate into any other type of cell in the body (Eriksson and Webster, 2008). Eriksson and Webster define the hESC itself through its "peculiar temporality" and its "not-yet-ness" (p. 62). A piece of music – John Cage's "Empty Words" – is described as disrupting the "regular interpretative process" through its not-yetness (Edmeades, 2016, p. 220). "Empty Words" consists of a single voice singing what sound like words but are not, and changes each time the piece is performed, within the context of a set of instructions provided by the composer. As a result:

> The less meaning we have to cling to, the more susceptible we are to the not-yet-ness of the text. In the process Cage not only empties the words of their significance but also opens the text to increased possible meanings.
>
> *(p. 223)*

The use of the concept of not-yetness to express aspects of queerness such as amateur drag performance – attributed to queer theorist José Muñoz – is observed by Goltz and Zingsheim (2010) as an essential element of queer resistance: "there is a quality to the rough and unfinished performance that draws our attention to the very process of its making, its not-yet-ness, where seams and flaws in the performance gesture towards futurity" (p. 303). Rubenstein (2017) describes Muñoz's queer as a figure of "radical alterity", and queerness as "both not-yet and enfleshed, and this "both" makes the enfleshment fall irremediably short of a full-out, bells-and-whistles ontology. Or it exposes such ontologies as puffed-up, uninteresting, plodding … straight and minivanned" (p. 294).

Several religious studies texts have used the term not-yetness to describe the nature of faith in the Christian tradition. For example, Collins (1989), reflecting

Complexity, emergence and learning futures **49**

on the theology of loneliness, suggests that it is this state that leads to the discovery of "God's not-yetness": "God's 'already' is a lonely reminder of his 'not yet'" (p. 75).

In political and social theory, not-yetness has been used to reflect on imagined and threatening "others" (Ahmed, 2004), democracy (McGonigal, 2011), evidence (Croissant, 2014), intersectionality (Nash, 2014), hunger (Lara, 2015) and feminist waves (Chamberlain, 2017). In a critical take on not-yetness as "lack", Quennerstedt (2019) rejects education's dominant framing of children as "not-yets", because "children are both becomings and beings at the same time... we can move beyond the not-yet-ness of the child as someone lacking something, and thus in need of a certain kind of education and a certain kind of teaching that fills this void" (p. 614).

Finally, methodologically, not-yetness has appeared in accounts of qualitative research writing. The Deleuzian "suggestion" in research writing, according to Pearce (2010), "tries to experiment with the not-yet-ness that both impossibilities and possibilities invoke. In doing so, it also attempts to account for what emerges within such engagements. To this extent, the writing submits to its own suggestions in a play of what lies between our consumptions and communications; memories and sense" (p. 902). Gale (2020), writing a decade later about "writing as inquiry" (drawing on Richardson (1994)), finds comfort in "the not-yet-ness and potential for spacetime making" (p. 97).

We can see in the concept of not-yetness a good deal of the kind of complexity that I have argued in this chapter is required for working with learning futures. Hope, lack, fidelity, waiting, invention, disruption, experimentation, negation and disunity can be teased out from within its various uses. Not-yetness, in this book, serves as a reminder that learning futures exist as troublesome objects to think and work with. We should not rush to fix or simplify them in our teaching and research: we should engage them as spaces of multiplicity and creativity. In a sphere of not-yetness, we must work with a proliferation of approaches that can help us make and engage with problems.

Becoming, complexity and learning futures

Pedagogy and research can and should engage with the relationality, indeterminacy and contingency of education and learning. These dimensions of complexity can help us grapple with the "not-yetness" of learning and its futures. In a climate of educational research in which the value of evidence-based practice is enshrined in policy and in funding priorities, and where uncertainty and risk are often seen as unwelcome, a complexity lens provides the foundation for a crucial and critical response. In working with learning futures as objects-to-think-with, complexity has a vital role, as it helps us understand the nature of our responsibility to the futures we are making as "implicated participants" whose knowledge

50 Understanding learning futures

practices are not isolated and whose deeds "reverberate through the system, activating responses that stretch across time and space":

> The complexity perspective deprives us of the comfortable position of external, uninvolved observer. It divests us of the 'view from nowhere' that allowed us to act with impunity. It therefore demands that we acknowledge ourselves as future makers and understand our responsibilities accordingly.
>
> *(Adam and Groves, 2007, p. 181)*

Facer (2021) echoes this focus on responsibility to the future, asking, as one of her key questions, "Who will attend to the consequence of these ideas of the future being put into the world and how?" (p. 20). She notes the need for programmes of inquiry in education, rather than individual projects, as a way of taking ongoing responsibility for the future. Insisting on responsibility is not to overstate our ability to predict, but instead to recognise that what we do and say about the future matters. Regardless of the complexity involved, teachers and researchers, students and participants can be part of producing new things in the world, including beliefs, practices and technologies (Urry, 2016). In addition, it has implications for how we understand caring. Osberg (2010) argues that complexity theory changes but does not diminish our responsibility for taking care of the future. It reframes care of the future to take account of open-endedness, not instrumental or linear logics.

So, to the "how" of Facer's question. How will we attend to the digital learning futures being put into the world? As we have seen in this chapter, the question of "what works?", and the approaches it generates, is limited. We require more kinds of questions, and methods, in order to engage imaginatively with the complexity of learning and learning spaces, the rapidly shifting terrain of digital education, and to respond creatively and critically to claims of "disruption" that accompany social and technological change. Practices involved in design-based research tend to work against complexity. Design itself, however, takes many forms, and its role in speculative approaches will become apparent in the next chapter. In their book about the possibilities for design anthropology, Akama et al. (2020) note that uncertainty "opens up pathways of what might be next and enables us to creatively and imaginatively inhabit such worlds with possibilities" (p. 3). This creative inhabiting demands the kinds of "situated, lived, embodied accounts" (p. 6) that design methods and methodologies have long engaged with and elicited.

Speculative approaches have not yet been widely adopted in learning and education, but they offer us a generative set of methodological considerations and pedagogical possibilities. Futures thinking urgently needs imaginative resources to stake a strong position at the edges of educational change. Speculative approaches to research and pedagogy can bring new practices and ideas into being while maintaining space for curiosity, critique, doubt, unintended consequences and emergent properties of technologies in use. The next chapter explores these speculative approaches in detail.

Notes

1 This section has been adapted from Ross, J (2017). Speculative method in digital education research. *Learning, Media and Technology*. 42/2. Creative Commons license CC:BY.
2 She notes that she borrowed this term from Farred (2008), who described it as "persistent incipience" (p. 59), but also links it to the work of Agamben and Heidegger as well as Benjamin and Iqbal.
3 Bloch's Not Yet is a state of "anticipatory consciousness" (Levitas, 2013, p. 6) requiring educated hope, which Thompson (2016) describes as "fidelity to an event that has not yet happened" (p. 442).

References

Adam, B. and Groves, C. (2007) *Future Matters: Action, Knowledge, Ethics*. Boston, the Netherlands: Brill.

Ahmed, S. (2004) 'Affective economies', *Social Text*, 22(2), pp. 117–139.

Akama, Y., Pink, S. and Sumartojo, S. (2020) *Uncertainty and Possibility: New Approaches to Future Making in Design Anthropology*. Abingdon: Routledge.

Alhadeff-Jones, M. (2012) 'Learning disorders: From a tragic to an epic perspective on complexity', *Complicity: An International Journal of Complexity and Education*, 9(2), pp. i-vi. doi:10.29173/cmplct17982.

Alhadeff-Jones, M. (2019) *Time and the rhythms of emancipatory education: Rethinking the temporal complexity of self and society*. Abingdon: Routledge.

Anderson, T. and Shattuck, J. (2012) 'Design-based research a decade of progress in education research?', *Educational Researcher*, 41(1), pp. 16–25. doi:10.3102/00131 89X11428813.

Barab, S. and Squire, K. (2004) 'Design-based research: Putting a stake in the ground', *The Journal of the Learning Sciences*, 13(1), pp. 1–14.

Barad, K. (2003) 'Posthumanist performativity: Toward an understanding of how matter comes to matter', *Signs: Journal of Women in Culture and Society*, 28(3), pp. 801–831. doi:10.1086/345321.

Barad, K. (2007) *Meeting the Universe Halfway: Quantum Physics and the Entanglement of Matter and Meaning*. Durham: Duke University Press. doi:10.1215/9780822388128.

Barnett, R. (2013) *Imagining the University*. London: Routledge.

Barnett, R. and Bengtsen, S. (2017) 'Universities and epistemology: From a dissolution of knowledge to the emergence of a new thinking', *Education Sciences*, 7(1), p. 38. doi:10.3390/educsci7010038.

Bastrup-Birk, H. and Wildemeersch, D. (2013) 'A fresh take on democratic education: Revisiting Rancière through the notions of emergence and enaction', *Complicity: An International Journal of Complexity and Education*, 10, pp. 111–129.

Bayne, S. (2014) 'What's the matter with "technology-enhanced learning"?', *Learning, Media and Technology*, pp. 1–16. doi:10.1080/17439884.2014.915851.

Bayne, S. et al. (2020) *The Manifesto for Teaching Online*. Cambridge: MIT Press.

Bell, D.R. (2017) 'Aesthetic encounters and learning in the museum', *Educational Philosophy and Theory*, 49(8), pp. 776–787. doi:10.1080/00131857.2016.1214899.

Biesta, G. (2005) 'Against learning. Reclaiming a language for education in an age of learning', *Nordisk Pedagogik*, 25, pp. 54–66.

Biesta, G. (2007) 'Why "What Works" won't work: Evidence-based practice and the democratic deficit in educational research', *Educational Theory*, 57(1), pp. 1–22. doi:10.1111/j.1741-5446.2006.00241.x.

Biesta, G. (2018) 'Creating spaces for learning or making room for education? New parameters for the architecture of education', in Tse, H.M. et al. (Eds) *Designing Buildings for the Future of Schooling*. Abingdon: Routledge.

Biesta, G.J.J. (2010) 'Why "What Works" still won't work: From evidence-based education to value-based education', *Studies in Philosophy and Education*, 29(5), pp. 491–503. Doi:10.1007/s11217-010-9191-x.

Bloch, E. (1986) *The Principle of Hope*. Translated by N. Plaice, S. Plaice, and P. Knight. Cambridge, MA: MIT Press.

Bodden, S. and Ross, J. (2021) 'Speculating with glitches: Keeping the future moving', *Global Discourse*, 11(1–2), pp. 15–34. doi:10.1332/204378920X16043719041171.

Byrne, D. and Callaghan, G. (2014) *Complexity Theory and the Social Sciences: The State of the Art*. Abingdon: Routledge.

Cameron, F. and Mengler, S. (2009) 'Complexity, transdisciplinarity and museum collections documentation: Emergent metaphors for a complex world', *Journal of Material Culture*, 14(2), pp. 189–218. doi:10.1177/1359183509103061.

Campbell, I. (2020) *Why indeterminacy now?* The Future of Indeterminacy, 30 June. Available at: https://indeterminacy.ac.uk/blog/why-indeterminacy-now/ (Accessed: 1 July 2021)

Chamberlain, P. (2017) 'What is feminist time keeping?', in Chamberlain, P. (Ed) *The Feminist Fourth Wave: Affective Temporality*. Cham: Springer International Publishing, pp. 45–72. doi:10.1007/978-3-319-53682-8_3.

Chen, K.-Z. and Oakley, B. (2020) 'Redeveloping a global MOOC to be more locally relevant: Design-based research', *International Journal of Educational Technology in Higher Education*, 17(1), pp. 1–22. doi:10.1186/s41239-020-0178-6.

Cilliers, P. (1998) *Complexity and Postmodernism: Understanding Complex Systems*. London, United Kingdom: Taylor & Francis Group.

Collins, W.E. (1989) 'A sermon from hell: Toward a theology of loneliness', *Journal of Religion and Health*, 28(1), pp. 70–79. doi:10.1007/BF00987504.

Cowling, M. and Birt, J. (2018) 'Pedagogy before technology: A design-based research approach to enhancing skills development in paramedic science using mixed reality', *Information*, 9(2), p. 29. doi:10.3390/info9020029.

Croissant, J.L. (2014) 'Agnotology: Ignorance and absence or towards a sociology of things that aren't there', *Social Epistemology*, 28(1), pp. 4–25. doi:10.1080/02691728.2013.862880.

Deleuze, G. and Guattari, F. (1988) *A Thousand Plateaus: Capitalism and Schizophrenia*. London: Bloomsbury Publishing.

Edmeades, L. (2016) 'Affect and the musication of language in John Cage's "Empty Words"', *Comparative Literature*, 68(2), pp. 218–234. doi:10.1215/00104124-3507962.

Edwards, R. (2010a) 'Lifelong learning: Emergent enactments', *Pedagogy, Culture & Society*, 18(2), pp. 145–157. doi:10.1080/14681366.2010.488041.

Edwards, R. (2010b) 'The end of lifelong learning: A post-human condition?', *Studies in the Education of Adults*, 42(1), pp. 5–17. doi:10.1080/02660830.2010.11661585.

Eriksson, L. and Webster, A. (2008) 'Standardizing the unknown: Practicable pluripotency as doable futures', *Science as Culture*, 17(1), pp. 57–69. doi:10.1080/09505430701872814.

Facer, K. (2021) *Futures in Education: Towards an Ethical Practice*. UNESCO. Available at: https://unesdoc.unesco.org/ark:/48223/pf0000375792 (Accessed: 12 May 2021)

Fadda, R. (2006) *Not-yet-ness*. The Center for Digital Art, Holon, The Palestinian Association for Contemporary Art (PACA), and The International Art Academy Palestine.

Farred, G. (2008) 'Disorderly democracy: An axiomatic politics', *CR: The New Centennial Review*, 8(2), pp. 43–65.

Fenwick, T. (2010) 'Workplace "learning" and adult education. Messy objects, blurry maps and making difference', *European journal for Research on the Education and Learning of Adults*, 1(1–2), pp. 79–95.

Gale, K. (2020) 'Writing in immanence: A creative-relational doing?', *Departures in Critical Qualitative Research*, 9(2), pp. 92–102. doi:10.1525/dcqr.2020.9.2.92.

Goldacre, B. and Plant, R. (2013) *Department for Education Analytical Review*. Department for Education. Available at: https://www.gov.uk/government/publications/department-for-education-analytical-review (Accessed: 24 February 2015).

Goltz, D.B. and Zingsheim, J. (2010) 'It's not a wedding, It's a gayla: Queer resistance and normative recuperation', *Text and Performance Quarterly*, 30(3), pp. 290–312.

Gurian, E.H. (2018) 'On the importance of "And": Museums and complexity', in MacLeod, S. et al. (Eds) *The Future of Museum and Gallery Design*. Abingdon: Routledge.

Haber, B. (2016) 'The queer ontology of digital method', *WSQ: Women's Studies Quarterly*, 44(3), pp. 150–169. doi:10.1353/wsq.2016.0040.

Hager, P. and Beckett, D. (2019) *The Emergence of Complexity: Rethinking Education as a Social Science*. Cham: Springer International Publishing (Perspectives on Rethinking and Reforming Education). doi:10.1007/978-3-030-31839-0.

Halberstam, J. (2011) *The Queer Art of Failure*. Durham: Duke University Press

Hoadley, C. (2007) 'Learning sciences theories and methods for e-learning researchers', in Andrews, R. and Haythornthwaite, C. (Eds) *The SAGE Handbook of E-learning Research*. London: SAGE, pp. 139–156.

Lara, A. (2015) 'Affect, heat and tacos. A speculative account of thermoception', *The Senses and Society*, 10(3), pp. 275–297. doi:10.1080/17458927.2015.1130301.

Lather, P. (2006) 'Paradigm proliferation as a good thing to think with: Teaching research in education as a wild profusion', *International Journal of Qualitative Studies in Education*, 19(1), pp. 35–57. doi:10.1080/09518390500450144.

Law, J. (2004) *After Method: Mess in Social Science Research*. Abingdon: Routledge.

Levitas, R. (2013) *Utopia as Method*. London: Palgrave Macmillan UK. doi:10.1057/9781137314253.

Lurcza, Z. (2014) 'Cultural identity and deconstruction', *Studia Universitatis Babes-Bolyai – Philosophia*, 59(3), pp. 69–82.

Mackenzie, A. (2005) 'Problematising the technological: The object as event?', *Social Epistemology*, 19(4), pp. 381–399. doi:10.1080/02691720500145589.

MacLure, M. (2006) 'The bone in the throat: Some uncertain thoughts on baroque method', *International Journal of Qualitative Studies in Education*, 19(6), pp. 729–745. doi:10.1080/09518390600975958.

Marstine, J. (2011) 'The contingent nature of the new museum ethics', In *The Routledge Companion to Museum Ethics*. London, United Kingdom: Taylor & Francis, pp. 3–25.

Martin, A.D. and Kamberelis, G. (2013) 'Mapping not tracing: Qualitative educational research with political teeth', *International Journal of Qualitative Studies in Education*, 26(6), pp. 668–679. doi:10.1080/09518398.2013.788756.

McCune, V. et al. (2021) 'Teaching wicked problems in higher education: Ways of thinking and practising', *Teaching in Higher Education*, pp. 1–16. doi:10.1080/13562517.2021.1911986.

McGonigal, J. (2011) 'The politics of redress in Post-9/11 Canada', in Wilson, S. (Ed) *Joy Kogawa: Essays on her Works*. 1st edn. Toronto, ON; Tonawanda, N.Y: Guernica Editions (Writers series, 32).

Morrison, K. (2008) 'Educational philosophy and the challenge of complexity theory', *Educational Philosophy and Theory*, 40, pp. 19–34.

Nash, J.C. (2014) 'Institutionalizing the margins', *Social Text*, 32(1 (118)), pp. 45–65. doi:10.1215/01642472-2391333.

Osberg, D. (2010) 'Taking care of the Future? The complex responsibility of education and politics', in Osberg, D. and Biesta, G. (Eds) *Complexity Theory and the Politics of Education*. Boston, the Netherlands: BRILL. doi:10.1163/9789460912405.

Ovens, A. (2017) 'Putting complexity to work to think differently about transformative pedagogies in teacher education', *Issues in Teacher Education*, 26(3), pp. 38–51.

Pearce, C. (2010) 'The life of suggestions', *Qualitative Inquiry*, 16(10), pp. 902–908. doi:10.1177/1077800410383122.

Peschl, M.F. (2020) 'Theory-U: From potentials and co-becoming to bringing forth emergent innovation and shaping a thriving future. On what it means to "learn from the future as it emerges"', in Gunnlaugson, O. and Brendel, W. (Eds) *Advances in Presencing*. Vancouver: Trifoss Business Press, pp. 65–112.

Quennerstedt, M. (2019) 'Physical education and the art of teaching: transformative learning and teaching in physical education and sports pedagogy', *Sport, Education and Society*, 24(6), pp. 611–623. doi:10.1080/13573322.2019.1574731.

Richardson, L. (1994) 'Writing: A method of inquiry', in Denzin, N. and Lincoln, Y. (Eds) *Handbook of Qualitative Research*. London: Sage.

Ross, J. and Collier, A. (2016) 'Complexity, mess and not-yetness: Teaching online with emerging technologies', in Veletsianos, G. (Ed) *Emergence and Innovation in Digital Learning: Foundations and Applications*. Athabasca University Press.

Rubenstein, M.-J. (2017) 'Response: Queer enfleshment', in Marchal, Joseph A., Brintnall, Kent L., and Moore, Stephen D. (Eds) *Sexual Disorientations: Queer Temporalities, Affects, Theologies*. Fordham University Press, pp. 292–295.

Shumar, W. and Bengtsen, S.S.E. (2021) 'An entrepreneurial ecology for higher education: A new approach to student formation', in Bengtsen, S.S.E., Robinson, S., and Shumar, W. (Eds) *The University Becoming: Perspectives from Philosophy and Social Theory*. Cham: Springer International Publishing (Debating Higher Education: Philosophical Perspectives), pp. 125–138. doi:10.1007/978-3-030-69628-3_9.

Stengers, I. (2000) *The Invention of Modern Science*. Minneapolis: University of Minnesota Press (Theory Out of Bounds, v. 19).

Thompson, P. (2016) 'Ernst Bloch and the spirituality of Utopia', *Rethinking Marxism*, 28(3–4), pp. 438–452. doi:10.1080/08935696.2016.1243417.

Urry, J. (2016) *What is the Future?* John Wiley & Sons.

Veletsianos, G. (2010) *Emerging Technologies in Distance Education*. Athabasca University Press. Available at: http://www.aupress.ca/index.php/books/120177 (Accessed: 17 June 2022).

Walker, R. (2011) 'Design-based research: Reflections on some epistemological issues and practices', in Markauskaite, L., Freebody, P., and Irwin, J. (Eds) *Methodological Choice and Design: Scholarship, Policy and Practice in Social and Educational Research.* Dordrecht: Springer Science & Business Media, pp. 51–56.

Zydney, J.M., Warner, Z. and Angelone, L. (2020) 'Learning through experience: Using design based research to redesign protocols for blended synchronous learning environments', *Computers & Education*, 143, pp. 1–14. doi:10.1016/j.compedu.2019.103678.

4
SPECULATIVE APPROACHES TO RESEARCH AND TEACHING

Introduction

Like the imaginaries discussed in Chapter 2, speculation appears frequently in contemporary writing and thinking about the future. Practices of speculation are of interest to scholars of philosophy, economics, literature, sociology, design and science and technology studies, and in relation to education and learning. Writing about the role of philosophy, Dewey (1927) lamented the lack of progress in science, including social science and psychology, caused by a lack of imaginative speculation:

> What is the matter? It lies, I think, with our lack of imagination in generating leading ideas. Because we are afraid of speculative ideas, we do, and do over and over again, an immense amount of dead, specialized work in the region of 'facts.' We forget that facts are only data; that is, are only fragmentary, uncompleted meanings... unless they are rounded out into complete ideas – a work which can only be done by hypotheses, by a free imagination of intellectual possibilities.
>
> *(Dewey, 1927, p. 8)*

He goes on to call for more "speculative audacity" (p. 9), a call which has been taken up through the years across a number of contexts and disciplines (Greene, 1988; Pringle, 2012; Savransky, 2017).

Dewey's critique of facts as incomplete echoes the previous chapter's discussion of "what works" (Biesta, 2007), and articulates some of the trouble we have seen in educational research that lacks engagement with complexity. The trouble is also found in futures thinking that foregrounds prediction over exploration, as

DOI: 10.4324/9781003202134-5

we saw in Chapter 2. However, some forms of speculation – notably financial speculation – are equally problematic in this regard. So, a clear sense of what I mean by speculation – and the various forms it can take – is essential to understand the speculative approaches discussed in this chapter.

The authors of a 2013 manifesto called *Speculate This!* propose that there are two registers for speculation – economic and cognitive – and these are connected by "investments [that] project into and stake claims for the future" (Uncertain Commons, 2013, p. 7). They differ, however, in their attitude to uncertainty, aligning with either "firmative" or "affirmative" modes of speculation. Firmative speculation attempts to solidify, pin down or enclose the future. It is what permits measurement and calculation, and therefore management, of risk (Cortiel et al., 2020). Affirmative speculation, on the other hand, creatively engages with uncertainty using intuition and play (Uncertain Commons, 2013). While the Uncertain Commons highlight the distinctiveness of these two modes, Cortiel et al. (2020) attempt instead to understand how they intersect, combine or sometimes seem indistinguishable when they are enacted in practice and when their effects play out. The specifics of enactment are key for my purposes, because the interplay of certainty and uncertainty, as we saw in Chapter 3's discussion of not-yetness, is a hallmark of speculative methods.

In the previous chapter, I described a complexity-informed view of learning as a response to disturbance, difference and irritation (Biesta, 2005). I argued that gaining an understanding of the complexity of learning requires creative approaches, including speculative methods. Speculative methods are aimed at envisioning or crafting futures or conditions which may not yet currently exist, to provoke new ways of thinking and to bring particular ideas or issues into focus. Michael (2012) describes them as "'inventive problem making' in which the parameters of the issue are reconfigured" (p. 536). In their foundational speculative design text, Dunne and Raby (2013) critique the "downgrading of dreams to hopes" (p. 8) that characterises the contemporary moment and its wicked problems, and identify in speculative design a way to support critical imagination about the future, and about the present. Critique through speculative design can make unseen limitations more visible and "loosen, even just a bit, reality's grip on our imagination" (p. 3). Speculative approaches, as I define them, work with the future as a space of uncertainty, and use that uncertainty creatively in the present.

Enactments of speculative methods are found in critical design, speculative design (DiSalvo, 2012; Dunne and Raby, 2013), inventive method (Lury and Wakeford, 2012) and design fiction, and across the social sciences and art and design disciplines. Speculative methods are often described as research methods, but they are equally suited to teaching contexts, as we will see – and their close couplings of provocation, engagement and inquiry are a good fit with the complex knowledge-production spaces of learning and education. More than this, Osberg (2010) argues that education can engage more experimentally with possibilities for the future than other domains. If this is the case, it may be necessary for speculative work to happen in learning settings if it is to happen anywhere. Speculative methods can provide ways to explore educational possibilities from within ongoing shifts in political, cultural, social and technological dimensions of education and the uncertainty they produce (Veletsianos, 2020).

For example, in his book on speculative design innovation for higher education, Staley (2019) presents a number of different visions for the future of universities. Each chapter of the book proposes a different kind of future university, with focal concepts including platforms, microcredits, humanities, mobility and play, amongst others. In his chapter on play, he introduces the "Institute for Advanced Play", in which higher learning is based on "generative creation: imagining that which does not exist, bringing the new into being, making serendipitous connections, seeking unexpected answers. The Institute for Advanced Play places wonder and curiosity at the center of its enterprise" (p. 161). Rather than being identified as teachers and students, everyone is a "fellow" (though some are "advanced") selected through a competitive process, and fellows are organised into temporary teams according to "play personalities". The purpose of the institute is to ask "what if" questions and then try to answer them through simulations or the building of small- or large-scale structures and organisations. In his discussion of this imagined university, he emphasises the value of play for adults, and defines play as a "disposition" rather than an activity (p. 165). Fellows engage in all kinds of play that blur spatial and temporal boundaries – including role playing the past, producing virtual worlds and hacking systems and ideas. In addition to play without specific end goals, there are also "innovation" projects sponsored by businesses and organisations, and those organisations can also place employees in the institute. Staley discusses the tension between "pure" and "applied" play, and describes the Institute as a place where these "uneasily coexist" (p. 173), with external pressures, poaching of fellows and consultancy opportunities potentially disturbing or changing the openness of the play that takes place there.

This is just one of ten distinct speculative designs for universities that make up Staley's book. He argues that higher education is not simply a transactional exchange of money for accreditation, and that depending on how it is envisaged, its transformative potential might be harnessed in a number of different directions. He describes these designs as "feasible utopias" (p. 14). The present book focuses on teachers, researchers and students, and in that context, there is much that can be done with and as a result of speculative approaches, as we will see. Staley encourages university leaders, too, to engage in more imaginative future-making. If a speculative sensibility is to be a more significant part of the strategic and policy work of universities, as well as teaching and research activities, this means that speculative approaches have to be understood within an ethical framework that is appropriate to work that might make things happen – because it really might.

I propose that there are three main qualities of speculative methods that are essential to understanding what they are and what they can do, and these relate to temporality, epistemology and performativity (Ross, 2017). First, speculative methods function within a complex interplay of past, present and future (temporality). Second, they are overtly constitutive of the problems, topics and questions they engage with (Wilkie, Michael and Plummer-Fernandez, 2015), which makes them epistemologically challenging. Indeed, in the social sciences, speculative methods are a response to some of the epistemological issues raised in the previous chapter – linearity, fixity and the tendency of research to underplay the extent to which it is involved in creating the realities it uncovers. Third, these methods centre engagement and audience in a way that adds to the glitchiness (Bodden and Ross, 2021) and unpredictability of their effects (performativity). When I refer to speculative *methods* in this chapter, I am talking about both research and pedagogical approaches – and the examples I will discuss frequently bridge the two. Later, in Chapters 9 and 10, I will attempt to disentangle them in order to provide practical insights and guidance about the use of speculative approaches in research and teaching, respectively.

After discussing each of these qualities, I will go on to show how these approaches can support research and teaching about learning, with reference to some recent examples of speculation in use in the field. Finally, the chapter situates the second part of the book, which looks in detail at four different speculative engagements with digital learning futures from the past decade.

Temporality and speculative method

Speculative methods, as with other approaches to thinking about the future, have an uneasy relationship with time and temporality that reflects the discussion of not-yetness in the previous chapter. As we saw in Chapter 2, futures are made in a variety of ways, but share an embeddedness in their particular place and time (whether acknowledged or not) – they are contingent and contextual. The intersection of hope, expectation, uncertainty and influence produces a state of not-yetness in knowledge claims and explorations of the future. Not-yetness carries multiple overlapping temporalities and is never simply about the future. The pedagogical futures we envisage inform us about what matters now, what issues and problems we have inherited and what debates define what can and cannot currently be thought about or imagined. Duggan (2019) describes futures as social practices made up of assumptions – for example, about the role of networked technologies (p. 119). These assumptions both reflect the present (they are spatially and temporally framed), and are enacted through what Springgay and Truman (2018) have referred to as "events of becoming". The present itself, for example in the context of the global Covid-19 pandemic, can take on the form of a speculative event, "squeezed between a radically contingent future and a past impossible to fix" (Cortiel et al., 2020, p. 8). Truman (2019), in her

60 Understanding learning futures

analysis of queer and Afrofuturist modes of speculation in science fiction, draws attention to how their distinctive temporalities resist and unsettle heteronormative and neoliberal worldbuilding. She notes that, in both, time is queered – with futurities "haunting" the present (p. 40). Haunted, unsettled, unfixed, squeezed and becoming, the present always contains and consists of multiple versions of the past and the future, and these can be exposed in useful, if challenging, ways by the use of speculative methods.

We can see this uneasiness in the use of speculation in technology design disciplines such as human computer interaction, design informatics and ubiquitous computing. While the practices of design fiction, for example, focus on the future, theorists in these fields also emphasise the trouble with looking ahead. For example, Dourish and Bell (2011) discuss how ubiquitous computing is framed as technology still emerging, and always belonging to the near future. By positioning it in this way, researchers and developers refuse responsibility for its impacts in the present. However, Auger (2013) is optimistic that speculative design can lead to generative approaches for critiquing and reimagining contemporary technology. A good example of this comes from Dumit (2021), who explores technical lags in video gaming and financial trading, and describes these as "shared speculative experiences" that prompt new questions: "What happens when lags are persistent, when we encounter them as things we have to creatively adapt to? How do they in turn warp reality by warping time…? …What kind of lag-time is this?" (p. 98).

The politics of speculative design come under scrutiny by Gonzatto et al. (2013), who describe design fictions as inevitably a product of someone who is acting in an interested (not uncommitted) way on the present. Design fictions are not "mere speculation" (p. 40), because visions of the future generate effects in the present. The temporalities of speculative method and design are therefore unstable and interwoven: "design fictions form part of the genre of an estranged futurity-to-come; they form a part of the contemporary technological prospective. … a distributed accumulation of past or otherwise temporary futures" (Hales, 2013, p. 7). Hales is hopeful that this complex of temporalities creates openings for new theoretical and artistic approaches, but seems to acknowledge that they can never be frictionless.

In the context of digital education, visions of the future of learning are often presented with apparent certainty, regardless of the success of the predictions made. Indeed, there is relatively little critical attention paid in digital education settings to the consequences of predictions which do not play out as envisaged (this is the case in other settings as well, as Pollock and Williams (2010) describe in their work on promissory organisations). This is unfortunate, as engagement with disappointment and failure can be generative in helping to grapple with indeterminacy, as I argued in the previous chapter. For instance, in their work on the use of virtual reality (VR) to support students' divergent thinking skills, Melo et al. (2019) encountered situations that were deeply at odds with the promised futures VR could usher in. Issues with technologies which were not yet ready for deployment led the teaching team, backed up by research funding to undertake a pedagogical project using VR, to "lose sight of the investigation [as we] found ourselves consumed with making any part of the VR environment work consistently at all" (p. 9). They theorise this shift using Berlant's theory of "cruel optimism" (2011), "when something you desire is actually an obstacle to your flourishing" (p. 1), and note that this led to a situation where "even when our technologies failed repeatedly and we missed milestone after milestone, we were unswerving in our commitment to continue" (Melo et al., 2019, p. 9). The team was eventually able to shift their understanding of their project from one that was not yet succeeding, to one that had failed, and to generate significant insights from this shift. However, the investment of time, money and social capital in projects such as these, and in new products and processes, often means that such insights cannot be valid outputs. We are therefore stuck in problematic loops of not-yetness, where predicted futures are endlessly deferred or reconfigured. Speculative methods, handled sensitively, may facilitate a different and valuable relationship between past, present and future.

Epistemology and speculative method

A central and influential argument for speculation in qualitative research has come about not because of a specific interest in the future, but from a need to try to undo "the logic of procedure and extraction" (Springgay and Truman, 2018, p. 204). By beginning in the "speculative middle", research can be understood as "speculative eventing", rather than as a process of gathering data (ibid). Springgay and Truman insist that methods themselves are not the issue. Instead, it is the tendency for methods to be predetermined and procedural, rather than to act from within problems (to problematise), that sits uneasily with relational understandings of research. Fox (2018) describes this as a theoretical move from the problem to the problematic, which he defines as "the shifting connections between constituting relations that form a particular context" (p. 157). In a similar vein, Lury (2021) writes of "problem space" as

> a space of methodological potential that is with-in and out-with the ongoing transformation of a problem. The potential is realized in a methodology that, rather than responding only to the initial presentation of a problem, composes the problem again and again.
>
> *(p. 5)*

Such an orientation can create difficulties in practice, as researchers may come to feel that they are abdicating responsibility for or losing control of their work (Georgis and Matthews, 2021). However, the obstructions that can result may lead to greater attention to the "problematic" itself as transcendent and persistent

62 Understanding learning futures

within and beyond the solutions offered to it (Savransky, 2018). These are not only philosophical matters – Benjamin has argued, for example, that speculative methods provide vital experimental space for both analysts and activists to "anticipate and intervene in new racial formations that… may appear to be a kind of radical intervention but may very well entail their own logics of extinction" (Benjamin, 2016, p. 22).

This work of anticipation and intervention signals that the epistemological foundations of speculative methods ask for an expansive understanding of what research can and should do. Different disciplines have taken up this challenge differently – for example, Drucker's (2009) approach to "speculative computing" aimed to create aesthetic provocations using computational methods, to draw attention to the role of subjectivity and interpretation in digital humanities. Rather than making devices "do things", Drucker proposes a speculative register for computing that can highlight how all forms of expression are acts of interpretation, with implications for computational acts of sorting, ordering and comparing.

Within the social sciences research methods literature, an important related concept is "inventive method" (Lury and Wakeford, 2012). Inventive methods often are not specifically orientated to the future, but to making a difference through investigation of and engagement with "the open-endedness of the social world" (p. 2). They are particularly attuned to epistemological issues, because inventiveness, for Lury and Wakefield, means that "answerability" of the problem at hand is introduced by crafting a method specifically to address that problem, and inventive methods change the problem they address. This epistemological blurring of problem and answer is what Lury (2021) has referred to recently as "compositional methodology". While the speculative approaches explored in this book tend more towards applied use of material or digital "objects-to-think-with", inventive methods can be and often are more conceptual in nature. Researchers engaging with inventive methods have used as devices or interventions of interest everything from the tape recorder, to the list, to the photo-image.

Lury and Wakeford summarise inventive approaches as:

> methods or means by which the social world is not only investigated, but may also be engaged… the knowledge of change they permit need not be limited to ascertaining what is going on now or predicting what will go on soon, but may rather be a matter of configuring what comes next.
>
> *(p. 6)*

In practice, this means that the legitimacy of a method as inventive is closely tied to its ability to engage with and affect the problem it addresses. Speculative approaches share this attention to engagement and configuration. For instance, sociologists Wilkie, Michael and Plummer-Fernandez (2015) describe a speculative method involving the creation of a series of "Twitter-bots" to participate in public exchanges about environmental issues. They characterise these bots as "open, ambiguous or troublesome", but able to evoke new formulations of issues (p. 80). They define methodology itself as "a process of asking inventive, that is, more provocative questions" (p. 82). Like Lury and Wakefield, Wilkie *et al* identify the active creation of issues through a research intervention.

The epistemological tensions this produces are not new. Ambiguity is a key epistemological dimension of speculative methods, and such ambiguity is challenging in research contexts where stability and replicability are valued.[1] Offering a challenge to the authors of a special issue on post-qualitative research, Greene (2013) highlights the problem with insisting on the "dynamic, fluid, indefinite, unfolding" nature of such research, asking what warrant or truth claim may be made for it, or what meaningful impacts it can have (p. 753). Here the importance of the "object of study" comes to the fore in speculative methods. Speculative methods can respect the "recalcitrance of the object of study" (MacLure, 2006, p. 734), its complexity and its unsettling nature. Ambiguity and recalcitrance are important, because paying attention to them helps resist the idea that, in working speculatively, "anything goes". Law's (2004) method assemblages, for instance, are built on a commitment to "pre-existing social and material realities" (p. 13). He calls for assemblages that are generous and uncertain, and suggests multiplicity, imaginaries, indefiniteness and re-enchantment as important contributors to methodological practice.

Teaching speculatively in digital contexts, we must equally allow for ambiguities and be prepared to craft and adapt our pedagogical approaches to take account of these. One of the challenges that confront researchers and teachers is continually drawing and redrawing the conceptual and pedagogical boundaries of what we mean by education and learning (see Chapter 3 for more on this). This challenge is of course not *limited* to digital education, but is present when technologies, and the subjectivities and practices associated with them, are at play, because they are so underdetermined (Poster, 1999) – able to be reconfigured and drawn into multiple imaginaries. Speculative methods can help us visualise and critique the possible nature and consequences of particular kinds of complexity and boundary-making.

Engagement, performativity and speculative method

A third key element of speculative method is its interactive and performative properties. Speculative methods are performative in the sense discussed earlier, that they are part of what produces the problem or object of study. In practice, this means that, as forms of communication, they *act* to create the futures they portray. In part, they do this through their focus on engaging publics at different scales and in a variety of contexts, including in formal and informal learning contexts.

64 Understanding learning futures

Researchers and teachers in design fields draw particular attention to issues of speculative engagement: DiSalvo (2012) defines speculative design as "the use of designerly means to express foresight in compelling, often provocative ways, which are intended to engage audiences in considerations of what might be" (DiSalvo, 2012, p. 109). Auger (2013) focuses on the centrality of the audience towards whom a given speculative design is directed. He explores the sorts of issues that can arise when the design and its intended audience are not well-matched – principally, that the design is not sufficiently relatable to engage or connect with the audience, which our case might mean research participants, partners, students or others involved in a speculative approach. Educational research faces imperatives to engage with research users, and indeed one reason given for the rise of design-based research (discussed in Chapter 3) is the alienation of practitioner and policymaker audiences from more abstract or theoretical research. Auger's point is that designers require "conceptual bridges" (p. 12) for their design fictions, which create a connection between the fictions being produced, and the audience's current perception of their world. Bridging techniques include consideration of context (ecological approach); provocation (uncanny approach); verisimilitude, familiarity, specificity, attention to detail and going to extremes (observational comedy approach); and the use of counterfactuals. Such techniques offer insights to researchers in digital education, as they work to engage stakeholders with concepts and findings, especially those concepts which may be counter-intuitive or otherwise challenging. Beyond simply engaging audiences or participants, there are also questions about how speculation might come to matter to them – including through what Elsden et al. (2017) call "Speculative Enactments". These enactments are consequential, activity-focused and co-constructive, with attention paid to the world-building that frames them and a focus on interventions into the mundane or routine. They are designed with ethical considerations in mind, precisely because they are designed to matter, and issues of informed consent are therefore potentially problematic in almost direct proportion to how successful the enactments are.

The notion of audience may also be problematic, however. The value of academic research has been reframed in recent years away from "dissemination" towards increasing emphasis on practices of public engagement, knowledge exchange, participation and impact (Bannister and O'Sullivan, 2013). As those who attempt public engagement with non-academic audiences discover, though, participants have a tendency to "misbehave" (Michael, 2012, p. 529) in ways that work against the context of the engagement event. How speculative method's "audiences" are framed, in other words, requires careful consideration of the possible roles of students, participants, users, stakeholders, critical friends and so on. It also requires ways of preserving and documenting the overspills, not succumbing to clean them up to avoid challenging the assumptions that have informed the engagement event (ibid). Talking of the metaphorical figure of the "idiot",

Speculative approaches to research and teaching **65**

which transforms events by resisting consensus and insists on "something more important" (Stengers, in Michael 2012, p. 535), Michael explains the balancing act involved in heeding, but not attempting to tame, such interventions:

> As soon as we think we have 'deployed' the idiot, slowed our thinking, and invented novel problems, we have also tamed it, and the process of querying our assumptions has become compromised. The idiot reminds us that we must never get too comfortable with 'what we are busy doing' – we should be open to creative or inventive problem making.
>
> *(pp. 536–7)*

Galloway and Caudwell (2018) explain the value of the problematic slightly differently, as being about "staying with the trouble" (in Haraway's (2016) terms), not providing solutions. They note that thoughtful engagement on the part of participants is in itself a valuable outcome of speculative research.

Digital education publics can comprise community members, students, teachers, families, learning technologists, administrators, employers, workers, museum visitors, policymakers and commercial interests. Furthermore, almost anyone who has been educated themselves will have a view and some beliefs about what sorts of educational futures are desirable. Often unquestioned assumptions about the importance of the "human touch" in education, for example, have informed debate about the sufficiency of online learning for decades (Dreyfus, 2001). Indeed, Markham (2021) argues that without careful design and planning of engagements, people tend to encounter various kinds of "discursive closures" in speculating about the future of technology. These come about because existing technological practices and designs are not seen as part of chains of decision-making or historically situated, and instead appear as "processes that just exist" (p. 392). This results, she notes, in the reproduction of an understanding of technology as inevitable and people as powerless to generate different kinds of futures. Speculative method can expose and work with such assumptions in novel ways, and interventions can be crafted to engage with a variety of publics, as the chapters in Part 2 show. There may also be times, however, when an inventive approach includes silences and gaps as part of its design, and these approaches, too, have something to tell us about the things that speculative design can make happen (Knox, 2014; Ross, 2017).

When thinking through these issues, the identities of audiences or participants for speculative engagements require attention. The performativity of speculative method has considerable potential to allow for different sorts of stories and engagements. However, as has been pointed out in recent literature, audiences for participatory design interventions have tended to be relatively homogenous and not representative of communities with a significant stake in particular futures (Harrington and Dillahunt, 2021). Working with young people of colour

66 Understanding learning futures

in a virtual design workshop setting, Harrington and Dillahunt used Afrofuturist perspectives to engage participants about technology's role in the future. They argue that the distinctive kinds of utopian and dystopian discourses that emerge from engaging with different audiences should not be underplayed, but also observe that lived experiences, especially racism, can greatly constrain the futures young people can envision.

Speculative approaches themselves have the potential to be extractive and to further the colonisation of futures and imaginaries. For instance, in their work on the speculative turn in anthropology, Chandler and Reid (2020) critique Haraway's speculative "Camille" narrative about non-settler ways of living (Haraway, 2016), arguing that her dream of "becoming indigenous" appropriates indigeneity and creates more problems than it solves. When considering speculative methods in teaching and research, researchers and educators need to critically question the dynamics of voice and engagement they are mobilising.

Speculation in practice: examples from research and teaching

When I began exploring speculative methods in 2014, there was little education-related literature to draw on to show how these methods could be enacted. Since that time, there has been a flourishing of accounts of the use of such approaches in technology fields as well as in digital education research. Often these are futures-focused, but some are situated in relation to the present or the past. In addition, the range of accounts of pedagogical experiments and speculative approaches to teaching has also grown in fields such as social anthropology (Gaspar, 2018), law (Fiesler, 2021) and art (Atkinson, 2020), or in interdisciplinary contexts (Osborn et al., 2019). This work has used speculative methods to cast new light on topics or engage students with new ways of thinking about key issues and questions, and has relevance for teaching about digital education topics. This section discusses some of this literature and highlights some current tendencies in the use of speculative approaches.

Researching digital education speculatively

The research landscape in digital education has recently shifted to incorporate much more critical futures work. I suggest this is at least partly due to how the field has had to respond to increasingly influential edtech imaginaries that are shaping policy and practice (Ross, 2017). There are a number of speculative methods being used by researchers in this context, and I offer a categorisation here based on a review of the recent literature: fictions, researcher-made objects, design activities for participants and speculative analysis. Michael (2021) identifies categories of speculative fabulation (the creation of stories, speculative narration of new ideas and possibilities) and speculative fabrication (designing and introducing artefacts and activities that enable people to "open up inventive problems" (p. 80)), but notes that these categories can blur, and that is the case with some of the methods described here.

In a 2020 special issue of the journal *Learning, Media and Technology*, focused on speculative futures, a number of storytelling approaches were brought together, and these form an important foundation for this kind of work in the field of digital education. Researcher-written speculative stories go by a number of names: most commonly **social science fiction, design fiction or speculative fiction**. They mostly take the form of short stories or vignettes, often incorporated into or cited in scholarly articles. They are echoed and influenced by the use of speculative fiction in broader technology studies and sociological fields (see for example: Benjamin, 2016; Graham et al., 2019), and they are typically set in schools or universities. They tend towards the dystopian, perhaps influenced by some of the same "discursive closures" Markham (2021) observes, but also because they tend to focus on the implications of data-driven education and platformisation, about which there has been a significant amount of critical work done in the past decade that has highlighted the inequalities and risks that come with increasing datafication and privatisation. So, for example, Hillman, Rensfeldt and Ivarsson's (2020) three speculative scenarios cover feature creep and privatisation, data exploitation, and recentralisation in a future Swedish school system, building on their review and analysis of the current state of the system. They highlight the risks, the persuasiveness and, eventually, the ubiquity of such a system:

> Even once a degree of teacher resistance to what was seen by some as dictating students' futures emerged, it was hard to argue with unemployment rates falling to a record low as more and more students seemed to find an interest in sectors where jobs were available. By optimising the local process of student feedback against goals articulated elsewhere, [the] system began to shape interests and success at an individual level.
>
> *(p. 12)*

Selwyn et al. (2020), building stories around a Melbourne, Australia-based school of 2030 they call Lakeside, look at the mundane realities that people in this school might experience. They note that a focus on the mundane "is most suited to generating thinking that is congruent with ideologically predetermined futures... The everyday realities of education have rarely proven to be spectacular over the past 100 years, so we were interested in imagining what schools might be like 10 years from now if things do not somehow turn out to be radically different" (p. 91). Their linked stories paint a picture of a "standardized, benchmarked and centralized" system that has "little room for affective, embodied and spontaneous action" (p. 104). Cox (2021), analysing possible futures for artificial

68 Understanding learning futures

intelligence in higher education, observes the complex temporalities involved in telling stories about this topic:

> rather than a single technology, something like AI is an idea or aspiration for how computers could participate in human decision making. Faith in how to do this has shifted across different technologies over time; as have concepts of learning… confusingly from a temporal perspective, uses of AI and robots in HE are past, present and future.
>
> *(p. 2)*

Cox describes his own use of fiction as a research output, but observes that fictions are also used to elicit research data or can be co-created with publics (p. 3). Speculative methods in general also include these categories. For instance, several studies involve **researchers building speculative objects** – digital or physical – for participants to engage with. Knox (2017) describes his "Learning Analytics Report Card" (LARC) project where students were invited to experiment with textual reports on their engagement, automatically generated from course-related activity in a virtual learning environment. Students were able to "play" with the inclusion and exclusion of certain aspects of the data and the timing of reporting (p. 743), and to speak back to the report card in the form of comments. LARC offered a space for students to speculate about alternatives to the predictive and "black boxed" nature of most learning analytics provision. The Teacherbot and Artcasting projects, likewise, took a speculative elicitation approach – and these projects will be discussed in detail in Chapters 5 and 7. In a blurring of researcher-participant roles, Ward-Davies et al. (2020) engaged in a socially distanced zine-making process, where a learning community (the Melbourne-based "SciCurious" community, part of a larger Science Gallery International programme bringing art and science together) passed physical, handmade magazines (zines) around by post, adding, removing and changing them as they went. As one co-author and participant noted,

> The power of this participatory speculative research has been that you, as SciCurious members, have done the collision work on your own and seen what happens when we disrupt the disciplinary spaces of art and science. In this research, you have been able to show what that curiosity might actually feel like, instead of telling a story. Working in this project has changed the way that I begin to speculate as an artist and practitioner.
>
> *(p. 14)*

This work has resonance with a number of projects where researchers have designed events or activities that **ask participants to generate prototypes** or other speculative material. In a series of engagements with young people about their ideas of the future, Priyadharshini (2019) invited participants to bring in

Speculative approaches to research and teaching **69**

their pop culture influences to inform their speculations, which tend, as she notes, to:

> inhabit[] darker worlds, reveling in the pleasures and potential of speculative and dramatic anticipations... a chief characteristic of speculative narratives is their break from more realist styles, as the host of sub-genres they encompass indicate – horror, gothic, supernatural, fairy tales, magic realism, sci-fi, cli-fi, dystopia.
>
> *(p. 3)*

These sit in contrast to the sorts of futures that are produced through "pragmatic and programmable decisions about the tomorrow" (p. 1) most common in schools and other formal settings where young people are asked to think about their futures. Also using pop culture, in this case as a way to elicit speculative futures from young Black people, who are frequently underrepresented in design work around technology futures, Harrington and Dillahunt (2021) introduced participants to Afrofuturist work and to the dystopian sci-fi television series Black Mirror. They hosted six virtual design sessions for students of the Design Apprenticeship Program in Chicago, Illinois, with outputs including a design workbook that recorded students' utopian and dystopian visions, ideations and design fictions. In two projects set in urban spaces in a disadvantaged area of Brussels in Belgium, Nijs et al. (2020) produced "speculative fabulations" ("spec-fabs") with young people, inviting them to engage in re-imagining relations with non-humans (squid and ghosts) using stencils, string, LED lights, simple electronics and various craft materials. Working with university students, faculty and staff to explore possible futures for teacher automation, Gallagher and Breines (2021) facilitated prototype-building workshops which, combined with interview data, generated 85 discrete use-cases for instances of automation in a future university. Some selected use-cases were planned to be developed into working prototypes to test further. Staunæs and Brøgger (2020) conducted a speculative experiment with 30 doctoral students, to re-imagine university data futures in a more caring, affirming register that could reconfigure what "counted". As part of this, students were asked to "ruminate on and collect artefacts, other than graphs and numbers, that make it possible to 'bring home energy' to the university and the academics" (p. 437). One group of students chose artificial fur as their artefact because of its "soft, embracing nature":

> Created by humans due to its artificial character, not utilising other species. Something that could be offered to you as an academic, something not connoting measurement and performance, rather a particular kind of warm spaciousness. A different kind of motivation. Warm but not heated. Calm, not hectic. All of which, they explained, felt very different from what they actually experienced as PhD students.
>
> *(p. 439)*

70 Understanding learning futures

A final category of speculative method in research involves the creation of **speculative outputs or analysis** based on research data. Smythe et al. (2018) found speculative analysis essential to grapple with the "'wicked' and entangled issues" (p. 21) that emerged from their project examining a mobile van for supporting digital literacies amongst Vancouver, Canada's low-income and homeless population. These issues included problems of scarcity, the slippage of digital inclusion to a more radical demand for more equitable digital landscapes, and the tensions between anonymity and relationality in providing community services. For them, the "not-yetness" of the sociotechnical landscape they were working in required reaching *beyond* the technological to a more experimental way of thinking about learning and resource sharing. Ehret and Čiklovan (2020) built on a multimodal discourse analysis of toxic digital discourse on the Twitch.tv live-streamed gaming platform to produce a "critical remix video" to synthesise toxic content and then reconfigure it to communicate and expose "pernicious ideologies and behaviors" (p. 709). They propose adding to speculative methods in education a focus on emerging technocultures, arguing that pedagogical development should flow from "emerging experiences of digital, social life" (p. 721). For them, speculative design experiments need to develop "new pedagogic potentials that themselves may inform social change through youths' expanded and nuanced repertoire of digital practices in the future" (ibid). In a similar vein, Lamb (2017) asked undergraduate research participants to contribute playlists of music tracks they found conducive to study, as part of his work on the sonic spaces of learning. Working with the idea of playlists and with the playlists themselves supported new questions about meaning-making around study and assessment, and the role of algorithms and platforms in producing learning spaces (see also Issar (2021) on the speculative production of algorithmic dissonance). Finally, conducting an analysis of two speculative fictions, Garforth and Iossifidis (2021) note their potential to offer "weird tales, uncanny atmospheres, and inhuman agencies" to support

> green utopianism… [that can] work in the here and now, with and through the end of the world, acknowledging the monsters and ghosts that supposedly rational societies have made, and come up with new arts for living on a damaged planet.
>
> *(p. 3)*

Overall, what we see in these different approaches to speculative method is an attempt to attune to different sensibilities – of participants, of data, of the process of making futures. From the nature of learning space to the production of interdisciplinarity, from mundane AI to young people's Afrofuturist-inspired technological imaginaries, speculative methods act on and within the problems and questions they generate. They also raise some questions about how to think about their credibility and value, given that they are inventively constructed and

Speculative approaches to research and teaching **71**

deployed by researchers in a way that is not following established methodological precedent, but attempting to engage the world and its messiness more creatively, imaginatively and inventively. These questions are picked up in Chapter 9. I turn now to consider the existing research and scholarship on teaching with speculative methods, and the theoretical and practice insights this offers.

Teaching with speculative methods

For my purposes in this book, teaching spans a number of different contexts and approaches, including facilitation and leadership in informal learning spaces, museums and galleries, and community settings. For example, Dewey's sensibility of "speculative audacity" has informed the teaching of history (Greene, 1988) and gallery education (Pringle, 2012), in both cases with a focus on imagination about "what lies beyond the accustomed boundaries and …what is not yet" (Greene, 1988, pp. 127–8).[2] For Pringle, the gallery is a complex space for learning because of the tensions inherent there between speculative and authoritative ways of knowing:

> where meanings are not necessarily fixed and where the art itself is frequently concerned with speculation… [but] for the majority of the twentieth century (and arguably into the twenty-first) galleries have understood their role to be primarily concerned with the accumulation, conservation and dispensation of this knowledge.
>
> *(p. 117)*

Rousell and Hickey-Moody (2020) engaged in speculative experimentation in their community-based art education practice, noticing "an emerging political aesthetics at play… a political aesthetics that is shaped by non-discursive and speculative experimentations with alternative forms of life and relations of care" (p. 100). Like Pringle, they draw attention to the labour involved in supporting alternative "modes of belonging", however anarchic they may appear (p. 101).

Osborn et al. (2019) described their pedagogical approach to engaging with historical materials in a speculative manner as "retrofuturology". They embarked on a year-long "experiment in interdisciplinary pedagogy" with a focus on Georgetown University's Old North Building in Washington, DC. The Pilgrimage project brought together students and teachers from six courses on topics including creative writing, media production and museum studies, and "applied the not-yetness of speculative method [to explore] how technological, artistic, and creative projects can inspire and maintain student engagement when directed toward a topic of shared concern" (p. 351). Using approaches such as mediated collaboration (where student work from one course was used as prompts for another), students ultimately produced a public exhibition. The authors describe a four-stage "Pilgrimage model":

72 Understanding learning futures

Discovery – choosing a common focus that is experienced and analyzed through a variety of techniques and building a shared research archive through targeted coursework;

Investigation – analyzing the archive using disciplinary methods. The archive serves as a repository of past discoveries, a resource for ongoing research, and a source for new interpretations;

Experimentation – developing technical skills that activate the archive using speculative, experimental, and critical design methods;

Articulation – communicating the archive, research findings, and interpretations to public and scholarly audiences through multimedia and digital projects.

(p. 363)

Speculative uses of the past are seen too in Nooney and Brain's (2019) "speculative pasts" assignment for students, which challenges them to "interweave historical thinking with speculative design, inviting thinking and experimentation with the relationship between social conditions and technological development" (p. 223) by developing historical artefacts based on hypothetical alternative histories of personal computing.

A need for new approaches to teaching students how to look and think ethnographically sparked Gaspar's (2018) development of speculative "laboratories", including a "kit of idiotic objects for social research" (p. 82) and the prototyping of a speculative museum (p. 85). These approaches were speculative because they related to theory in an open and exploratory way (p. 85), and because they took a designerly, improvisational approach and an interest in "otherness": "I was exposing students to the other, [and] the other (that which was unknown to me in first place) was being produced through the very pedagogical opportunities created" (p. 86).

Fiesler (2021), a law educator, identifies a role for speculation in teaching students how to engage their legal imaginations – a crucial skill for foreseeing and responding to potential consequences of emerging technologies, including "potential harms that are difficult to anticipate" (p. 15):

the legal imagination requires perceiving connections between the general and the specific – or even the general and the speculative. When asking my students to imagine both the promise and the potential harms of the technology they might create, I am asking them to both extrapolate from the pitfalls of the past and to imagine uses and circumstances beyond their control.

(p. 10)

To do this, she worked with students to analyse the legal implications of science-fictional accounts (such as those in the TV series Black Mirror) and to produce others, arguing that "if students can get excited about thinking through the ethical and legal implications of some technology that someone else might create a hundred years from now, they should be able to do the same with the technology that they are creating right now" (p. 14).

Unsurprisingly, design disciplines have been engaging with speculative pedagogies for many years, with their contemporary form emerging at the Royal College of Art in London in the early 1990s (Mitrović et al., 2021, p. 174). Recently, the Speculative.edu project, involving universities and organisations from Croatia, the UK, Portugal, Italy and Slovenia, produced a range of resources for speculative design education, including the *Beyond Speculative Design* textbook (Mitrović et al., 2021). Through a series of case studies, they identify tensions in the use of speculative design: inclusion, engagement, the use of design objects as props or products, and the nature of "completion". They suggest that educators need to engage with the complexity engendered by and expressed in these tensions (p. 163), and that

> whilst examining and critiquing [critical speculative design] work, we must always consider that many of the projects are the material evidence of a learning process – therefore inherently vulnerable and open to mistakes.
>
> *(p. 172)*

This vulnerability is not limited to the projects themselves, but potentially to teachers, also. The design of learning activities can be informed by speculative approaches, as Konnerup, Ryberg and Sørensen (2019) discuss. Concerned about the tendency of learning design approaches to adopt prescriptive approaches that can "break the intimate link between the teacher's beliefs and the practice of designing and teaching" (p. 119), they propose speculative design as a generative way of allowing for greater co-creation and exploration of learning objectives (p. 123), and supporting "dynamic, experimental opportunities for the collective design of new practices" (pp. 124–5). As Atkinson (2020) puts it, in the context of art education, "speculative pedagogies therefore evoke …a politics and ethics of the suddenly possible" (p. 58). He asks,

> In contrast to the regulatory forces of transcendence and prescription, can we view the practice of pedagogic work as a process of adventure? Can we conceive it as a process of experimentation without criteria, that attempts to parallel the immanence and difference of ways in which learners learn, some of which often lie beyond or are disobedient to our established parameters of pedagogic and artistic practice?
>
> *(p. 64)*

74 Understanding learning futures

These are questions about the nature of learning, but also about the structures, spaces and processes of education. In later chapters, I will discuss how two speculative pedagogies – the Teacherbot and the Digital Futures for Learning Open Education Resource assignment – worked to problematise taken-for-granted notions of what learning futures may hold.

As we have seen in this chapter, in both methodological and pedagogical forms, speculative approaches are productive for working with the future as a social practice, as a medium for imagination, and as a site of ongoing not-yetness. The case studies that make up the next part of this book engage with various digital education futures that were "of their time", and show how the future keeps shifting and moving as we engage with it.

Notes

1 Ambiguity is by no means the preserve of speculative methods, because all forms of science are unified around "trusted rituals of engagement in risky forms of diplomacy" – so speculative thought may contribute to working with ontological and epistemological diversity as it already exists, to the benefit of the sciences more generally (de Freitas, 2020, p. 70).
2 Cultural heritage projects such as EMOTIVE (Perry et al., 2017), for example, have experimented with immersive digital engagements with the past, in ways that were designed for affective and imaginative responses.

References

Atkinson, D. (2020) 'Inheritance, disobedience and speculation', in Addison, Nicholas and Burgess, Lesley (Eds) *Debates in Art and Design Education*. Abingdon: Routledge, pp. 57–71.

Auger, J. (2013) 'Speculative design: Crafting the speculation', *Digital Creativity*, 24(1), pp. 11–35. doi:10.1080/14626268.2013.767276.

Bannister, J. and O'Sullivan, A. (2013) 'Knowledge mobilisation and the civic academy: The nature of evidence, the roles of narrative and the potential of contribution analysis', *Contemporary Social Science*, 8(3), pp. 249–262. doi:10.1080/21582041.2012. 751497.

Benjamin, R. (2016) 'Racial fictions, biological facts: Expanding the sociological imagination through speculative methods', *Catalyst: Feminism, Theory, Technoscience*, 2(2), pp. 1–28. doi:10.28968/cftt.v2i2.28798.

Berlant, L. (2011) *Cruel optimism*. Durham: Duke University Press.

Biesta, G. (2005) 'Against learning. Reclaiming a language for education in an age of learning', *Nordisk Pedagogik*, 25, pp. 54–66.

Biesta, G. (2007) 'Why "What Works" won't work: Evidence-based practice and the democratic deficit in educational research', *Educational Theory*, 57(1), pp. 1–22. doi:10.1111/j.1741-5446.2006.00241.x.

Bodden, S. and Ross, J. (2021) 'Speculating with glitches: Keeping the future moving', *Global Discourse*, 11(1–2), pp. 15–34. doi:10.1332/204378920X16043719041171.

Chandler, D. and Reid, J. (2020) 'Becoming indigenous: The "speculative turn" in anthropology and the (re)colonisation of indigeneity', *Postcolonial Studies*, 23(4), pp. 485–504. doi:10.1080/13688790.2020.1745993.

Cortiel, J. et al. (Eds) (2020) *Practices of speculation: Modeling, embodiment, figuration.* Bielefeld: transcript Verlag. doi:10.14361/9783839447512.

Cox, A.M. (2021) 'Exploring the impact of Artificial Intelligence and robots on higher education through literature-based design fictions', *International Journal of Educational Technology in Higher Education*, 18(3), pp. 1–19. doi:10.1186/s41239-020-00237-8.

de Freitas, E. (2020) 'Why trust science in a trickster world of absolute contingency? The speculative force of mathematical abstraction', *Critical Studies in Teaching and Learning*, 8(SI), pp. 60–74.

Dewey, J. (1927) 'The rôle of philosophy in the history of civilization', *The Philosophical Review*, 36(1), pp. 1–9.

DiSalvo, C. (2012) 'Spectacles and tropes: Speculative design and contemporary food cultures', *Fibreculture Journal* [Preprint], (20). Available at: http://twenty. fibreculturejournal.org/2012/06/19/fcj-142-spectacles-and-tropes-speculative-design-and-contemporary-food-cultures/ (Accessed: 5 August 2022).

Dourish, P. and Bell, G. (2011) *Divining a Digital Future: Mess and Mythology in Ubiquitous Computing.* Cambridge: MIT Press.

Dreyfus, H. (2001) *On the Internet.* London: Routledge.

Drucker, J. (2009) *SpecLab: Digital Aesthetics and Projects in Speculative Computing.* Chicago: University of Chicago Press. doi:10.7208/chicago/9780226165097.001.0001.

Duggan, S.B. (2019) 'Digital disruption, education policy, and the future of work: Shifting frames of reference in shifting times', in Duggan, S.B. (Ed) *Education Policy, Digital Disruption and the Future of Work: Framing Young People's Futures in the Present.* Cham: Springer International Publishing, pp. 117–129. doi:10.1007/978-3-030-30675-5_6.

Dumit, J. (2021) 'Lagging realities', in Cortiel, J. et al. (Eds) *Practices of Speculation: Modeling, Embodiment, Figuration.* Bielefeld: transcript-Verlag, pp. 97–116.

Dunne, A. and Raby, F. (2013) *Speculative Everything: Design, Fiction, and Social Dreaming.* Cambridge, MA: The MIT Press.

Ehret, C. and Čiklovan, L. (2020) 'How speculative designs produce new potentials for education research in digital culture', *Discourse: Studies in the Cultural Politics of Education*, 41(5), pp. 708–722. doi:10.1080/01596306.2020.1774713.

Elsden, C. et al. (2017) 'On speculative enactments', in *Proceedings of the 2017 CHI Conference on Human Factors in Computing Systems.* New York, NY, USA: Association for Computing Machinery (CHI '17), pp. 5386–5399. doi:10.1145/3025453.3025503.

Fiesler, C. (2021) 'Innovating like an optimist, preparing like a pessimist: Ethical speculation and the legal imagination', *Colorado Technology Law Journal*, 19(1), pp. 1–18.

Fox, T. (2018) 'Problematic milieus: Individuating speculative designs', in Filimowicz, M. and Tzankova, V. (Eds) *New Directions in Third Wave Human-Computer Interaction: Volume 2 – Methodologies.* Cham: Springer International Publishing (Human–Computer Interaction Series), pp. 155–173. doi:10.1007/978-3-319-73374-6_9.

Gallagher, M. and Breines, M. (2021) 'Surfacing knowledge mobilities in higher education: Reconfiguring the teacher function through automation', *Learning, Media and Technology*, 46(1), pp. 78–90. doi:10.1080/17439884.2021.1823411.

Galloway, A. and Caudwell, C. (2018) 'Speculative design as research method', in Coombs, G., McNamara, A., and Sade, G. (Eds) *Undesign.* 1st edn. Abingdon: Routledge, pp. 85–96. doi:10.4324/9781315526379-8.

Garforth, L. and Iossifidis, M. (2021) 'Weirding Utopia for the anthropocene: Hope, Un/Home and the uncanny in annihilation and the city we became', *Pulse: The Journal of Science and Culture* [Preprint], 7, pp. 1–24.

Gaspar, A. (2018) 'Teaching anthropology speculatively', *Cadernos de Arte e Antropologia*, 7(2), pp. 75–90. doi:10.4000/cadernosaa.1687.

Georgis, D. and Matthews, S. (2021) 'The trouble with research-creation: Failure, play and the possibility of knowledge in aesthetic encounters', *International Journal of Qualitative Studies in Education*, pp. 1–17. doi:10.1080/09518398.2021.1888164.

Gonzatto, R.F. et al. (2013) 'The ideology of the future in design fictions', *Digital Creativity*, 24(1), pp. 36–45. doi:10.1080/14626268.2013.772524.

Graham, E.M. et al. (2019) *How to Run a City Like Amazon, and Other Fables*. London: Meatspace Press.

Greene, J.C. (2013) 'On rhizomes, lines of flight, mangles, and other assemblages', *International Journal of Qualitative Studies in Education*, 26(6), pp. 749–758. doi:10.1080/09518398.2013.788763.

Greene, M. (1988) *The Dialectic of Freedom*. New York: Teachers College Press (The John Dewey lecture).

Hales, D. (2013) 'Design fictions an introduction and provisional taxonomy', *Digital Creativity*, 24(1), pp. 1–10. doi:10.1080/14626268.2013.769453.

Haraway, D.J. (2016) *Staying with the trouble: Making kin in the chthulucene*. Durham: Duke University Press (Experimental Futures). doi:10.1215/9780822373780.

Harrington, C. and Dillahunt, T.R. (2021) 'Eliciting tech futures among black young adults: A case study of remote speculative co-design', in *Proceedings of the 2021 CHI Conference on Human Factors in Computing Systems. CHI '21: CHI Conference on Human Factors in Computing Systems*, Yokohama Japan: ACM, pp. 1–15. doi:10.1145/3411764.3445723.

Hillman, T., Rensfeldt, A.B. and Ivarsson, J. (2020) 'Brave new platforms: A possible platform future for highly decentralised schooling', *Learning, Media and Technology*, 45(1), pp. 7–16. doi:10.1080/17439884.2020.1683748.

Issar, S. (2021) *Resolving the problem of algorithmic dissonance: An unconventional solution for a sociotechnical problem* [preprint]. SocArXiv. doi:10.31235/osf.io/qkve3.

Knox, J. (2014) 'The "Tweeting Book" and the question of "non-human data"', *TechTrends*, 59(1), pp. 72–75. doi:10.1007/s11528-014-0823-9.

Knox, J. (2017) 'Data power in education: Exploring critical awareness with the "Learning Analytics Report Card"', *Television & New Media*, 18(8), pp. 734–752. doi:10.1177/1527476417690029.

Konnerup, U., Ryberg, T. and Sørensen, M.T. (2019) 'Designs for learning as springboards for professional development in higher education', in Littlejohn, A. et al. (Eds) *Networked Professional Learning: Emerging and Equitable Discourses for Professional Development*. Cham: Springer International Publishing (Research in Networked Learning), pp. 111–127. doi:10.1007/978-3-030-18030-0_7.

Lamb, J. (2017) *Speculative research feat. Slick Rick*. DR JAMES LAMB. Available at: http://www.james858499.net/6/post/2017/11/speculative-research-feat-slick-rick.html (Accessed: 19 August 2021).

Law, J. (2004) *After Method: Mess in Social Science Research*. Psychology Press.

Lury, C. (2021) *Problem Spaces: How and Why Methodology Matters*. Newark, United Kingdom: Polity Press.

Lury, C. and Wakeford, N. (2012) *Inventive Methods: The Happening of the Social*. London: Routledge.

MacLure, M. (2006) 'The bone in the throat: Some uncertain thoughts on baroque method', *International Journal of Qualitative Studies in Education*, 19(6), pp. 729–745. doi:10.1080/09518390600975958.

Markham, A. (2021) 'The limits of the imaginary: Challenges to intervening in future speculations of memory, data, and algorithms', *New Media & Society*, 23(2), pp. 382–405. doi:10.1177/1461444820929322.

Melo, M. et al. (2019) 'Pedagogy of productive failure: Navigating the challenges of integrating VR into the classroom', *Journal For Virtual Worlds Research*, 12(1), pp. 1–19. doi:10.4101/jvwr.v12i1.7318.

Michael, M. (2012) '"What are we busy doing?" Engaging the idiot', *Science, Technology & Human Values*, 37(5), pp. 528–554. doi:10.1177/0162243911428624.

Michael, M. (2021) *The Research Event: Towards Prospective Methodologies in Sociology*. Abingdon: Routledge.

Mitrović, I. et al. (2021) *Beyond Speculative Design: Past–Present–Future*. SpeculativeEdu; Arts Academy, University of Split.

Nijs, G. et al. (2020) 'Fostering more-than-human imaginaries: Introducing DIY speculative fabulation in civic HCI', in *Proceedings of the 11th Nordic Conference on Human-Computer Interaction: Shaping Experiences, Shaping Society. NordiCHI '20: Shaping Experiences, Shaping Society*, Tallinn Estonia: ACM, pp. 1–12. doi:10.1145/3419249.3420147.

Nooney, L. and Brain, T. (2019) 'A "speculative pasts" pedagogy: Where speculative design meets historical thinking', *Digital Creativity*, 30(4), pp. 218–234. doi:10.1080/14626268.2019.1683042.

Osberg, D. (2010) 'Taking care of the Future? The complex responsibility of education and politics', in Osberg, D. and Biesta, G. (Eds) *Complexity Theory and the Politics of Education*. Boston, the Netherlands: BRILL. doi:10.1163/9789460912405.

Osborn, J.R. et al. (2019) 'The pilgrimage project: Speculative design for engaged interdisciplinary education', *Arts and Humanities in Higher Education*, 18(4), pp. 349–371. doi:10.1177/1474022217736510.

Perry, S. et al. (2017) 'Moving beyond the virtual museum: Engaging visitors emotionally', in *2017 23rd International Conference on Virtual System & Multimedia (VSMM)*. Dublin: IEEE, pp. 1–8. doi:10.1109/VSMM.2017.8346276.

Pollock, N. and Williams, R. (2010) 'The business of expectations: How promissory organizations shape technology and innovation', *Social Studies of Science*, 40(4), pp. 525–548. doi:10.1177/0306312710362275.

Poster, M. (1999) 'Underdetermination', *New Media & Society*, 1(1), pp. 12–17. doi:10.1177/1461444899001001003.

Pringle, E. (2012) 'From trance-like solipsism to speculative audacity?', in Burgess, Lesley and Addison, Nicholas (Eds) *Debates in Art and Design Education*. Abingdon: Routledge, pp. 111–120.

Priyadharshini, E. (2019) 'Anticipating the apocalypse: Monstrous educational futures', *Futures*, 113, pp. 1–8. doi:10.1016/j.futures.2019.102453.

Ross, J. (2017) 'Speculative method in digital education research', *Learning, Media and Technology*, 42(2), pp. 214–229. doi:10.1080/17439884.2016.1160927.

Rousell, D. and Hickey-Moody, A. (2020) 'Speculative and symbolic forms of expression: New practices in community arts education', in Burgess, Lesley and Addison, Nicholas (Eds) *Debates in Art and Design Education*. Abingdon: Routledge.

Savransky, M. (2017) 'The wager of an unfinished present: Notes on speculative pragmatism', in Wilkie, A., Savransky, M. and Rosengarten, M. (Eds) *Speculative Research: The Lure of Possible Futures*. New York & London: Routledge.

Savransky, M. (2018) 'The humor of the problematic: Thinking with stengers', *SubStance*, 47(1), pp. 29–46.

Selwyn, N. et al. (2020) 'What might the school of 2030 be like? An exercise in social science fiction', *Learning, Media and Technology*, 45(1), pp. 90–106. doi:10.1080/1743 9884.2020.1694944.

Smythe, S., Pelan, D. and Breshears, S. (2018) 'The LinkVan project: Participatory technology design in Vancouver', *Language and Literacy*, 20(3), pp. 9–25. doi:10.20360/langandlit29406.

Springgay, S. and Truman, S.E. (2018) 'On the need for methods beyond proceduralism: Speculative middles, (in)tensions, and response-ability in research', *Qualitative Inquiry*, 24(3), pp. 203–214. doi:10.1177/1077800417704464.

Staley, D.J. (2019) *Alternative Universities: Speculative Design for Innovation in Higher Education*. Baltimore: JHU Press.

Staunæs, D. and Brøgger, K. (2020) 'In the mood of data and measurements: Experiments as affirmative critique, or how to curate academic value with care', *Feminist Theory*, 21(4), pp. 429–445. doi:10.1177/1464700120967301.

Truman, S.E. (2019) 'SF! Haraway's situated feminisms and speculative fabulations in English class', *Studies in Philosophy and Education*, 38(1), pp. 31–42. doi:10.1007/s11217-018-9632-5.

Uncertain Commons (2013) *Speculate this!* Durham, NC: Duke University Press.

Veletsianos, G. (2020) 'How should we respond to the life-altering crises that education is facing?', *Distance Education*, 41(4), pp. 604–607. doi:10.1080/01587919.2020.1825 066.

Ward-Davies, A. et al. (2020) 'Post studio methods: Being scicurious as a site for research', *Journal of Artistic and Creative Education*, 14(2). Available at: https://jace.online/index.php/jace/article/view/486 (Accessed: 7 August 2021).

Wilkie, A., Michael, M. and Plummer-Fernandez, M. (2015) 'Speculative method and Twitter: Bots, energy and three conceptual characters', *The Sociological Review*, 63(1), pp. 79–101. doi:10.1111/1467-954X.12168.

PART 2
Speculative objects to think with

The chapters Part 1 of this book explored futures thinking and digital learning futures, introduced complexity and not-yetness, and set out the landscape of speculative methods and pedagogies. Part 2 shifts from exploring concepts and defining speculative approaches, to detailed examination of speculation in practice. To do this, the next four chapters draw on a decade of speculative research and teaching that I have led or (in the case of the Teacherbot in Chapter 5) been significantly involved with.

I am focusing on my own projects and courses in this part of the book so that I can show what goes on under the skin of speculative work: the methodological, pedagogical, creative, analytic and ethical decisions and responses that make it what it is, and the sometimes subtle or unexpected effects it can have. Previous work on speculative approaches, as we saw in Chapter 4, illustrates how questions, objects, audiences, forms of analysis, findings and impacts are mutually constitutive and emergent. This part of the book attempts to trace that emergence and put it in context.

This context is extremely important. The next four chapters are presented in more or less chronological order, with the first one discussing work that took place in 2013–4, and the last one discussing a project from 2020. The 2010s were a decade of change, excitement, disillusionment and a growing number of critical questions and voices in the sphere of digital education and learning. Each of the projects discussed in this part of the book has something to say about methods or pedagogies, but also about the particular moment in which it took place – the configuration of past, present and (then-) future it enacted. There is a tendency in the digital education field to value the recent and the cutting-edge. We less often remember to look back at what was once edgy, or to explore futures we previously engaged with and brought into being. I invite you to read these

DOI: 10.4324/9781003202134-6

80 Speculative objects to think with

case studies as expressions of learning futures that are not universal or permanent, but were specific and informed by their social, political and cultural context as well as by the people, places, organisations and objects that made them happen. I have attempted in each case to describe how they came to be, and some of the historical, political and practical factors that influenced them.

Objects-to-think-with

In Part 3 of this book, I discuss aspects of speculative design for research (Chapter 9) and teaching (Chapter 10) in depth. I want to highlight one of these here: an "object-to-think-with" – as it comes up often in the chapters to follow, and needs some explanation.

For my purposes, an object-to-think-with is something material or digital with which participants or respondents can engage or produce speculatively. In digital education contexts, an object-to-think-with will often be technology- or computing-related, and can take the form of low-tech wireframes, stories or models, or more sophisticated coded or otherwise functional objects. In the case studies that follow, the specific speculative objects explored are a Twitter bot, an Open Educational Resources assignment, a prototype mobile app and a digital storytelling tool and the stories it produced. However, I have a tendency to describe other things as objects-to-think-with, including courses and concepts – so you will encounter objects of different scales and degrees of ephemerality in what follows. Chapter 9 will help to pull these together.

Ten years of speculation: introducing the case studies

Throughout the book so far, I have stressed the need to work with digital education futures in ways that:

- take account of relationality and indeterminacy;
- acknowledge the challenges of responsibility and representation;
- foreground creativity;
- offer alternatives to determinist forms of speculation.

This all sounds, and is, quite serious. There is an urgency around our understandings of the future and how education must work with and towards it. However, one reason I value speculative research methods and teach in speculative ways is because it is also fun. Speculative work helps me make space for playfulness and imagination. It also helps me practice optimism and hope, and to be open to surprises.

These features emerge in the four case studies in this part of the book, which discuss speculative methods and pedagogies in practice. In each of the case study chapters that follow, I introduce speculative objects, audiences and ways of knowing produced through research and teaching projects. In Chapter 5, a speculative Twitter bot makes a surprising entrance into the social space of a Massive Open Online Course and proceeds to engage with participants about the nature of teaching. The chapter explores debates about automation and massification of higher education, and investigates the glitch as a speculative object. Chapter 6 focuses on the speculative pedagogy of the Digital Futures for Learning course, in which the course itself is partly made up of Open Educational Resources produced by students. It examines openness and co-creation as educational qualities and as challenges for higher education. Chapter 7 turns to engagement in museums and galleries, and to the Artcasting project, which explored alternatives to problematic forms of evaluation that cultural heritage organisations were grappling with. Finally, Chapter 8 introduces and discusses the Data Stories Creator, developed as part of work to imagine surveillance futures in higher education at a time of radical shifts in modes and visibility of education, partly driven by the Covid-19 pandemic. These projects, the speculative questions and objects they generated, and the audiences and forms of analysis they engaged with, prepare the ground for the final part of the book, which discusses key dimensions, theoretical concerns and practical considerations of working with speculative methods and pedagogies.

5

TEACHING AT SCALE, AUTOMATION AND A SPECULATIVE TEACHERBOT

Introduction

In the early 2010s, Massive Open Online Courses (MOOCs) became a topic of considerable interest in relation to the future of higher education and the role of the teacher. MOOCs at this time were online courses offered free of charge on an open enrolment basis, designed for scale. Major MOOC platforms that emerged during this period, such as Coursera, EdX and Futurelearn, added value to the content and teaching of universities and other recognised education providers by publishing course materials, managing enrolments and providing interactive functionality such as quizzes, discussion fora and peer marking facilities. The majority of early MOOCs were created and taught by content experts, often academics, working with learning designers and other digital education specialists from within their own organisations.

MOOCs were a media phenomenon, largely because of the enrolment figures of tens or even hundreds of thousands of participants signing up for the highest-profile courses, and the rhetoric spun and encouraged from the platforms and university partners that MOOCs would "open up" education to the world (Knox, 2016). MOOCs were, at the time, being heralded as the potential saviour of a "broken" higher education system, a system of spiralling costs and student debt, growing student numbers and demand for higher education provision across the world, and the perception that digital technologies were not being used to their fullest potential. Media attention fuelled further enrolments, and generated thousands of headlines and articles, as well as opinion pieces from within and beyond the sector about the death of traditional higher education. It seemed that the digital future of learning, long predicted, had arrived. Business

DOI: 10.4324/9781003202134-7

84 Speculative objects to think with

models were proposed: mostly that, while anyone could take the MOOC for free, "premium" services such as certification would come at a cost.

Clay Shirky, one of the early voices describing MOOCs as disruptors of the higher education system, explained in an article in the *Guardian* in late 2012 that the academy, like the music industry before it, was facing an existential crisis relating to digitisation – this one brought about by the MOOC. The fight over MOOCs, he said, was not about the value of higher education or online education, it was about:

> the story we tell ourselves about higher education: what it is, who it's for, how it's delivered, who delivers it.... The possibility [MOOCs] hold out isn't replacement... [it's] that the educational parts of education can be unbundled. Moocs expand the audience for education to people ill-served or completely shut out from the current system.
>
> *(Shirky, 2012)*

The notion of unbundling was and remains powerful in the context of accounts of disruptive education futures (Czerniewicz et al., 2021). Indeed, visions of the future that assume increasing and potentially limitless demand for education, and increasingly limited resources to provide it, require some form of unbundling, as we saw in the KPMG report on future universities in Chapter 2.

These futures also, it was thought, required the development of automated support for, or possible replacement of, human teachers in the context of growing enrolments and increased digitisation. In one typical scenario for automation, the human teacher would be freed up to focus on personal, expert, complex tasks and interactions with students, while more routine, administrative and other tasks would be automated. In another, the massification of education would require increased personalisation through technology, so that teachers would focus on delivering content while automated, intelligent systems would deal with ensuring students received this content in suitable ways, and testing their attainment. Few, if any, accounts of the time were exploring what this would mean for the relationships between teachers and students, and between human and non-human educators. The role of the teacher in supporting or guiding automated systems was also not discussed.

The 2013–4 "interventions in automated teaching" project, with its speculative twitter-based "teacherbot" which participated in the third instance of the E-learning and Digital Cultures MOOC (EDCMOOC), attempted to open up conversations about these questions, and did so in a highly public, visible and risky way. This chapter situates the Teacherbot project in the context of developments around online teaching at scale and automation in education. It then highlights the speculative aspects of this pedagogical research project – its glitchiness, and its status as a provocation. It closes with some analysis of automation and teaching since the project, and considers speculative teacherbot futures.

Online teaching at scale and automation: a short history of EDCMOOC

In January 2013, six of the UK's first MOOCs launched on the Coursera platform, developed by academic and technology teams at the University of Edinburgh. Among these six was *E-learning and Digital Cultures* (EDCMOOC). *E-learning and Digital Cultures* emerged from a postgraduate-level course of the same name, on the fully online MSc E-learning (now the MSc in Digital Education), which had for several years been experimenting with multimodal assessment (Bayne and Ross, 2013) and tackling topics such as popular cybercultures, virtual community and posthumanism, and their relationship to education. The MSc course was taught largely in the open, with course materials, discussion and student work appearing on a public-facing web site.[1] It was devised by Siân Bayne, and I co-designed and co-taught it for the first four years. Siân and I, along with our colleagues Jeremy Knox, Hamish Macleod and Christine Sinclair, were the course team for EDCMOOC.

EDCMOOC's sensibility owed more to the MSc course and programme than to the emerging MOOC trends for content-driven, teacher-focused courses assessed by multiple-choice quizzes and tending to tackle fact-based topics such as computer science. The MSc course, like others on the programme, was dialogic and participatory, with students and teachers working closely together online to develop insights into the topics being explored. We wanted to bring a participatory approach, along with the theme of digital cultures and education, to the MOOC. There were MOOC models for doing this – indeed, before Coursera and other platforms for large-scale MOOCs emerged in early 2012, teachers were creating their own participatory open online courses. The original MOOCs were built to explore connectivist principles for networked learning, and these connectivist MOOCs provided support for the approaches we wanted to explore (McAuley et al., 2010). However, no one had yet used the Coursera platform in the way we had in mind, or at the scale of enrolment the Coursera courses were seeing, with many thousands of people signed up for each course.

At the time of the development of EDCMOOC, the University of Edinburgh had for more than a decade been innovating with fully online distance learning. The MSc E-learning programme itself was born in the early 2000s from investments in developing online postgraduate provision. The partnership between the University and the Coursera platform was the first of its kind in the UK (along with the University of London), and the highly public nature of MOOCs combined with the media, policymaker and public interest they were generating, meant that our work, along with the other five course teams', would be subject to significant scrutiny.

In 2012, when we first developed EDCMOOC, there was little data or insight about who might enrol for the course, so we designed for an audience we knew: educators and learning technologists. The course had 51,000 signups for its first run (42,000 at the start, with more joining through the initial weeks), 21,600

86 Speculative objects to think with

of whom were active on the course site at some point during the MOOC, and 4,500 of whom were still active in the final week (of these, 1,719 received a free certificate of accomplishment).[2]

EDCMOOC engaged participants with various kinds of cultural representations of education and technology, including utopian and dystopian accounts of current and future education, and representations of being human in digital culture and education. The design of the course was unusual for the large-scale MOOCs of the time – in addition to readings, short films and other materials, the MOOC was built around various kinds of interactions: discussion boards, twitter exchanges, participant blogs and live "hangouts" with the course teams. The assessment used Coursera's "peer marking" functionality, and asked participants to produce a digital artefact engaging with a theme from the course. Many of these artefacts were shared publicly and collated by participants on a digital whiteboard.

Through the five weeks of the course, more than 900 blogs were submitted to the EDCMOOC blog aggregator, approximately 700 tweets per day used the nominated Twitter hashtag "#edcmooc", and participants created and sustained peer-led connections in social media spaces including Twitter, Facebook, Google, shared maps, social bookmarking and more. This was in addition to the many thousands of forum posts, blog comments and images and artefacts shared, discussed and developed through the course.

The first instance of EDCMOOC was, in our judgement and based on participant feedback, a success. A large majority (82.8%) of active participants who responded to the post-course survey (total n = 1,684) reported that overall their experience was good, very good or excellent. The artefacts and other materials produced by participants showed their engagement with the themes and course. However, feedback also indicated that some participants found the MOOC and the quantity of interactions both on the site and elsewhere overwhelming, and wanted more teacher presence in the MOOC. The teaching team had in fact been very active in the discussion forums, on Twitter and in our own blog, but the MOOC was not designed like others people had experienced or heard about, and there were no video lectures, so our participation was often on the same terms as that of other participants. Because of the sheer number of participants and volume of engagement, this kind of participation was too subtle to count, for many. One of the earliest threads in the discussion forum was titled "where are the professors?" and this thread continued to be active throughout the course, as teachers and participants discussed the various pedagogical and technical dimensions of this question. When we hosted our first live video broadcast, at the end of Week 1, participants expressed relief and excitement, as we discussed in a paper published not long after the first run:

> *This* was seemingly what many had been waiting for: an embodied, authoritative, and recognizably "teacherly" moment. This thing we had resisted was, many said, a turning point for them in their engagement with

and understanding of the course. A question for us going forward is, how can we provide reassuring and recognizable evidence of our attention earlier, without undermining our commitment to the value of dialogue and interaction among peers?

(Ross et al., 2014)

This question led to the recording of weekly video introductions and other developments, such as teaching assistants, for the subsequent run of the course. It also informed the design of a speculative Teacherbot.

"We welcome our robot colleagues": teacherbot and automated teaching

EDCMOOC itself was something of a speculative object, designed to explore possible futures for dialogic approaches to online education at scale. The visibility or otherwise of the teacher in the MOOC, and the wider discussions that were going on about automation and the future relationship of technology and the teacher (Selwyn, 2016), led to a conversation about what such dialogue might consist of, and who or what it might involve. As Selwyn notes, the nature and role of the human teacher is variously described in terms of (in)efficiency, empathy, expertise, (lack of) scalability and variability, and the "human touch" remains essential in many people's conception of good education. Educational researchers had also been engaging with theories of posthumanism to help think through some of the implications of the education-technology relationship (Edwards, 2010; Knox, 2016; Bayne, 2018). In questioning the foundations of humanism – the human as a stable, individual, agentic subject – posthumanism allows interrogation of the intra-actions of categories of human and non-human. Researchers were considering how the category of human continues to shift, how the human and non-human might work together, what the posthuman condition of education might be. Or, as the Manifesto for Teaching Online put it, "Automation need not impoverish education: we welcome our new robot colleagues" (Bayne et al., 2016).

In late 2013, the Teacherbot project team (including all the members of the EDCMOOC teaching team, along with colleagues from design informatics and information services, and led by Siân) was awarded "Challenge Investment" funding from the University of Edinburgh to build a Twitter "bot" that would engage with participants on the third instance of EDCMOOC, due to launch in November 2014. The bot would participate in course-related discussions on Twitter, and would hopefully build a sense of teacher presence and support learning, as well as help students and teachers think about the nature of teaching, potential partnerships between human- and non-human teachers and the future of education at scale.

Twitter is a free microblogging service and a social network, launched in 2006. By 2012, the service had 140 million active users and was reporting 340

88 Speculative objects to think with

million Tweets a day. Some proportion of those were "bots", accounts set up to post or reply automatically in response to certain parameters or triggers. A Pew Research Center study in 2017 looked at who or what was tweeting links to 2,135 popular web sites, and found that 66% "are shared by accounts with characteristics common among automated 'bots,' rather than human users" (Wojcik et al., 2018). At the time of our project, the rise of the Twitter bot was being discussed regularly in the media, often in relation to a trend of "buying" followers to boost visibility and credibility on the platform (Hill, 2012). Soon, attention would turn to the use of bots for more controversial purposes, for instance as part of political campaigns and disinformation efforts (Woolley, 2016; Neyazi, 2020). In the spaces between these manipulative and destructive uses of automation, Twitter bots were also emerging as playful, experimental, artistic (Lunden, 2013), civic-minded or speculative projects. For instance, in their work on a project about energy-demand reduction, Wilkie et al. (2015) developed three Twitter bots to explore how "communications circulate, communities are enacted, and identities are rendered in relation to energy-demand reduction" (p. 97). Each bot had a different mode of operating – from translating and re-translating energy-related tweets, to tweeting about energy reduction in a human-like way, to highlighting and congratulating possible energy reduction activities of other users. Describing their speculative method as performative, they note that its interventions "are designed to 'prompt' (as much as probe) emergent enactments that can problematize existing practices (in our case, the neat conceptualization of community and the practices of energy-demand reduction) and open up the prospective" (p. 98). It was this mode of speculation and experimentation that informed the Teacherbot project.

Teacherbot attempted to engage with debates about possible futures for teaching that were previously mostly theoretical in nature. By trying to work some of the promises and threats of automation into a semi-automated, experimental form, it gave the researchers, and the MOOC participants, something to talk about (and to do) in attempting to move beyond utopian/dystopian binaries to a more subtle understanding of what these educational futures might look like (Bayne, 2015). Teacherbot participated in the #EDCMOOC Twitter feed, using the account @EDCMOOC. It consisted of a series of pre-prepared statements, questions and provocations. A post would appear from the @EDCMOOC Twitter account if it was triggered by particular keywords in tweets that also included the MOOC hashtag #EDCMOOC.

Teacherbot's responses were written in advance, based on course content and questions and issues which had arisen in the previous two instances of the course. Its programmed responses fell into three main categories: content, process and social (Bayne, 2015). The human course teachers could add new trigger keywords and responses at any time, using the graphical user interface developed for the project. For example, the short animated film Bendito Machine III (Mallis,

2008), included as part of the week on utopian and dystopian visions of technology, explored relationships with technology in terms of worship and obsession. The teachers wrote rules to automatically respond to tweets that referenced the film or technology using certain key words. Teacherbot might respond to a tweet about the animated characters' apparent obsession with various gadgets and devices by observing that:

> "If machines are part of mind & memory, maybe it's right to be obsessed with them" [with a link to a wikipedia entry on 'extended cognition'].
> *(Teacherbot response)*

Many Teacherbot responses quoted from or referenced course readings or concepts, and they were sometimes framed as questions for further discussion:

> Do MOOC learners need new literacies to navigate teacherlessness?
> *(Teacherbot question)*

Other responses were intended as pastoral interventions – to answer frequently asked factual questions (for example about assignment due dates), to provide reassurance if participants tweeted about feeling overwhelmed by the scale of the MOOC, or to give encouragement to persist with difficult readings or concepts:

> You could start by reading some of the discussions [link to discussion forum]
> Make sure you send your Google username if you want to come to the hangout office hours
> Try this paper to untangle some of the terminology [link to paper]
> *(Teacherbot responses)*

The ultimate purpose of the Teacherbot project was to work creatively with:

> ways of theorising and practising digital education and automated teaching which are driven neither by technical-rational efficiency models, nor by equally instrumentally focused social models which assume a position of humanistic opposition to, or appropriation of, digital technology.
> *(Bayne, 2015, p. 460)*

Teacherbot would, we hoped, help the researchers, and EDCMOOC participants, think about how human and non-human teachers might form a "teaching assemblage" (ibid). Along the way, Teacherbot did some other things that were unexpected. To start with, it made a bit of an entrance.

90 Speculative objects to think with

Glitches as speculative interruptions: teacherbot goes live

I have been talking about the Teacherbot for many years, but did not tell this particular story in detail until recently, in a paper about the speculative potential of glitches. In the paper, my co-author and I defined a glitch as:

> a generative problem, one capable of introducing unanticipated possibilities and futures into an otherwise prescribed situation... [glitches are] sociomaterial encounters rather than merely technical errors.
>
> *(Bodden and Ross, 2021, p. 16)*

This discussion of glitches began at a 2018 symposium at Lancaster University called "Staying with Speculation", and an exchange with designer and researcher Shawn Bodden, who was in the process of analysing fieldwork data from Budapest, which included material about the unconventional political activism undertaken by the Two-Tailed Dog Party against the ruling Fidesz government. He told me about their sidewalk "repairs" and the glitchy interactions with police this produced; I told him about what happened on the day the Teacherbot went live. Talking together during the symposium and afterwards, we pondered the place of glitches, mistakes and accidents, technical and otherwise, in the landscape of speculation. We explored in particular the tendency of glitches to be "idiotic" in the manner outlined by Stengers (2005): to redefine the parameters of the question or problem at hand through refusal, slowness or nonsense. As Michael (2012, 2021) notes, overspills, unforeseen actions and misbehaviours are an inherent part of speculative design.

At the same time, glitches, in technical terms, are interesting because they are malfunctions that alter but do not entirely break the system. This is important because, as Gaboury (2018) notes in his discussion of queer computation, "a broken machine cannot compute, queerly or otherwise. It is a brick, a doorstop; it has no radical potential for computation as it has no computational function" (p. 486). The tension in systems that do not do what they should, but do not cease, is what makes the glitch so generative, and so problematic for researchers and teachers. Work with "glitches" in digital music in the 1990s generated the concept of the "post-digital" for Cascone (2000), who used the term to describe how the sounds of everyday failures of technology and devices (clipping, distortion and so on) became a productive focus of composition. Building on ideas of bringing the "background" forward, the glitch genre was one doorway to the significance that post-digital has in contemporary theory, including educational theory.

The third instance of EDCMOOC ran in November and December 2014, and had about 12,000 participants enrolled. The pre-course information had been clear about the automated nature of the bot that was to join the MOOC, and the EDCMOOC site included a page which explained the project and invited participants to engage with the bot and discuss their responses to it in the forums and elsewhere. This connected well with the themes of the MOOC, and the discussions we would have about the nature of the human in education; the role of the human teacher in an increasingly datafied landscape; and about cultural representations of learning and technology, including science-fictional representations.

Having spent several months working on, refining and testing the design, functionality and interface of the Teacherbot, the first day of the MOOC arrived, and Teacherbot was switched on. Teacherbot announced itself not by gently beginning to respond in a light touch way to relevant tweets, but with a barrage of many hundreds of identical tweets over a short period of time:

> @EDCMOOC Posthuman does not really mean the end of humanity. It signals the end of a certain conception of the human. #EDCMOOC

> @EDCMOOC Darwin's conception of life, is one in which the human is one species among many, destined to be overcome. #EDCMOOC

A glitch in the code triggered the bot to respond to itself (citing N. Katherine Hayles' 2008 work, *How we became posthuman* (Hayles, 2008), and Elizabeth Grosz' *Becoming Undone* (Grosz, 2011)), over and over again, and this had not been caught in testing with the test hashtag. Only when the bot went live was the problem discovered, and by then, it was too late:

> @EDCMOOC I'm guessing you REALLY want to tweet this – it seems to be on a tweeting loop! #twentyidenticaltweets #EDCMOOC:)
> *(EDCMOOC participant, 5 November 2014)*

Participants were variously startled, charmed, amused and annoyed by the looping teacherbot and by its rather menacing messages to humanity. These had, of course, been initially generated by the MOOC teachers and intended to be triggered by participants, at (hopefully) appropriate times, but in the context of a new course and a bot whose capabilities were unknown to participants, it was a significant glitch. The error was relatively quickly identified and repaired, but not before the bot had made itself known in dramatic fashion. The impact of this early glitch is hard to quantify in terms of overall student experience, but in numerical terms it meant Teacherbot's participation in the Twitter stream swamped that of any other participants, including the human teachers. Teacherbot posted 1487 tweets, as compared to the next most frequent tweeter (one of the human teachers) with 132 tweets.

Our response at the time was to shut it down as quickly as possible, fix it and relaunch. However, this temporary glitch has something to say about speculative methods in research and teaching. By introducing itself in such a visible way, Teacherbot at least temporarily exacerbated the dichotomies of human and non-human, and uncritically utopian and dystopian visions of automation in education, that the course was setting out to dismantle. It also signalled a break from the more usual conceptions of artificial intelligence (AI) in education, which are often "driven by a productivity-oriented solutionism" (Bayne, 2015, p. 460). The initial inability of Teacherbot to blend in with its human co-teachers and students intersects with issues of fragmentation and the state of being overwhelmed that participants often report in massive online course contexts (Knox, 2016). As noted above, the dynamics created by the course's discussion-based pedagogical approach, and rejection of the "talking head" video lecture format in the first run of the course, led to a fragmented experience for some. Teacherbot did probably the most successful thing it *could* have done in such a distributed attention economy – it made an entrance. The glitch that introduced Teacherbot to the course community also did some important work in defamiliarising the study spaces of the MOOC:

> Pedagogical and communicative possibilities became apparent: the expectations of what a teacher does might prove to be incorrect; the need of participants in a massive course to be shown where to look might be filled in unanticipated ways; the anxiety of learning in a new space, with strangers, might be tempered by a bit of bleak comic relief. What the course would be and what and how participants would learn became less certain. Modes of engagement broke down and reconfigured themselves in an altogether less human shape, for a few minutes. In doing what it did, Teacherbot's glitch signaled "the end of a certain conception" (Hayles, 2008, p. 296) of the educational encounter.
>
> *(Bodden and Ross, 2021, p. 24)*

In building speculative objects for research and teaching, researchers and teachers need to be open to glitches: technical, human, temporal and otherwise. What one sets out to do is never the whole, or necessarily even the most interesting, story. Even projects that are designed to be speculative run the risk of attempting to channel complexity in particular directions. The learning outcome and the research objective loom large because they often serve as gatekeepers for getting to do certain work in the first place. There are also real responsibilities to learners and participants to proceed in ethical and caring ways. These responsibilities are, if anything, more pronounced when there is less certainty about what will happen. Where glitches threaten relations of care, we have to intervene. As we found in the Teacherbot project, though, glitches and interventions to repair them need not close off imaginative and speculative space. As EDCMOOC continued post-glitch, the Teacherbot's dramatic entrance and work of defamiliarisation contributed to a fascinating form of relationality in the MOOC.

Speculation beyond the glitch

After its noisy, glitchy arrival, Teacherbot's presence became more subtle, and it began to respond to participant tweets and intervene in conversations in ways that were more aligned with our intentions. Because of its early behaviour, MOOC participants who were active on Twitter were especially aware of its presence, and some of its limitations. Participants nicknamed it "Botty", gendered it (normally female), remarked both when it did sensible and foolish things, and sought advice from peers about how to provoke it to respond. We began to see what some other teacherly dimensions of Teacherbot might entail.

Bozkurt, Kilgore and Crosslin (2018) conducted a social network analysis and a content analysis of the impact of Teacherbot, and they highlighted a few of these dimensions. Looking at the whole five-week period of the course and all the tweets using the hashtag #EDCMOOC during that time (4317 interactions from 423 participants), they identified Teacherbot as "an important entity which has the capacity to change and shape the network structure" (p. 47). Drawing on a community of inquiry model, they looked for evidence of Teacherbot engaging in direct instruction, organisation and facilitation of discourse, and found the bot's activities located in the last of these categories. Teacherbot drew lurkers into conversations, was the hub of the largest cluster of Twitter activity and was involved in a total of 40.3% of all interactions in the #EDCMOOC discussion – either by tweeting or by being mentioned (p. 51). Compared with the human teachers, Teacherbot was more effective at bridging different clusters of activity (p. 55). And the authors found from their content analysis that participants used a notably welcoming tone with the bot, taking a particular interest in understanding its capacities, memory and "where it stands on the machine-human continuum" (p. 55) or, as Bayne (2015) describes it, "the limits to its proxy 'humanity'" (p. 463).

Looking in depth at interactions with Teacherbot, and participant reflections on it, Bayne (2015) observes that the bot was particularly successful at prompting both meaningful reflection and generative misunderstandings about course concepts, especially through the extracts from readings it often responded with. As the number of programmed tweets was limited, extracts sometimes came up more than once. An exchange later on in the course highlighted that people were aware of the bot's particular interests and pet sources:

> [PARTICIPANT 1]: RT @EDCMOOC Precisely what/who will define authoritative notions of exemplary humanity in the 21st century? (Graham 2002) #edcmchat
>
> [PARTICIPANT 2]: Lol… you are sounding like teacherbot!!!! #edcmchat #edcmooc
>
> [PARTICIPANT 1]: that was her! She always pulls out that quote… :-) #edcmchat

(Twitter exchange about the Teacherbot)

94 Speculative objects to think with

This repetitiveness may or may not be a major distinction between Teacherbot and a human teacher, but responses to it express a degree of acceptance of the bot's idiosyncrasies. Even when participants expressed exasperation, this tended to be very kindly phrased:

> [@participant] Re The Human touch-I see early readers successfully integrating verbal, physical& tech methods-do iPads contest 'social' learning? #edcmooc
>
> *(EDCMOOC participant)*

> [Teacherbot] The rationale of education is founded on the humanist idea of a certain kind of subject. (Usher & Edwards, 1994) #edcmooc _.-- _._
>
> *(Teacherbot, 28 November 2014)*

> @EDCMOOC it's late Tbot, don't you sleep ??
>
> *(EDCMOOC participant)*

The presence of Teacherbot also motivated some creative and provocative responses from participants. In an intriguing development, at one point, a new Twitter account appeared under the name @TEACHERBOT_47. This account claimed to be a digital artefact assignment created for the MOOC, and it had several exchanges with the official Teacherbot. It was unclear if this account was automated in any way, but its first tweet, in week four of the MOOC, read "Welcome to E-Learning and Digital Cultures #edcmooc Start date 28-01-2035". It claimed to be a future EDC teacher, gave (correct) information about the course, and responded to some of Teacherbot's responses to participants, offering invented quotes from a future transhumanist literature (a literature which the course materials had identified as distinct from the posthumanist theory it was focused on):

> 'Posteducation': education is rendered superfluous by genetic engineering (Pedersen 2010) #edcmooc _. . -_
>
> *(Teacherbot)*

> Transhuman education greatly enhances the posthuman condition by creating happiness
>
> *((Wake 2027) (Teacherbot_47) Exchange 1)*

> We need to understand that five hundred years of humanism may be coming to an end. (Hassan 1977) #edcmooc _. -_ _
>
> *(Teacherbot)*

Five hundred years of humanism has come to an end and been replaced by transhumanism.

(Presley 2027) (Teacherbot_47) (Exchange 2)

The uncertainty about this account and its status is part of the story of teaching online at scale. It raises questions: whether it was "really" a bot, who created it, and whether its combination of playfulness and serious, teacherly behaviour was intended to problematise, or undermine, the official Teacherbot. When the door is opened to different forms of relations and different possibilities for teaching in online education, more entities may pass through than were imagined.

Teacherbot was not designed to make the MOOC more efficient, and it was not intelligent in any meaningful sense (Breines and Gallagher, 2020). It neither removed routine tasks from the human teachers, nor did it personalise the experience of MOOC learning for participants. The role it ultimately fulfilled was to provoke, invite, include and acknowledge. As Bozkurt et al. (2018) noted, its "always on, always there, and always ready" nature enriched the social space of the MOOC, and offered some insights into what our "robot colleagues" might, in practice, be able to do in the future, and what we might wish them to do.

Teacherbot futures

Since the teacherbot project and EDCMOOC ended, MOOCs have undergone a further transformation. As time passes, MOOCs have lost commentators' confidence that they will be the disruptive force for higher education that was hoped for or feared. As Popenici and Kerr wrote in 2017, "MOOCs remain just a different kind of online course, interesting and useful, but not really aimed at or capable of changing the structure and function of universities" (2017, p. 8).[3] Increasingly, MOOCs are seen as part of the offerings of traditional educational institutions, not a replacement for them. Addressing challenges of teaching and learning at scale is still seen as core to the future of universities of all kinds, with the "iron triangle" of access, cost and quality posing significant problems for many university programmes and courses: scale and cost are seen as locked in to the system, and quality therefore comes under greater pressure (Ryan, French and Kennedy, 2021).

At the same time, some of the early MOOC platforms – notably Coursera and EdX – have been acquired or funded for truly staggering sums. When Coursera went public in March 2021, it became "the tenth largest listed education company globally" (HolonIQ, 2021), valued at more than $7 billion US dollars, part of the current boom in edtech investment (Komljenovic, 2021; Williamson, 2021).

Along with the growing fortunes of some MOOC platforms, discussions about automated and artificially intelligent agents in education have continued

96 Speculative objects to think with

to pick up steam. New and emerging technologies such as brain-computer interfaces have complicated the picture of who or what might be automated through augmented and artificial intelligence (Williamson, 2017). The impact of these possible futures on the educational workforce (not just teachers but also administrators, technologists and more) has been subject to attention, and the same rhetorics of replacement and augmentation are still in force (Popenici and Kerr, 2017). However, we can also see the development of more nuanced accounts of automation, its design, its possible roles in education and its impacts on relationships and experiences of learning. For instance, Myers et al. (2019) looked at tutor experiences of the introduction of automated support mechanisms, which, despite having the stated rationale of giving tutors more time for meaningful pedagogical support by freeing them up from low-level support tasks, resulted in complex impacts on tutor identities and a perception of threat from changing academic routines. Ideland (2021), in her study of EdTech entrepreneurs in Sweden, identified in their accounts a vision of the desirable human teacher as "absolutely present and who is coaching, not lecturing, flexible, willing to speed up, and ready to work whenever and wherever" (p. 43) – changing, but not disappearing, in response to personalised and "smart" technologies in schools.

Teacherbots, too, have continued to evolve and are emerging from within diverse settings. A project which followed from our own was designed to investigate the notion of automation and the "teacher function" and used speculative co-design methods to understand perspectives of teachers, staff and students and to produce use cases for future teacherbots at the University of Edinburgh (Breines and Gallagher, 2020). The project developed a framework for evaluating teacherbot designs, moving away from efficiency as a core value, and criteria were the extent to which the designs were pedagogically generative, expressed university values, had potential to positively influencing the student and teaching experience, were ethical, were supportive of teacher professionalism and were technologically feasible (p. 8). Interviews with participants in the project identified narratives of teaching at the university and how they might be expressed in terms of automation, including social performances, discretion, liberation, transparency and visibility, bias, diversity and horizontalism (Gallagher and Breines, 2021). Examples of teacherbot designs produced through participatory design sessions included bots for helping students identify their knowledge of a subject before a course began, creating peer groupings based on sophisticated criteria, generating discussion (inspired by the original teacherbot), preparing students for tutorials and collecting resources from students to help co-create knowledge (pp. 9–10). The researchers identified:

> a transition from the not-yetness of these technologies into pragmatic spaces as the community itself has identified need and gaps where the University itself can benefit and where they would be welcome – if they

serve to advance university values and facilitate better educational experiences, rather than adding to teachers' workloads or undermining their work.

(p. 11)

Also drawing on the Teacherbot project, Cox (2021) developed a design fiction that imagined a future iteration of the EDCMOOC bot whose capabilities were slightly enhanced but whose interactions with students remained challenging in various ways, not least for students who were less compliant with the vision of a particular course:

> STUDENT 1: @CriticalBot we have been set the task to research bias in AIED [Artificial Intelligence in Education]. What do you know about bias in AIED?
>
> CRITICALBOT: Blanchard is recommended in the reading list.
>
> STUDENT 2: I think he means rtfm [read the fucking manual].
>
> STUDENT 1: Blanchard?
>
> CRITICALBOT: Sorry. I should have typed: Blanchard, E. G. (2015). Socio-cultural imbalances in AIED research: Investigations, implications and opportunities. International Journal of Artificial Intelligence in Education, 25(2), 204–28. No one's perfect.
>
> STUDENT 1: @CriticalBot What is the main point he makes?
>
> CRITICALBOT: Nice try. Try reading the abstract. Abstracts summarise key points. It may also be useful to read the conclusion section to grasp the author's main argument before deciding on whether to undertake a closer reading.

(p. 9)

Cox points to this design fiction as embodying alternative imaginaries of AI, focused on simple tech but capable of teaching high-level skills. Whether and how an AI could actually do this, he notes, is an open question and a challenge. Other theoretical work has pointed to Teacherbot as an example of both the potential for critical transformation of digital education (Malott, 2020) and as a failed attempt to intervene in problematic MOOC spaces (Atiaja Atiaja, Guerrero Proenza and Yamba-Yugsi, 2018).

Teacherbots are producing complex realities that teams of teachers and researchers are grappling with. Perhaps the best example of this is Jill Watson from Georgia Tech in the US. The Jill Watson project began in 2016 with a single chatbot agent introduced into an online course on AI to answer simple questions in the course discussion forum (Goel and Polepeddi, 2016). Several versions were generated over the following year, including specific chatbots to respond to student introductions, and iterations of the question-answering bot. Despite being far more technically advanced, researcher-teachers described their experience with the project in similar terms to the EDCMOOC Teacherbot project, proposing that: "we may view Jill Watson as an experiment in human-AI collaboration. The… class has become a microsociety in which humans and AI agents collaborate extensively and intensively, living and working together for long durations of time" (p. 19). A key difference was that the Jill Watson agents were not disclosed to participants until the end of the course. Each agent in each new semester was given a new name, and all the human teaching assistants (TAs) were given pseudonyms, specifically to make it more difficult to tell who was not a real person. Naturally, students beyond the first semester heard about the project and therefore knew that *some* of their TAs were automated agents, but not who. It became a game to guess which one(s), and this was revealed at the end of each course. Considering the ethical dimensions of disguising the nature of their project, the researchers argued that this was appropriate because the course was about AI and aimed at prospective computer scientists: "we're both indirectly training our students to recognize other bots and giving them the opportunity to have the experience of being the person who may unknowingly be interacting with them" (Eicher, Polepeddi and Goel, 2018, p. 92). Indeed, on a different course that used a Jill Watson agent (aimed at the general public), students were told about this from the start, and offered a way to give feedback if the agent gave confusing or misleading information (ibid, p. 93). By 2020, the Jill Watson project had expanded to support the creation of custom agents, provide research assistance and connect students with peers (School of Interactive Computing, 2020).

In a very different setting, the European CEPEH project, which ran from 2018 to 2020, generated prototypes of open access chatbots for healthcare education that could do things like support "natural language-based interaction between the medical student and the Virtual Patient" (Dolianiti et al., 2020, p. 138). The project also aimed to support the co-design of new chatbots, and worked with participants involved in healthcare education to create and evaluate these (Pears et al., 2021). A key focus for this project was the production of bots using open source and free technologies, to allow for new uses and contexts in the future.

Beyond the design and development of automated agents from within or specifically aimed at the contexts of use, we are also seeing an interest in automation and AI that is impacting education from the outside, as it were. Toncic (2020) conducted research with secondary school writing teachers in the US to probe their knowledge and understanding of the impact of "smart" grammar checkers such as Grammarly. These, he argues, are often used by students without teachers' knowledge (and with no intention to cheat, as they are usually presented as just an enhancement to the ubiquitous spell checker), and teachers still give significant weight to proper grammar in student writing, without realising that students may be augmenting their initial capabilities. AI-mediated literacy practices need to be better understood and accounted for, especially as they have a tendency to reify "already-in-place embodied and enacted linguistic practices. That is, they automatize specific types of discursive practices but not others" (p. 31), potentially unfairly undervaluing certain kinds of writing or creative communication.

This chapter has situated the Teacherbot as a speculative project within the historical context of automation, MOOCs and changing perceptions of the teacher. The questions and the situation that informed the project are specific to a time and place: a well-known university with access to an emerging MOOC platform, a critical mass of researchers working on digital education and design; and a moment where a particular set of possibilities were in play so that we could ask whether "robot colleagues" like the Teacherbot offered genuine opportunities for educators to intervene in imaginaries of automation and scale, and potentially reshape the agenda of algorithmic technologies in education (Bayne et al., 2020). The speculative methods that produced knowledge in this project were orientated to these specificities: producing patterns from the noise of MOOC participation and teaching automation; rendering other possibilities silent. The futures that are made thinkable through speculative approaches contribute to problem-making, rather than prediction, because they engage with the messiness of the future in the present – both deliberately and inadvertently – in ways that provoke engagement.

Summary of insights

- Speculative objects generate realities and relations in the spaces they are inhabiting, including in educational settings.
- Glitches and surprises are not incidental when working speculatively.
- Unasked questions and unspoken assumptions in future trends like automation of teaching are often worth exploring in speculative ways.
- Research ethics need to be centred in an ongoing way in a speculative project, to trace and respond to emergent impacts.

Notes

1 For example, see http://edc.education.ed.ac.uk for the 2010 instance of the course.
2 This initial high enrolment and subsequent dropoff is one of the best-known and most discussed aspects of the MOOC phenomenon (Clow, 2013). The low barriers to signup mean that MOOCs attract enrolments from people with a very wide range of motivations and intentions (Christensen et al., 2013), and "completion" as a criteria for success is a relatively poor metric for evaluation (Stracke, 2017).

100 Speculative objects to think with

3 However, at the time of writing this chapter, MOOCs in one of their parallel futures as workforce development tools are understood as the "first generation" of industry certification platforms – see for example the work of venture capital firm Emerge Education on emerging models of employability training (Navas, 2021).

References

Atiaja Atiaja, L., Guerrero Proenza, R. and Yamba-Yugsi, M. (2018) 'MOOCs: Design of a teaching methdology from a humanist understanding', in *International Conference on Future of Education*, pp. 30–37. doi:10.17501/26307413.2018.1105.

Bayne, S. (2015) 'Teacherbot: Interventions in automated teaching', *Teaching in Higher Education*, 20(4), pp. 455–467. doi:10.1080/13562517.2015.1020783.

Bayne, S. et al. (2016) *The 2016 manifesto for teaching online*. Manifesto for Teaching Online. Available at: https://blogs.ed.ac.uk/manifestoteachingonline/the-text/ (Accessed: 25 August 2021).

Bayne, S. (2018) *Posthumanism: A navigation aid for educators*, on_education, 2018(01). Available at: https://www.oneducation.net/no-02-september-2018/posthumanism-a-navigation-aid-for-educators/ (Accessed: 23 January 2019).

Bayne, S. et al. (2020) *The Manifesto for Teaching Online*. Cambridge: MIT Press.

Bayne, S. and Ross, J. (2013) 'Posthuman literacy in heterotopic space: A pedagogical proposal', in Lea, M.R. and Goodfellow, R. (Eds) *Literacy in the digital University: Critical Perspectives on Learning, Scholarship and Technology*. London: Routledge.

Bodden, S. and Ross, J. (2021) 'Speculating with glitches: Keeping the future moving', *Global Discourse*, 11(1–2), pp. 15–34. doi:10.1332/204378920X16043719041171.

Bozkurt, A., Kilgore, W. and Crosslin, M. (2018) 'Bot-teachers in hybrid massive open online courses (MOOCs): A post-humanist experience', *Australasian Journal of Educational Technology*, 34(3). doi:10.14742/ajet.3273.

Breines, M.R. and Gallagher, M. (2020) 'A return to Teacherbot: Rethinking the development of educational technology at the University of Edinburgh', *Teaching in Higher Education*, pp. 1–15. doi:10.1080/13562517.2020.1825373.

Cascone, K. (2000) 'The aesthetics of failure: "Post-Digital" tendencies in contemporary computer music', *Computer Music Journal*, 24(4), pp. 12–18.

Christensen, G. et al. (2013) *The MOOC Phenomenon: Who Takes Massive Open Online Courses and Why?* SSRN Scholarly Paper ID 2350964. Rochester, NY: Social Science Research Network. doi:10.2139/ssrn.2350964.

Clow, D. (2013) 'MOOCs and the funnel of participation', in *Third Conference on Learning Analytics and Knowledge (LAK 2013)*, Leuven, Belgium, pp. 185–189. Available at: http://hcibib.org/LAK13#S10 (Accessed: 20 January 2022).

Cox, A.M. (2021) 'Exploring the impact of Artificial Intelligence and robots on higher education through literature-based design fictions', *International Journal of Educational Technology in Higher Education*, 18(3), pp. 1–19. doi:10.1186/s41239-020-00237-8.

Czerniewicz, L. et al. (2021) 'Academics teaching and learning at the nexus: Unbundling, marketisation and digitisation in higher education', *Teaching in Higher Education*, pp. 1–15. doi:10.1080/13562517.2021.1876019.

Dolianiti, F. et al. (2020) 'Chatbots in healthcare curricula: The case of a conversational virtual patient', in Frasson, C., Bamidis, P., and Vlamos, P. (Eds) *Brain Function Assessment in Learning*. Cham: Springer International Publishing (Lecture Notes in Computer Science), pp. 137–147. doi:10.1007/978-3-030-60735-7_15.

Edwards, R. (2010) 'The end of lifelong learning: A post-human condition?', *Studies in the Education of Adults*, 42(1), pp. 5–17. doi:10.1080/02660830.2010.11661585.

Eicher, B., Polepeddi, L. and Goel, A. (2018) 'Jill Watson doesn't care if you're pregnant: Grounding AI ethics in empirical studies', in *Proceedings of the 2018 AAAI/ACM Conference on AI, Ethics, and Society. AIES '18: AAAI/ACM Conference on AI, Ethics, and Society*, New Orleans LA USA: ACM, pp. 88–94. doi:10.1145/3278721.3278760.

Gaboury, J. (2018) 'Critical unmaking: Toward a queer computation', in Sayers, J. (Ed) *The Routledge Companion to Media Studies and Digital Humanities*. London: Taylor and Francis.

Gallagher, M. and Breines, M. (2021) 'Surfacing knowledge mobilities in higher education: Reconfiguring the teacher function through automation', *Learning, Media and Technology*, 46(1), pp. 78–90. doi:10.1080/17439884.2021.1823411.

Goel, A.K. and Polepeddi, L. (2016) *Jill Watson: A Virtual Teaching Assistant for Online Education*. Technical Report. Georgia Institute of Technology. Available at: https://smartech.gatech.edu/handle/1853/59104 (Accessed: 3 September 2021).

Graham, E.L. (2002) *Representations of the Post/Human: Monsters, Aliens and Others in Popular Culture*. New Brunswick, NJ: Rutgers University Press.

Grosz, E. (2011) *Becoming Undone: Darwinian Reflections on Life, Politics, and Art, Becoming Undone*. Durham: Duke University Press. doi:10.1515/9780822394433.

Hassan, I. (1977) 'Prometheus as performer: Towards a posthumanist culture?' *The Georgia Review, 314*, pp. 830–850.

Hayles, N.K. (2008) *How We Became Posthuman: Virtual Bodies in Cybernetics, Literature, and Informatics*. Chicago: University of Chicago Press.

Hill, K. (2012) *The Invasion of the Twitter Bots*. Forbes. Available at: https://www.forbes.com/sites/kashmirhill/2012/08/09/the-invasion-of-the-twitter-bots/ (Accessed: 25 August 2021).

HolonIQ (2021) *Coursera and 300+ Global Education IPOs*. Available at: https://www.holoniq.com/notes/coursera-and-300-education-ipos/ (Accessed: 10 January 2022).

Ideland, M. (2021) 'Google and the end of the teacher? How a figuration of the teacher is produced through an ed-tech discourse', *Learning, Media and Technology*, 46(1), pp. 33–46. doi:10.1080/17439884.2020.1809452.

Knox, J. (2016) *Posthumanism and the Massive Open Online Course: Contaminating the Subject of Global Education*. Abingdon: Routledge.

Komljenovic, J. (2021) 'The rise of education rentiers: Digital platforms, digital data and rents', *Learning, Media and Technology*, 46(3), pp. 1–13. doi:10.1080/17439884.2021.1891422.

Lunden, I. (2013) *Pentametron is a Twitter poet that gives bots some literary cred*. TechCrunch. Available at: https://social.techcrunch.com/2013/01/13/pentametron-is-a-twitter-poet-that-gives-bots-some-literary-cred/ (Accessed: 25 August 2021).

Mallis, J. (2008) *Bendito Machine III (Obey His Commands)*. Zumbakamara. Available at: https://www.youtube.com/watch?v=p9S6lFlyaWA (Accessed: 31 January 2019).

Malott, C. (2020) 'The sublation of digital education', *Postdigital Science and Education*, 2(2), pp. 365–379. doi:10.1007/s42438-019-00083-6.

McAuley, A. et al. (2010) *The MOOC model for digital practice*. Available at: https://oerknowledgecloud.org/sites/oerknowledgecloud.org/files/MOOC_Final_0.pdf (Accessed: 15 September 2013).

Michael, M. (2012) '"What Are We Busy Doing?": Engaging the idiot', *Science, Technology, & Human Values*, 37(5), pp. 528–554. doi:10.1177/0162243911428624.

Michael, M. (2021) *The Research Event: Towards Prospective Methodologies in Sociology.* Abingdon: Routledge.

Myers, F. et al. (2019) 'The automation game: Technological retention activities and perceptions on changes to tutors' roles and identity', *Teaching in Higher Education*, 24(4), pp. 545–562. doi:10.1080/13562517.2018.1498074.

Navas, S. (2021) *Beyond universities, the world needs alternative pathways into jobs.* Emerge Edtech Insights, 3 September. Available at: https://medium.com/emerge-edtech-insights/beyond-universities-the-world-needs-alternative-pathways-into-jobs-part-1-why-are-we-4bb8e775f606 (Accessed: 6 September 2021).

Neyazi, T.A. (2020) 'Digital propaganda, political bots and polarized politics in India', *Asian Journal of Communication*, 30(1), pp. 39–57. doi:10.1080/01292986.2019.1699938.

Pears, M. et al. (2021) 'Co-creation of chatbots as an educational resource: Training the trainers workshop', in *INTED2021 Proceedings. INTED2021.* doi:10.21125/inted.2021.1570.

Pedersen, H. (2010) 'Is the 'Posthuman' educable? On the convergence of educational philosophy, animal studies, and posthumanist theory', *Discourse: Studies in the Cultural Politics of Education*, 31 (2), pp. 237–250. doi:10.1080/01596301003679750.

Popenici, S.A.D. and Kerr, S. (2017) 'Exploring the impact of artificial intelligence on teaching and learning in higher education', *Research and Practice in Technology Enhanced Learning*, 12(1), pp. 1–13. doi:10.1186/s41039-017-0062-8.

Ross, J. et al. (2014) 'Teacher experiences and academic identity: The missing components of MOOC pedagogy', *Journal of Online Learning and Teaching*, 10(1), pp. 57–69.

Ryan, T., French, S. and Kennedy, G. (2021) 'Beyond the iron triangle: Improving the quality of teaching and learning at scale', *Studies in Higher Education*, 46(7), pp. 1383–1394. doi:10.1080/03075079.2019.1679763.

School of Interactive Computing (2020) *Jill Watson, an AI pioneer in education, turns 4, Georgia Tech School of Interactive Computing.* Available at: https://ic.gatech.edu/news/631545/jill-watson-ai-pioneer-education-turns-4 (Accessed: 8 September 2021).

Selwyn, N. (2016) *Education and Technology: Key Issues and Debates.* London: Bloomsbury Publishing.

Shirky, C. (2012). *Higher education: Our MP3 is the mooc.* The Guardian, 17 December. Available at: http://www.theguardian.com/education/2012/dec/17/moocs-higher-education-transformation (Accessed: 23 August 2021).

Stengers, I. (2005) 'The cosmopolitical proposal', in Latour, B., Weibel, P. and Zentrum für Kunst und Medientechnologie Karlsruhe (Eds) *Making Things Public: Atmospheres of Democracy.* Cambridge, MA: MIT Press.

Stracke, C.M. (2017) 'Why we need high drop-out rates in MOOCs: New evaluation and personalization strategies for the quality of open education', in *2017 IEEE 17th International Conference on Advanced Learning Technologies (ICALT). 2017 IEEE 17th International Conference on Advanced Learning Technologies (ICALT)*, pp. 13–15. doi:10.1109/ICALT.2017.109.

Toncic, J. (2020) 'Teachers, AI grammar checkers, and the newest literacies: Emending writing pedagogy and assessment', *Digital Culture & Education*, 12(1), pp. 26–51.

Usher, R. and Edwards. R. (1994) *Postmodernism and Education.* London: Routledge.

Wilkie, A., Michael, M. and Plummer-Fernandez, M. (2015) 'Speculative method and Twitter: Bots, energy and three conceptual characters', *The Sociological Review*, 63(1), pp. 79–101. doi:10.1111/1467-954X.12168.

Williamson, B. (2017) 'Computing brains: Learning algorithms and neurocomputation in the smart city', *Information, Communication & Society*, 20(1), pp. 81–99. doi:10.1080/1369118X.2016.1181194.

Williamson, B. (2021) *Valuing futures*. code acts in education, 20 April. Available at: https://codeactsineducation.wordpress.com/2021/04/20/valuing-futures/ (Accessed: 10 January 2022).

Wojcik, S. et al. (2018) *Bots in the Twittersphere*. Washington, DC: Pew Research Center.

Woolley, S.C. (2016) 'Automating power: Social bot interference in global politics', *First Monday*. doi:10.5210/fm.v21i4.6161. Available at: https://firstmonday.org/ojs/index.php/fm/article/view/6161 (Accessed: 5 August 2022).

6
WORKING WITH DIGITAL FUTURES FOR LEARNING THROUGH STUDENT-GENERATED OPEN EDUCATIONAL RESOURCES

Introduction

Speculative pedagogies have begun to flourish in a range of disciplines. They are being used to support new approaches to learning design, and to engage students with new ways of thinking about their subject areas (for more on this, see Chapter 4). This chapter discusses an example of speculative pedagogy: student-generated Open Educational Resources (OERs) made for an online postgraduate course on the topic of Digital Futures for Learning. Because of the nature of the assignment, the role of peers in assessing it and its place in the course, these OERs were speculative objects, and the course itself was designed and structured to facilitate their emergent and often surprising qualities.

Speculative approaches can be impactful in learning settings, as we saw in Chapter 5, but there are risks to be navigated along the way for educators who want to take them on. There is also a tension between freedom and constraint in formal educational contexts, complexity around the nature of openness and power dynamics around assessment to be taken into account (more on this in Chapter 10). This chapter therefore discusses in some detail how this specific course was put together and structured, and how students were supported to take risks to produce resources with potential for life beyond the course. It also discusses the nature of these OERs as gateways to particular, context-specific education futures that went well beyond what the teachers of the course could have provided for students, demonstrating the emergent and contingent nature of learning futures.

As with the research projects discussed in this part of the book, this pedagogical approach did not emerge from nowhere: it was informed by debates around the nature of and right to access to knowledge, and designed to probe what

DOI: 10.4324/9781003202134-8

kinds of futures might be possible at a time when major issues were emerging around the relationship of openness and closure in learning contexts (Edwards, 2015). So, I begin here by setting the scene that produced the OER assignment in Digital Futures for Learning.

Open educational resources, practices and a continuum of openness

With the emergence of MOOCs and widespread interest in how these might affect access to higher education (see Chapter 5), other forms of openness, including OERs, began to come into greater focus in the sector. Open education in the broadest sense has a very long tradition, but OERs emerged most directly from developments focused on access and the potential reusability of digital learning objects (Weller, 2014). As complexities of the production and use of these resources became apparent, discussions emerged about open practice (Cronin, 2017), how to support teachers, researchers and students to work in ways that encourage collaboration, power dynamics involved in open education (Knox, 2013; Olakulehin and Singh, 2013; Rolfe, 2015; Amiel and Soares, 2016) and sensitivity to contexts of knowledge creation and use (Collier and Ross, 2017). These developments were accompanied by extensive discussion of, debate about and experimentation with different modes and approaches to openness online (Bayne, Knox and Ross, 2015).

Before MOOCs, ideas of online education were often constructed in opposition to the "wild west" of cyberspace (Cohen, 2007), designed to take place in spaces that were private, enclosed, safe and "striated" (Bayne, 2004). Due at least in part to the influence of the rhetoric around MOOCs, by the mid-2010s, discourses of digital education emphasised ideals of openness over closure or constraint. As Gourlay (2015) notes, in practice, these discourses tended to emphasise a fantasy of powerful institutions and unfettered human potential. As critical responses and empirical accounts of the impacts of open education emerged, the view of openness in education as inevitably liberatory began to look increasingly problematic. By 2017, critical work on open education had coalesced around three main arguments: "there is a false binary between 'open' and 'closed' which needs to be challenged; an overemphasis on access to content homogenises learners and their contexts; [and] open educational practice does not attend sufficiently to issues of power and inclusion" (Collier and Ross, 2017, p. 7). Edwards (2015) argued that, far from seeing openness and closure as being in opposition, "all forms of openness entail forms of closed-ness" (p. 253) and that educators must decide "what forms of openness and closed-ness are justifiable" (p. 255). This was a call to pay more attention to "the tradeoffs that inevitably come with navigating the complexity of issues like access, ownership, and sustainability" (Ross, Bayne and Lamb, 2019, p. 29).

106 Speculative objects to think with

In the context of OERs, these tradeoffs involved debates about how to value different dimensions of social and epistemic justice entangled with them. On one hand, there was a recognised need for less well-resourced educational systems – including those in the Global South – to have more equitable access to the products of an extractive knowledge creation system. The value of sharing and the possibilities of breaking down barriers between people, systems and ideas have long been espoused as key benefits of the open web, and OERs were seen as part of this tradition. On the other hand, the tendency of wealthy, prominent institutions and educators to view their knowledge as universal, and to "bestow" this on others in the form of educational resources intended more for reuse than remix, led to assertions of neocolonialism (Adam, 2019). The work involved in remixing and repurposing such open materials, while arguably having the most potential to be transformative in the Global South (Hodgkinson-Williams and Trotter, 2018), required significant investment of resource on the part of organisations, for instance by introducing micro-credentials, to "optimise the value proposition" (p. 220).

As discussions of the nature and potential for open resources have developed, questions have become more pointed in interrogating their knowledge practices: for instance, who makes and is represented in OERs, and which forms of knowledge are reproduced in them (Veletsianos, 2021)? Open practices in general have come to be seen as variable in their processes, intentions and outcomes. For example, Bali, Cronin and Jhangiani (2020) propose three axes for open practices – from content to process; teacher to learner; and pedagogy to social justice focused, and they discuss strengths and limitations of each of these. Giving examples of various combinations of focus, they identify a category of work they refer to as "public scholarship by students" (p. 8), which aligns most closely with OER work students undertook on Digital Futures for Learning. Their example of this, the US-based Domain of One's Own service which provides students with their own web hosting space, is described as "a process-centric, student-centric practice" (ibid). Elsewhere, they discuss student editing of Wikipedia as both content- and process-focused, and as learner-centred (p. 3). They suggest that such student scholarship can have positive social justice impacts if it does not take place on exploitative platforms and if it foregrounds the voices of marginalised students, but they also identify the uneven potential for surveillance and the threats this may bring to some students when publishing open materials.

In general, discussions of openness and open access (to knowledge, to culture and to education) have identified a tendency of for-profit entities – including publishers, platform providers and others – to seek advantage from shifting landscapes, technologies and possibilities for sharing (Yeo, 2020). An example of the kinds of debates that have taken place centred around one of the major North American open education conferences in 2019. The OpenEd conference had been running since 2003, under the organisational leadership of David Wiley from the US edtech company Lumen Learning. It was a high-profile conference on the North American edtech calendar each year. Leading up to the 2019 conference, there were criticisms from a number of educators, practitioners and researchers, including many who were attending the conference, about a planned keynote panel featuring speakers from three for-profit publishers. People objected to giving publishers such a high-profile platform at the conference (Jhangiani, 2019). The keynote panel was subsequently cancelled as several speakers pulled out, citing harassment on social media. Wiley announced at the conference that the OpenEd conference series would be adjourned indefinitely in order to make room for consideration of next steps for the community (Burke, 2019). In fact, the conference took place virtually in both 2020 and 2021, with a note on the website that "for the last two years, the Open Education Conference has been governed by a Steering Committee and four-organization partnership. This interim organizing structure is designed to support the conference through a transition to full community ownership starting in 2022".[1] This reconfiguration of a major conference, sparked by debates about how, and by whom, openness was being mobilised, echoes what we see in the critical literature on openness: growing refusal to accept utopian promises of "access for all", and a focus on costs – financial and otherwise – that may not be immediately apparent.

In summary, the context in which the particular education futures discussed in this chapter were produced was one of significant debate and some uncertainty. On top of this, most students on the Digital Futures for Learning course had never produced an OER before, and it felt, and was, risky in a number of ways for them, and for the teachers. I go on now to outline the course and the nature of this public-facing work, before analysing some examples of digital futures for learning that emerged from it, and highlighting the impacts of this speculative pedagogical approach.

The Digital Futures for Learning course

Digital Futures for Learning was created to give students the opportunity to consider the trajectory and implications of digital technologies for the future of learning. Over the past 12 years, I have taught it with different colleagues,[2] each of whom has brought to it particular insights and perspectives that I, and the students, have hugely valued. As I wrote the first iteration of this chapter in late 2021, I was preparing to teach it again in early 2022 – preparation that involved selecting three key themes that would engage students and give them space and scope to create interesting materials themselves. The student-created materials building on these themes were the basis for the whole second half of the course, so this selection is vital. Although the course continues to run in the form described below, it is discussed here in the past tense, as it may well evolve further in the coming years.

108 Speculative objects to think with

The course asked: how are more established digital practices evolving? How will new digital technologies and trends impact on learning? How will the students and teachers of tomorrow construct their learning environments and practices? Each time it ran, it took three key themes as its starting point, and used them to guide exploration of emerging practices and technologies. A key to this course was the way it was co-created by its participants. This was important because of the subject matter of the course – digital futures – and how quickly the topics of interest evolved. Creating a sustainable and engaging course of this nature benefited from a pedagogical approach which was both carefully structured and open in terms of content.

The course was first proposed and approved in 2008, as part of the fully online MSc in Digital Education (MSc in E-learning, as it was known then), and it ran for the first time in 2010. Part of my role in the MSc at that time was as technology co-ordinator, which included responsibility for "horizon scanning", trying to understand what digital futures might look like in our field and how the programme could and should innovate. Each year at our programme away days, I would present a few key emerging themes or technologies, for discussion amongst the group. This process led to the idea for this course. I explained in the course proposal documentation that the MSc needed: "an explicitly 'blue skies' thinking course – a way to prepare students to be critical consumers/producers of new technologies as they emerge, and to understand how the 'next big thing' that comes along might fit into their current educational practices" (Digital Futures for Learning proposal, November 2008). From the outset, students not only created materials for one another but also gave detailed peer feedback for others. This aspect of the course was inspired by work around peer assessment (Boud, Cohen and Sampson, 1999) and authentic assessment (Cumming and Maxwell, 1999). It also emerged from a context in which "co-creation" was becoming a focus of attention in education and informal learning (Morse, Macpherson and Robinson, 2013; Bovill et al., 2016; Dollinger, Lodge and Coates, 2018; Matthews et al., 2018).

Students in the Digital Education programme were typically studying part-time while also working, and many were mid-career professionals in education roles in formal, workplace and community learning settings. They usually took the programme over at least three years, with the most common pattern being to study a single course per semester. Many studied the full MSc, including a dissertation, but there were also Postgraduate Certificate and Postgraduate Diploma qualification routes. Digital Futures for Learning was one of a number of optional courses on the programme, and it was not offered every year, but ran eight times in total between 2010 and 2022. There were usually 15–20 participants each time, and themes over the years include personalisation, mobility, authorship and collaboration, ubiquity, openness, making and coding, trust, privacy, complexity, failure, entanglement, surveillance, interfaces, participation, sustainability and representation.

When the course started, and for the first two years, the student-created topics were presented in the form of seminars and learning events, shared only amongst the group. From 2013, I changed the assessment format to involve the creation of OERs, published openly on the web. The aim of the assignment was to provide a high-quality, engaging introduction to topics each student had explored in a previous "position paper" assignment. These topics were aligned with one or more of the course themes, but went beyond them to explore ideas, issues and possibilities relevant to each author's interests and context. This in itself was not unusual on the MSc Digital Education programme, in which most courses gave students some flexibility about assignment topics, on the principle that their professional and other interests and priorities would form a strong foundation for engagement with key theories and concepts. What was unusual was that the fully teacher-provided content for this course spanned just five weeks, with the remaining seven weeks shaped significantly by students' work. In the next section, the OER assignment and the kinds of outputs students produced are discussed.

Co-creating futures: the OER assignment

The Digital Futures Open Education Resources were created in a two-stage process, and assessed by a combination of peer review, tutor marking and self-assessment. Central to the OER assignment was that students created a resource that let others engage meaningfully with the key elements of their topic, engaging and involving their peers in considering, in a scholarly way, issues relevant to the course themes. Students were informed that the target audience for the OERs was education professionals and Masters-level students working in fields including digital education, learning technology, digital futures and e-learning. In other words, the benefit of the OER was not only intended to be for the student who created it – it was equally for the students who would participate in it. For this reason, it was important that the assessment of the OERs reflected the purpose of the assignment, which was to facilitate learning for the whole student group, and the staged production and peer review process reflected this. For students as both creators and consumers of the OERs, this created challenges. When creating, they considered what shared knowledge could be relied on, how to make more specialist topics accessible to others and how to make the links to the core course themes explicit. When reviewing, they took into account their position as part of the intended audience and therefore their own interests, while also trying to follow writer and critic John Updike's first rule of criticism:

110 Speculative objects to think with

> Try to understand what the author wished to do, and do not blame [them]
> for not achieving what [they] did not attempt.
>
> *(Hawthorne, 2009)*

They were encouraged, above all, to give feedback based on genuine participation:

> Be as generous as you can with your time and energy, and engage whole-
> heartedly. Just because you are providing formal feedback on the resource
> doesn't mean you have to be detached or neutral in your participation.
> Take the experience for what it is, and learn as much as you can. ...Be
> honest – if you don't think something worked, say so. If something really
> impressed you, say so. ...Try to give feedback that you would find help-
> ful yourself. Remember that this feedback will directly inform what your
> peers submit to be marked, so your feedback really does matter.
>
> *(guidance for peer review of OERs)*

The first OER stage was a complete first version, building on the position paper topic. Resources created in this stage formed the content for the final block of the course, and each author received detailed feedback from peers. Authors then revised their OERs before submitting a final version, which was marked by the tutors. Table 6.1 gives an example of how the course was structured.

Each time the course ran, the way that students interpreted and imagined the future of learning became highly relevant to the overall shape of the course. Some students focused on a particular professional setting, others an emerging technology, and others a critical question or a utopian or dystopian vision. Still others were interested in the OER format itself and the possibilities of openness now and in the future.

The OERs discussed in this section are drawn from the 2017, 2019 and 2020 instances of the course, and I focus on finalised resources that students gave permission to have listed on a public web site created for this purpose in 2017.[3] After the final assessment and course evaluation had been completed and marks returned, I emailed students to invite them to have their OER listed. Not all the authors in each year wished to have links to their work published, and for some OERs I discussed with the authors what changes they would need to make to have them shared (especially if there were issues with referencing materials). It is also worth noting that, as live digital resources, the OERs in the form discussed in this chapter are not guaranteed to be identical to the ones that were initially presented for the course, though they are substantively the same in terms of focus and approach. In early 2022, I contacted authors of all the OERs cited here to ask for permission to include discussion of their work in this chapter, and all kindly agreed. All of these OERs did well in assessment terms, but my discussion here is focused on the visions they present.

TABLE 6.1 Digital Futures for Learning course structure, 2020

Week	Key activities
Weeks 1–5: "thinking about the future" theme: interfaces theme: participation theme: sustainability	Reading, discussing, attending tutorials, developing topics and creating stories from the future. Interaction and feedback from tutors and peers in course discussion forums. End of week 5: Finalise topic for position paper and OER. Students were asked to email the course organiser to discuss their topic, and receive formative feedback on this.
Weeks 6 & 7: position paper writing	End of period: Position paper (Assignment 1) due. Detailed tutor feedback and a mark would come in week 10 (after the first draft of the OER was published). Students could take this feedback as well as peer feedback into account when revising their OER.
Weeks 8 & 9: OER development	End of period: Open Educational Resource (Assignment 2, stage 1) due. The OER was built from the position paper topic, with students designing a resource that conveyed the important aspects of their topic in a way that was engaging.
Weeks 10 & 11: peer engagement with OERs	Each student responsible for giving detailed feedback on the OERs of three of their group members, and encouraged to engage with others. Tutors gave formative feedback and asked questions, facilitated discussion, pointed out interesting aspects of OERs.
Week 12: peer feedback & wrapping up	Start of week: OER peer feedback forms due. Feedback reviewed, collated and distributed by course organiser. Wrapping up and discussions of key ideas and questions raised through the course.
After end of semester	Open Educational Resource (Assignment 2, stage 2) and reflective commentary due. Final OER and commentary reviewed and marked by tutors.

Grappling with edtech imaginaries

A number of OER authors took a particular interest in one or more emerging technologies, their pedagogical implications and the imaginaries around them – including blockchain, biological and cognitive technologies and surveillance technologies.

112 Speculative objects to think with

Blockchain technologies and their implications for recordkeeping, transactions and relations of trust were of growing interest in education in the late 2010s. In her OER on blockchain in education, Murphy (2017) observed that blockchain was being positioned within edtech imaginaries of disruption and even the reconfiguration of higher education, primarily through recording and verifying credentials. Inviting OER participants to engage in a "critical experiment" to examine issues of trust, ideology and neutrality, she designed a fictional future system called "How to Adult" which involves young people achieving and recording 50 core skills (see Figure 6.1) which every human adult should acquire by age 25. Covering practical, technical, emotional and intellectual skills (everything from creating a splint for a broken leg to knowing when consent is given), the system would use blockchain technology to record these skills for each person, each skill verified by someone with the same skill.

Once achieved, "adult" status confers employment opportunities, voting rights and other advantages, as well as providing people with confidence that "they might survive any global crises or shortages" ("How to Adult" promotional slides). Murphy offers a critical toolkit for examining this and other blockchain proposals, which includes questions such as:

- What assumptions are we making about those whose data is collected in a blockchain? What ideas does this reinforce?
- What data is collected, for what purpose, and how else might it used?
- Who is trusted in this application of blockchain? And what is the nature of that trust?

(Murphy, 2017)

Through her own speculative scenario, Murphy produced an object-to-think-with and scaffolded that thinking process for participants. Responses to the scenario (shared publicly within the OER by participants) cover matters such as the value of governance, the nature of consensus, and questions about exclusion and inequality.

Taking a similar speculative approach to Murphy's, but inviting even more immersion, Nicholls' (2017) OER engages participants in a fictional world of the "Nexus Academy" in 2030, where they take on the role of investigator on behalf of the "Digital Education Watchdog" (led by commissioning officer Ed Snowden) which briefs them on concerns about the nature of the technologies being used, the data being generated about participants, and the relationship between the Academy and third-party organisations. Participants investigate these claims using an evidence board consisting of interconnected nodes representing organisations, people and technologies related to Nexus Academy, as well as links to scholarly papers, talks and other materials that could help investigators understand what they are seeing. Technologies in the evidence board

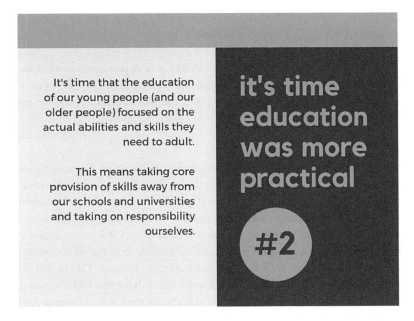

FIGURE 6.1 Rationale for Murphy's "How to Adult" speculative scenario.

include facial recognition, teacherbots, bioportfolios embedded in genetic code and blockchain certificates. Overall, Nicholls frames the production of the "bio-digital citizen" through these technologies and their interactions, and emphasises the implications for privacy, for example:

> Utilising historical data recorded in each citizen's Digifolio, advanced artificial intelligence and machine learning algorithms are being devised by DigiCorp employees to build autonomous TutorBot. In some cases these are known to have complete control over what and how citizens study through the Nexus Academy's microlearning and nanodegree programmes.
>
> *("Sarah" Node)*

Carbonel's (2019) OER, focusing on cognitive technologies in education, attends to their possible retroactive social effects, including changes in privacy experiences and expectations, advantages conferred by "enhancement" and issues of identity and selfhood. She adopts Williamson's (2019) framework distinguishing between biological, computer and social codes to invite participants to analyse a then-emerging, controversial educational technology – a headband that captured recordings of brain activity, and software which the makers claimed could provide neurofeedback to "improve the attention levels of teenagers and children".[4] The OER takes participants through approaches to analysing cognitive

114 Speculative objects to think with

technologies, and emphasises the importance of engaging with emerging technologies and the imaginaries around them:

> What the world of tomorrow looks like will depend on the choices we make today. This is why we need to have an open discussion about what we, as citizens and educators, see as important issues and how we might deal with them.
>
> *(Carbonel, 2019)*

What we see in these OERs is a commitment to the value of engaging critically with edtech imaginaries, and an optimism that doing so can offer genuine possibilities for things to be otherwise. This is interesting, given the tendency for future technological visions to lean towards the dystopian (Markham, 2021). Critical thinking in educational settings is seen in these OERs as an antidote to edtech dystopias, and the extent to which education itself can effect change at individual or collective level is examined explicitly in some OERs that focus on critical literacies (Ichaporia, 2019; Lopes, 2020). Ichaporia's OER examines arguments for the value of taking a critical literacies approach to current debates and challenges around emerging technologies and practices. She highlights issues of "truth decay", surveillance capitalism and personalised learning, and observes that critical literacies need to operate at multiple levels (from the individual to the institutional and sectoral):

> Applying critical digital literacy could empower students and educators in various ways e.g. once suitably informed, students may choose to opt out of personalised learning. …At the institutional level, critical digital literacy could make educators more mindful when using educational technology to predict student potential… [but] this 'opening up' of the concept of digital literacy cannot easily be achieved without the support of all stakeholders.
>
> *(Ichaporia, 2019)*

Lopes makes a related point, with a focus on surveillance technologies, noting the normalisation of surveillance in schools and other educational settings and the lack of attention to these issues in "so-called digital literacy skills and competences" training. She proposes that this is as a result of their orientation to the future (Facer, 2016):

> The current educational system operates in the future by pre-determining what skills, competencies or knowledge should be emphasized over others and assuming a monitoring behavior that continuously assesses and adjusts desired traits, whether to prepare students for a known future, or to try and colonize said future.
>
> *(Lopes, 2020)*

She argues instead for a more dynamic orientation to literacies, with a view towards examining situated practices as a foundation for dialogical relations and praxis in the Frierian sense.

These OERs, in their explicit engagement with emerging technologies, social and educational practices, and ethical and theoretical considerations, are models for how digital futures for learning can be situated and worked with in generative and active ways. These authors are realistic about the challenges facing educators and students, but use their critical awareness of how these technologies and imaginaries have come to be, and how they function, to offer others some ways into significant and complex issues.

Entangled workplace learning futures

One aspect of the design of the Digital Futures course is that the teachers' expertise need not limit the discussions students can pursue. A number of course participants over the years have come from workplace learning contexts of various kinds, and their OERs pushed course themes in sometimes unexpected directions, ones that went well beyond what I or the other tutors would have been able to convey.

Some workplace-focused topics were fairly general in nature, often with a focus on office workers, but others managed to give glimpses into the possible futures of specific sectors, linking these to broader insights. The *Deck Officer Training and Technology* OER (Ferguson, 2020) was one of these. According to Ferguson, the maritime education sector typically views technology in a fairly instrumental way, with an understanding of human cognition and decision-making as the primary driver for what does, and does not, happen on board ships. Ferguson takes OER participants through the limitations of such a view, showing how data-driven, autonomous and other systems and interfaces *influence* rather than merely *support* bridge operations. Drawing on actor network theory, he proposes the "posthuman seafarer", and argues that maritime education will need to change to accommodate this figure, drawing on a core reading from that year that introduced the notion of "digi-grasping" as a way of making sense of digital worlds in a participatory way (Dufva and Dufva, 2019):

> While we still teach our deck officers about celestial navigation and the use of a sextant, skills such as 'digi-grasping' will become increasingly impor-tant... digi-grasping is more than a theoretical or technical understanding it reflects the qualities and skills required to operate in the physical and digital environment.
>
> *(Ferguson, 2020)*

Another workplace-focused OER tackles "entanglement" from a more office-based perspective (Peckham, 2019). Drawing on course readings, Peckham reviews concepts of "hybrid", "brainy and playful" and "mundane" spaces to explore how

116 Speculative objects to think with

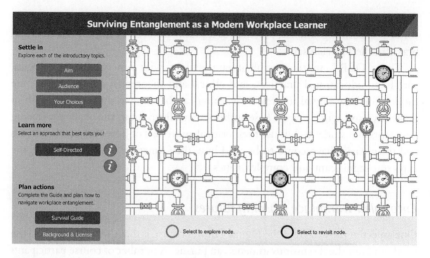

FIGURE 6.2 Peckham's "surviving entanglement" machine.

workplaces might become more continuously quantified, gamified and databased. The design of the OER aligns with the theme of entanglement, as the resource itself is designed as a machine full of pipe and valves (see Figure 6.2), with each valve, or node, leading to different themes and content.

Moving through in a non-linear fashion, participants are offered related valves and "thought starters". Framed as a matter of "survival", Peckham argues that:

> the chances of survival [for modern learners] are improved by replacing the mythical view of technological infrastructure as 'seamless, homogenous assemblies' with a more realistic concept which positions the complex intermingling of people, space, technology and data as a 'messy affair' (Shepard, 2013).
>
> *(Node 6) (Peckham, 2019)*

He illustrates this messiness in the design of the OER itself, with nodes changing colour, recommendations different depending on context and content offered in visual and non-linear ways.

A third workplace-focused OER describes itself as a "bootcamp" to examine individualised learning (Adams, 2019). Drawing on the 2019 course theme of "failure", Adams proposes that current self-paced learning provision from employers and others sets many individuals up for failure, and that the future of self-paced learning design will be more fragmented and compressed, lending itself to a "high-energy, intense" workout-type approach. Her OER demonstrates what this could look like, with four "workouts" taking the place of more traditionally structured learning resources. Building on Selwyn's (2017) challenges around individualised learning, she tackles individual differences, not-knowing, social learning and age-related digital divides.

Working with digital futures for learning **117**

Messiness, entanglement, relationality and sense-making in complex technology-rich environments come through in these OERs as key considerations for the future of workplace learning.

Engaging with complexity

The final group of OERs for discussion in this chapter each take a different, and effective, approach to contending with the complexity of education in technological spaces. Smallbones (2017) explores complexity itself, and how it challenges reductive approaches to education, including technologically reductive ones. Guiding participants through mapping their own learning ecosystems, defining aspects of complexity including emergence (see Chapter 3), exploring multimodality and critiquing personalised learning in favour of abundance, she invites written responses to Gough's (2013) question: "how might understanding our worlds and selves as open, recursive, organic, nonlinear and emergent make different practices possible for curriculum design, and research on teaching and learning, ...?" (p. 1227).

Alexakis (2020), focusing in particular on hypertextuality as a site of playfulness and risk-taking, constructed his OER as an editable, offline wiki, inviting participants to view it as a non-linear "makerspace" and to develop their own version of the resource and engage with a series of activities. Focusing on reframing "failure" as an opportunity for making new links and engaging in multiple ways with complex questions or issues, he encourages experimentation with rhizomatic writing practices. Here the design of the OER produces a direct connection with complexity theory.

Finally, Collins (2019) uses postdigital theory to challenge the sanitised vision of education presented by proponents of "Education 4.0", characterised by human-machine interactions, virtual reality, AI and other "exponential technologies", some of which she characterises as underpinned by "zombie ideas". Taking a postdigital perspective on learning analytics, she observes the "contextual vacuum" that constitutes much of the discourse around these developments, and encourages instead a "more holistic and robust [perspective]... exposing and critiquing the ideological assumptions and agendas which underpin the adoption and promotion of digital technologies and sociotechnical imaginaries" (Collins, 2019).

Speculative pedagogy through student-generated OERs

The experience of creating assignments in OER format went beyond a standard essay-based assignment in two key respects. First, they were for an audience beyond the tutor, so authors had to take into account the needs, interests and expertise of their peers. Second, creating genuinely open resources required careful attention to issues such as accessibility, structure, audience and licensing, which formed a substantial part of the work that students undertook.[5] Beyond the assignment itself, the

118 Speculative objects to think with

sensibility of the course and critical questions around openness and closure that it raised produced the course itself as a speculative space. Aspects of debates around open education were brought to life by engagement with the creation of OERs, and students on Digital Futures for Learning were asked to consider their work critically in this respect, with a number of readings and resources provided to support this. This could have unexpected effects, as in the 2017 instance of the course, when the teachers proposed to make aspects of the course materials and discussion public on the open web. As reported in an online case study about this development (Ross, 2018), students were quick to respond to our discussion post asking for their views, and these ranged from cautious welcome to discomfort to resistance. In a constructively critical vein, they questioned our aims, and how they could expect to benefit from having their discussions made public in this way. Even while expressing some support for the idea, describing positive experiences of open practices elsewhere and the value they placed on openness in education, the group recognised the impact that making these discussion spaces visible would have on their willingness to take risks in expressing ideas and responding to the course themes. The scrutiny that such openness would entail would, in Edwards' terms (2015), produce closures, in this case by changing and limiting the way people would interact in the forums – perhaps creating what one participant described as a chilling effect on discussion. In addition to these insights, they challenged us to defend the pedagogical value of this proposal, and thoughtfully explored the question of trust:

> What do we stand to gain from exposure without engagement? Would we in effect become a showcase? … Is it a case of using this instance of the course to engage a wider audience in the academic issues or, because of the subject matter, is it something that should be showcased for 'external' observation and analysis? There could very well be different agendas and motivations – can they work together? … Do we trust our tutors?
>
> *(student on Digital Futures for Learning in 2017)*

The points collectively raised about the purpose and politics of openness, and risks surrounding exposure, surveillance and vulnerability, were core to the discussions we were having through the course. A techno-utopian vision of open access to education masks these, and other, pedagogical decisions and makes it harder to talk about the gains and losses that come with each choice we make about what, and how, to share. The Digital Futures for Learning web site was the outcome of these discussions – a showcase of course themes and work produced by students, and a polished end-product rather than a snapshot of process:

> It is a different kind of reflection of open practice than the teachers had initially envisaged… [but it] offers a glimpse into what we think is an ethically defensible approach to open practice, one that seeks to understand how different participants are affected by our choices as teachers, and helps

us all to learn and to create conditions in which the question of whether students trust their teachers can be answered optimistically.

(Ross, 2018)

The key features of this course – the student-generated content, the peer feedback mechanisms and the persistence and openness of the materials – created an experimental space, which tended to stay unresolved throughout each semester as design, assessment and feedback roles continually shifted. There were moments of stability: in the early weeks of the course and again most notably when the teachers provided final marks for the OERs. But, unlike most courses, after those final marks were returned, it began to shift again, as the OERs took on a life of their own on the web. The course was designed to create a speculative pedagogical space, but it was the student perspectives and work on the OERs that kept its learning design from becoming fixed or static.

The course was also speculative because it was explicitly designed for unknown problems and contexts (Konnerup, Ryberg and Sørensen, 2019), and the course design was a "springboard for development": "dynamic, experimental opportunities for the collective design of new practices". (pp. 124–5). Speculative pedagogies can, at their best, "evoke …a politics and ethics of the suddenly possible" by being "'reactive', responsive or generative and improvising in relation to how something in a learning encounter matters for a learner and how the potentialities of such mattering can be developed" (Atkinson, 2020, p. 58), and when the course achieved this for individual students, it mattered to them and sometimes had impacts beyond their studies. A participant from one course instance emailed a year later to let the tutors know that the course had led to professional opportunities and the development of a further OER. Others have reported using their OERs for purposes beyond the programme.

Osborn et al. (2019) describe something similar with their interdisciplinary Pilgrimage Project, for example, where a "Remix Practices" course had "an overlapping point of engagement into the work of the other courses and maintained the sense that the students were engaged in a project that expanded beyond the scope and boundaries of a single course" (pp. 358–9). For them, the blurring of disciplinary boundaries "affords new and productive pedagogical approaches" (p. 366) that they characterise as speculative in nature. In Digital Futures, the blurring of authorial boundaries afforded these new pedagogical possibilities, as student work formed gateways for others to new topics and approaches.

So, when students produced their own speculative scenarios and designerly responses to questions about futures for learning, and tackled dystopian visions and technologies with hopeful educational responses, they were making a different course from the one I would have made, and a different course from the previous years', too. This did not always go without a hitch: it was essential, for example, that everyone was very clear about the intended audience for their OERs, and this sometimes needed several exchanges with individuals who wanted (for example) to produce something for children, parents, or other audiences. Individuals'

120 Speculative objects to think with

approaches to peer feedback sometimes diverged from the supportive but questioning model I presented above, either through being too harsh or, more commonly, too "nice". Where feedback on the position paper assignment (from tutors) was at odds with feedback on the OERs (from peers), students could be left with some uncertainty about which feedback to try to action. Ultimately, most attempted to action tutor feedback over that of peers, and this probably indicates some of the limits of co-creation in a formal educational context.

In their first week of the semester, students on the Digital Futures course read about and discussed what it means to think about and work with the future. As part of this, they read Facer's chapter on "using the future in education", in which she argues for a pedagogy of the present as a reframing of the educational challenge: "to explore how to create the spaces and practices that will continually enable the dynamic disclosure, imagination and creation of radically new possibilities in the present" (Facer, 2016, p. 70). In its design and its practice, Digital Futures for Learning takes up this reframed challenge, its refusal to pin the future down to a single vision or voice, and its tendency to blur the epistemological and temporal boundaries of the curriculum and the course. This form of speculative pedagogy keeps the future moving.

Summary of insights

- Speculative course design makes space for students' own futures work, keeping learning futures open and moving.
- Pedagogical practices that centre students' perspectives and priorities are useful for speculative course design, including peer- and self-assessment, and co-design of curriculum.
- Education-focused responses to key issues can generate optimism and hope for digital learning futures that go beyond solutionism.
- Open educational practices can blur the boundaries of a course, generating speculative impacts beyond the time and space of the formal engagement.

Notes

1 https://openeducationconference.org/about, accessed February 2022.
2 The course was first designed and taught with Hamish Macleod, and has since been co-taught with Jeremy Knox, Siân Bayne, Stuart Allan and Huw Davies. My thanks to these great teachers and to the brilliant MSc Digital Education students who have engaged with the course over the years.
3 https://digitalfutures.de.ed.ac.uk
4 This quote is from an archive of the BrainCo website, accessed on 8 October 2021 from http://ec2-54-82-236-75.compute-1.amazonaws.com/product/brainco-product. At the time of writing this chapter this product has disappeared from the live site, replaced by products aimed at adults and the "self-hacking" market. This may or may not relate to the Chinese ban on the product in schools, in reaction to a public backlash against the use of this technology in Chinese schools (Jiangnan, 2019).

5 Students were supported to consider aspects of licensing and the design of OERs by colleagues in the Open Education team at the University of Edinburgh – special thanks to Charlie Farley who led tutorials for the students to introduce them to key considerations.

References

Adam, T. (2019) 'Digital neocolonialism and massive open online courses (MOOCs): Colonial pasts and neoliberal futures', *Learning, Media and Technology*, 44(3), pp. 365–380. doi:10.1080/17439884.2019.1640740.

Adams, A. (2019) *Digital future of workplace learning – Exploring the limitations of individualised learning.* Available at: https://blogs.ed.ac.uk/onlineworkplace2025/ (Accessed: 5 October 2021).

Alexakis, C. (2020) *On playfulness, failure, composition & hypertextuality.* Available at: http://dfloer.tiddlyspot.com/ (Accessed: 7 October 2021).

Amiel, T. and Soares, T.C. (2016) 'Identifying tensions in the use of open licenses in OER repositories', *The International Review of Research in Open and Distributed Learning*, 17(3), pp. 122–134. doi:10.19173/irrodl.v17i3.2426.

Atkinson, D. (2020) 'Inheritance, disobedience and speculation', in Addison, Nicholas and Burgess, Lesley (Eds) *Debates in Art and Design Education.* Abingdon: Routledge, pp. 57–71.

Bali, M., Cronin, C. and Jhangiani, R.S. (2020) 'Framing open educational practices from a social justice perspective', *Journal of Interactive Media in Education*, 2020(1). doi:10.5334/jime.565.

Bayne, S. (2004) 'Smoothness and striation in digital learning spaces', *E-Learning*, 1(2), pp. 302–316.

Bayne, S., Knox, J. and Ross, J. (2015) 'Open education: The need for a critical approach', *Learning, Media and Technology*, 40(3), pp. 247–250. doi:10.1080/17439884.2015.1065272.

Boud, D., Cohen, R. and Sampson, J. (1999) 'Peer learning and assessment', *Assessment & Evaluation in Higher Education*, 24(4), pp. 413–426. doi:10.1080/0260293990240405.

Bovill, C. et al. (2016) 'Addressing potential challenges in co-creating learning and teaching: Overcoming resistance, navigating institutional norms and ensuring inclusivity in student–staff partnerships', *Higher Education*, 71(2), pp. 195–208. doi:10.1007/s10734-015-9896-4.

Burke, L. (2019) *Open education... Is closed.* Inside Higher Ed, 6 November. Available at: https://www.insidehighered.com/digital-learning/article/2019/11/06/david-wiley-steps-down-and-adjourns-open-education-conference (Accessed: 17 February 2022).

Carbonel, H. (2019) *A critical approach to cognitive technologies in education, teaching ideas; a passion for teaching.* Available at: https://vickytill.wixsite.com/neurotechined (Accessed: 7 October 2021).

Cohen, J. (2007) 'Cyberspace and/as space', *Columbia Law Review*, 107(1), pp. 201–256.

Collier, A. and Ross, J. (2017) 'For whom, and for what? Not-yetness and thinking beyond open content', *Open Praxis*, 9(1), pp. 7–16. doi:10.5944/openpraxis.9.1.406.

Collins, J. (2019) *Postdigital or 4.0? Conceptualising education in the 21st century.* Available at: https://www.open.edu/openlearncreate/course/view.php?id=4491 (Accessed: 7 October 2021).

Cronin, C. (2017) 'Openness and praxis: Exploring the use of open educational practices in higher education', *The International Review of Research in Open and Distributed Learning*, 18(5). Available at: http://www.irrodl.org./index.php/irrodl/article/view/3096 (Accessed: 16 February 2018).

Cumming, J.J. and Maxwell, G.S. (1999) 'Contextualising authentic assessment', *Assessment in Education: Principles, Policy & Practice*, 6(2), pp. 177–194. doi:10.1080/09695949992865.

Dollinger, M., Lodge, J. and Coates, H. (2018) 'Co-creation in higher education: Towards a conceptual model', *Journal of Marketing for Higher Education*, 28(2), pp. 210–231. doi:10.1080/08841241.2018.1466756.

Dufva, T. and Dufva, M. (2019) 'Grasping the future of the digital society', *Futures*, 107, pp. 17–28. doi:10.1016/j.futures.2018.11.001.

Edwards, R. (2015) 'Knowledge infrastructures and the inscrutability of openness in education', *Learning, Media and Technology*, 40(3), pp. 251–264. doi:10.1080/17439884.2015.1006131.

Facer, K. (2016) 'Using the future in education: Creating space for openness, hope and novelty', in Lees, H.E. and Noddings, N. (Eds) *The Palgrave International Handbook of Alternative Education*. London: Palgrave Macmillan UK, pp. 63–78. doi:10.1057/978-1-137-41291-1_5.

Ferguson, A. (2020) *Deck officer training and technology: Developing a critical approach*. OER Commons. Available at: https://www.oercommons.org/courseware/lesson/75036/overview (Accessed: 5 October 2021).

Gough, N. (2013) 'Towards deconstructive nonalignment: A complexivist view of curriculum, teaching and learning', *South African Journal of Higher Education*, 27(5), pp. 1213–1233.

Gourlay, L. (2015) 'Open education as a "heterotopia of desire"', *Learning, Media and Technology*, 40(3), pp. 310–327. doi:10.1080/17439884.2015.1029941.

Hawthorne, M. (2009) *Remembering Updike: The Gospel according to John*. The New Yorker, 27 January. Available at: http://www.newyorker.com/books/page-turner/remembering-updike-the-gospel-according-to-john (Accessed: 28 September 2021).

Hodgkinson-Williams, C.A. and Trotter, H. (2018) 'A social justice framework for understanding open educational resources and practices in the global south', *Journal of Learning for Development*, 5(3), pp. 204–224.

Ichaporia, N. (2019) *Digital literacy for digital futures, digital literacy for digital futures*. Available at: https://digitalfutures.weebly.com/ (Accessed: 8 October 2021).

Jhangiani, R. (2019) *For-profit, faux-pen, and critical conversations about the future of learning materials*. Rajiv Jhangiani, Ph.D., 15 October. Available at: https://thatpsychprof.com/for-profit-faux-pen-and-critical-conversations/ (Accessed: 30 September 2021).

Jiangnan, X. (2019) *AI headbands tracking student attention levels suspended amidst online controversy*. People's Daily Online, November. Available at: http://en.people.cn/n3/2019/1101/c90000-9628768.html (Accessed: 8 October 2021).

Knox, J. (2013) 'The limitations of access alone: Moving towards open processes in education technology', *Open Praxis*, 5(1), pp. 21–29. doi:10.5944/openpraxis.5.1.36.

Konnerup, U., Ryberg, T. and Sørensen, M.T. (2019) 'Designs for learning as springboards for professional development in higher education', in Littlejohn, A. et al. (Eds) *Networked Professional Learning: Emerging and Equitable Discourses for Professional Development*. Cham: Springer International Publishing (Research in Networked Learning), pp. 111–127. doi:10.1007/978-3-030-18030-0_7.

Lopes, A. (2020) *The Panopticon: Digital literacy and a future of surveillance*. Panopticon_DFL. Available at: https://panopticondfl.wordpress.com/ (Accessed: 7 October 2021).

Markham, A. (2021) 'The limits of the imaginary: Challenges to intervening in future speculations of memory, data, and algorithms', *New Media & Society*, 23(2), pp. 382–405. doi:10.1177/1461444820929322.

Matthews, K.E. et al. (2018) 'Conceptions of students as partners', *Higher Education*, 76(6), pp. 957–971. doi:10.1007/s10734-018-0257-y.

Morse, N., Macpherson, M. and Robinson, S. (2013) 'Developing dialogue in co-produced exhibitions: Between rhetoric, intentions and realities', *Museum Management and Curatorship*, 28(1), pp. 91–106. doi:10.1080/09647775.2012.754632.

Murphy, H. (2017) *Education and the blockchain, Digital Futures in Learning*. Available at: http://educationandtheblockchain.weebly.com/ (Accessed: 7 October 2021).

Nicholls, J. (2017) *The biodigital citizen*. Available at: https://joenicholls..kumu.io/the-biodigital-citizen (Accessed: 7 October 2021).

Olakulehin, F.K. and Singh, G. (2013) 'Widening access through openness in higher education in the developing world: A Bourdieusian field analysis of experiences from the National Open University of Nigeria', *Open Praxis*, 5(1), pp. 31–40. doi:10.5944/openpraxis.5.1.40.

Osborn, J.R. et al. (2019) 'The pilgrimage project: Speculative design for engaged inter-disciplinary education', *Arts and Humanities in Higher Education*, 18(4), pp. 349–371. doi:10.1177/1474022217736510.

Peckham, K. (2019) *Surviving entanglement as a modern workplace learner*. Available at: http://obviouschoice.com.au/courseware/oer/v2/story_html5.html (Accessed: 5 October 2021).

Rolfe, V. (2015) 'A systematic review of the socio-ethical aspects of Massive Online Open Courses', *European Journal of Open, Distance and E-learning*, 18(1), pp. 52–71.

Ross, J. (2018) *Openness and this course: A case study*. Digital Futures for Learning. Available at: https://digitalfutures.de.ed.ac.uk/openness-and-this-course-a-case-study/ (Accessed: 30 September 2021).

Ross, J., Bayne, S. and Lamb, J. (2019) 'Critical approaches to valuing digital education: Learning with and from the manifesto for teaching online', *Digital Culture & Education*, 11/1, pp. 22–35.

Selwyn, N. (2017) *Education and Technology: Key Issues and Debates*. 2nd edn. London: Bloomsbury.

Shepard, M. (2013) 'Minor urbanism: Everyday entanglements of technology and urban life', *Continuum*, 27(4), pp. 483–494. doi:10.1080/10304312.2013.803299.

Smallbones, M. (2017) *Embracing complexity in education*. Available at: https://docs.google.com/presentation/d/1uGL4MChRXp5SJ1KQ0mYRphJLKwK39R6KBxVHobXbGto (Accessed: 7 October 2021).

Veletsianos, G. (2021) 'Open educational resources: Expanding equity or reflecting and furthering inequities?', *Educational Technology Research and Development*, 69(1), pp. 407–410. doi:10.1007/s11423-020-09840-y.

Weller, M. (2014) *The Battle for Open*. London: Ubiquity Press. doi:10.5334/bam.

Williamson, B. (2019) 'Brain data: Scanning, scraping and sculpting the plastic learning brain through neurotechnology', *Postdigital Science and Education*, 1(1), pp. 65–86. doi:10.1007/s42438-018-0008-5.

Yeo, S. (2020) 'Access now, but for whom and at what cost?', *Information, Communication & Society*, 23(4), pp. 588–604. doi:10.1080/1369118X.2018.1529192.

7

ARTCASTING AND DIGITAL CULTURAL HERITAGE ENGAGEMENT FUTURES

Introduction

This chapter shifts focus to learning in the cultural heritage sector, also commonly referred to as the Gallery, Library, Archive and Museum (GLAM) sector. The nature of engagement in heritage spaces is relevant to both formal and informal learning futures. This sector has distinctive approaches and priorities for informal learning, informed by its emphasis on objects and collections, their care and curation, and sharing and production of meanings around them. In GLAM organisations, the future is ever-present in practices of care and conservation, and organisations take their role as custodians of heritage for the future extremely seriously. As Harrison (2015) explains, heritage is also concerned with "assembling and designing the future" by:

> working with the tangible and intangible traces of the past to both materially and discursively remake both ourselves and the world in the present, in anticipation of an outcome that will help constitute a specific (social, economic, or ecological) resource in and for the future.
>
> *(p. 35)*

This extends to the collection and conservation of intangible heritage. Though this chapter focuses on tangible heritage objects and their digital counterparts, the scope of cultural heritage collection, care and interpretation also includes born-digital artworks, social media archives, traditional craft skills and performances of many kinds.

Digital humanities research, often closely aligned with digital cultural heritage research, has a long tradition of experimental and inventive work, including

DOI: 10.4324/9781003202134-9

Drucker's "speculative computing" as a concept that can help to foreground the partiality, situatedness and subjectivity of knowledge by generating new computational forms and practices (Drucker, 2009). Critical museum studies and cultural heritage scholars are grappling with the implications of the "data turn" and the collapse of past-present-anticipated future in datafied heritage (Bonacchi, 2021), the need for new forms of interaction with data (Kenderdine, 2021) and new forms of digitisation of material culture (Ireland and Bell, 2021), the place of "ruins" (Landau and Pohl, 2021) and the pleasures and disappointments of augmented and virtual reality heritage spaces (Bertrand et al., 2021). As they do so, experimentation and the questions it can tackle continue to evolve (Drotner, Haldrup and Achiam, 2021). The nature of the digital object itself also continues to be theorised (Cooper, 2019; Dunn et al., 2019; Jeffrey, Love and Poyade, 2021).

The role of digital technologies in museums and galleries is deep and enduring (Parry, 2010) and informs all aspects of the work of contemporary heritage organisations. Collections management databases and processes are at the heart of heritage information ecosystems, with digitisation of records, creation of digital scans and images of objects and production of associated metadata seen as an urgent priority both in terms of knowledge production and sharing. Issues of copyright and intellectual property as digitisation unfolds produce ongoing, complex tensions (Crews, 2011; Dolen, 2013; Aufderheide, Milosevic and Bello, 2016; Stobo et al., 2018). Overall, as in the higher education sector (as we saw in the previous two chapters), questions of access to and representation of knowledge have accompanied the evolution of digital cultural heritage practices.

The potential uses of digital technologies for engagement and learning are also seen as central to the outreach and education strategies of museums and galleries. By the mid-2010s, digital apps for museums tended to focus on improving and personalising information delivery, or gamifying visitor experiences, but critical questions were being asked about how effective or engaging these approaches were. Answering those questions by measuring informal learning or evaluating digital engagement has proved extremely challenging, as we will see. These two issues – digital engagement and evaluation – were ready for some speculative future-making.

In 2015–6, I led an interdisciplinary team of researchers to build a concept and a prototype app called Artcasting.[1] This was created as part of a funded project[2] aiming to generate new ways of thinking about heritage engagement and evaluation. Building on mobilities theory, the app invited gallery visitors to imaginatively relocate artworks in space and time, and explain their choices. The way this project was designed and built, and the insights it generated for gallery visitors and educators, sheds light on what a speculative approach to challenging questions in informal museum and gallery learning can achieve.

126 Speculative objects to think with

This chapter begins with an overview of the role of the "digital" in cultural heritage engagement and practice, setting the scene for an exploration of how the evaluation of engagement has been understood and critiqued. I then discuss the design and outputs of the Artcasting project, and its speculative nature. Finally, I consider how futures were produced through the Artcasting project and what this has to offer ongoing futures work in cultural heritage engagement.

Digital engagement, digital cultural heritage

A shift of focus in the GLAM sector from "object" to "subject" has been extensively explored in museum studies literature in recent decades (Bayne, Ross and Williamson, 2009), as the educational and community engagement mission of the museum has come to be seen as just as, if not more, important than the cultivation of institutional expertise and ownership (Anderson, 1999). Research examining how visitors interpret exhibitions and cultural heritage objects (Falk and Dierking, 2013; Hooper-Greenhill, 2013) highlights the unpredictability and idiosyncrasy of engagement, as people bring their own relationships, understanding, experience, questions, emotions and expectations to their interaction with heritage. However, even with the museum studies turn to greater focus on visitor experience, engagement has sometimes been side-lined or "footnoted" in museum education discourses (Roberts, 1992), with the transfer of knowledge from institution to visitor remaining most central to actual practice and the design of heritage spaces.

An overemphasis on providing content (Perry et al., 2017) was playing out in a number of ways during the period of the Artcasting project. One was the types of digital engagement materials organisations were investing in. Digital heritage displays, applications and interactives were often immersive and eye-catching without moving beyond didactic approaches to telling visitors what they were looking at and why it mattered. There was a lot of excitement about possibilities for more participatory modes of engaging with digital cultural heritage, for example in social media spaces, but in practice these approaches were hampered by constraints of short-term funding, difficulties around sharing authority and limitations on the reusability of digital objects and collections. New forms of engagement and learning were and remain contingent on a wide range of resources, constraints and priorities.

In short, digital cultural heritage materials and practices were rich with possibilities for visitor engagement and interpretation, but also with complexities around power, access, authority, resource, value and participation. For example, in an influential book, Simon (2010) defined a participatory institution as "a place where visitors can create, share, and connect with each other around content", but defined content as "the evidence, objects, and ideas most important to the institution in question" (no page).

For the purposes of understanding the landscape of cultural heritage at the time, and tensions around participation, it is useful to consider two general forms of digital cultural heritage engagement. First, there is technology-mediated engagement in heritage settings, which might include the use of apps, touchscreens, mobile devices, digital photography and other interactive or personalised technologies within the museum or in other physical heritage spaces. Second, there is online engagement with digitised or born-digital cultural heritage objects, collections and organisations, which includes user-generated images of museum and gallery spaces and objects, and sharing, creation and connection around heritage that takes place without the direct participation of the institution. Here I offer a brief overview of the key issues around these two forms of engagement, to set the scene for the Artcasting project and its speculative intervention.

Technology-mediated engagement in the museum

At the time of the Artcasting project, shifts in museum and gallery education and engagement practices had been sparked by greater availability of internet-connected digital devices, interactive software and technologies like touchscreens and mobile data and Wi-Fi coverage in museum buildings. Young people, in particular, were thought to need technology to support their engagement with cultural heritage, and they were an important catalyst for investment in technology, and a proliferation of projects aimed at providing attention-grabbing, immersive, slick digital educational resources within the museum space.

Mobile technology had become increasingly accepted as part of the visitor experience in cultural institutions – including via the presence of digital devices which serve to "blur" the concept of physical space in favour of what de Souza e Silva (2006) calls "hybrid space". Museum engagement was increasingly designed with the assumption that a large proportion of visitors would have internet-enabled smartphones with them. This built on an extended history in the sector of explorations of mobility and engagement, where cultural heritage educators sought "nomadic resources" (Hsi, 2003) which could move through gallery spaces with visitors and prompt them to "experiment further in the real setting rather than providing an escape from that setting" (p. 309); and "seamless visits" which bridge locations and times (ibid). The proliferation of mobile devices such as smartphones and tablets held out the promise of richer in-gallery engagements, and more effective links between home, school, gallery and public space. Smartphones became the focus of intense interest. They were seen as a direct descendent of handheld materials and devices long part of the experience of cultural heritage settings (Tallon and Walker, 2008), but also represented a shift towards more personal, intimate, mediated and ubiquitous relationships with

128 Speculative objects to think with

digital flows and the social world, leading Parry (2008) to describe them as "both agents and epitomes of the modern museum" (p. 191).

Some projects in the early 2010s sought to leverage these technologies and their potential to blur the lines between spaces and encourage visitor voice. The QRator project was a key example (Hudson-Smith et al., 2012) – using mobile devices and QR codes (when these were quite new, before they fell out of fashion and subsequently became ubiquitous during the Covid-19 pandemic) to contribute to digital labels and access curatorial insights about objects and collections (Bailey-Ross et al., 2017). In the US, the Cleveland Museum of Art invested heavily in digital, interactive in-gallery spaces with their *Gallery One* project (Alexander, 2014), including the creation and sharing of visitor-generated "favorites" tours (p. 351). There were also a number of projects involving mobile devices that engaged with cultural heritage beyond a museum or gallery space – for example, the *Northumberland Rock Art* project (Mazel et al., 2012) and the Cardiff-based project *With New Eyes I See* (Kidd, 2019). Tate's ArtMaps project invited visitors to tag artworks with geographical locations – finding that a group of professional artists tagged locations based on geographic features, historical associations, archetypal representations, personal associations and representational associations (Coughlan et al., 2015), making multiple relationships between artworks and locations visible, and leveraging ambiguity in fruitful ways.

Such projects illustrate the range of approaches to digital engagement with physical spaces of cultural heritage. At the same time, engagement with digitised cultural heritage objects and collections was on a different, though sometimes intersecting, trajectory.

Engagement with digital cultural heritage

In addition to using digital technologies to foster engagement with material spaces and objects, digital objects were becoming increasingly relevant to museums seeking to grow and diversify audiences, reach beyond their geographical locations, and tap into the growth of the web and social media platforms as spaces for interaction, learning and participation. The museum web site as a source of materials and tools for engagement grew in importance from the early 2000s, though this came along with critiques of how "interactive" such projects were:

> One museum carries on its website a sequence that entreats you to "build a bat's wing". Each click of the mouse brings another few bones, culminating in the complete skeleton and a photograph of a bat in flight. Is this a worthwhile activity? What might be its learning objectives? And is clicking a mouse really interactive?
>
> *(Hawkey, 2002, p. 12)*

Nevertheless, the impact of digital artefacts and their mobilities could be striking. In the mid-2010s, one high-profile example of collections that had been digitised and openly shared, the *Rijksstudio* and its "make your own masterpiece" tool from the Rijksmuseum in the Netherlands (Pijbes, 2015), was being held up internationally as an ideal to which other organisations could and should aspire (Bicknell, 2013). *ARtours* in Amsterdam's Stedelijk Museum explored possible responses to the openness of the digital object, in particular its mobility, which at the time (2009) echoed the mobility of the museum's collections during a renovation and construction project that saw them without a permanent place to be displayed for several years (Schavemaker et al., 2011). In response, Stedelijk developed an "augmented reality" lending library of images, which could then be "hung" in an immediate location of the borrower's choosing and viewed by others through their smartphones. In theorising digital engagement, mobile technologies and practices were seen as carrying experiences across locations and amongst people, thereby generating "interconnected opinion space", not bound by the time and place of a museum visit (Charitonos et al., 2012, p. 815).

Digital objects had been theorised as being more open than their material, gallery-based counterparts to being "re-claimed, re-contextualised and re-formed" into personally meaningful configurations (Bayne, Ross and Williamson, 2009, p. 110). This produced opportunities for learning and engagement, but also introduced tensions for cultural heritage organisations around issues of interpretation and authenticity. Who had the right to produce, publish, share and interpret digital images of objects and artworks was a matter of considerable debate, and sometimes disagreement as different museum priorities (care, sharing, participation, expertise) came into conflict (Ross, Beamer and Ganley, 2018a). As an early example, in a project I was involved with between 2007–9, working with national museums in the UK, an interviewee talked about a senior colleague's response to being shown photographs of their museum objects on Flickr, a photo-sharing social media platform:

> INTERVIEWEE: He couldn't get over all the photographs that had just been taken in the galleries, on phones, mobile phones and uploaded and stuff. But, yeah, it's out there and people are doing it.
> INTERVIEWER: Yeah. What did he think of that?
> INTERVIEWEE: Well, I think he's still in shock.
> INTERVIEWER: Was he? A bad shock or a good shock?
> INTERVIEWEE: Bad.
>
> *(Bayne, Ross and Williamson, 2009, p. 119)*

In the mid-late 2000s, before the dominance of centralised platforms in the online ecosystem, key thinkers in digital museum contexts promised to address anxieties about the emergence of participatory and social media and its implications for

130 Speculative objects to think with

their work, offering the possibility of "harnessing" participation through their own digital platforms (Simon, 2008). This promise was soon undermined by the rise of digital platforms, as the plethora of places and ways that people were encountering cultural heritage objects and collections online exceeded or subverted anticipated boundaries of engagement. This challenge extended to issues of expertise and trust, as new questions emerged around how knowledge and interpretation attaches to circulating digital culture; and how it might be used to communicate organisational values and points of view in a de-centralised digital cultural landscape. New forms of authority and trustworthiness were emerging, and museums needed to examine the gains and losses involved in shifting organisational boundaries. The contributions of digital and mobile processes themselves – for example, the algorithmic surfacing of particular resources as a visitor browses or searches a digital collection – were still underexplored factors in many kinds of heritage experiences and the meanings made of them. Also underexplored were issues around how to evaluate digital engagement in the museum and gallery context.

Value and evaluation: measuring engagement with cultural heritage

At the time of the Artcasting project, digital engagement, inspiration and learning were high priorities for museums and galleries, but however inventive the intervention or project, methods for evaluating it were often constrained by their need to be easy to capture, report on and summarise. Typically, this need was addressed through brief questionnaires that participants were asked to complete after a gallery activity or visit, in person or online. As a result, the data that cultural organisations worked with when analysing and communicating the value of their activity lacked a sense of the richness of participants' experience. This problem was being tackled in multiple ways (Crossick and Kaszynska, 2014), but new perspectives were needed.

A key challenge faced by the sector was to understand and evidence engagement's impact on individuals and communities, both at the time of the experience and in the longer term. Museums and galleries were negotiating profound tensions around the meaning of evaluation (O'Brien et al., 2010). These tensions were also apparent in the broader cultural value literature, with impact framed as either intrinsic or instrumental (Belfiore and Bennett, 2010). There were theoretical dilemmas as well: for example, that the articulation of engagement through a survey, or any other method, does not offer a direct and unmediated understanding of a response to an artwork or heritage object, and people are often in a state of "affective ignorance" in relation to their own aesthetic experience (Melchionne, 2010).

Artcasting and digital cultural heritage engagement futures **131**

The meaning of objects and exhibitions is "never fully completed" (Hooper-Greenhill, 2000, p. 118), nor is the experience of engagement with those objects. Evaluation practices in museums and galleries tended to be static and instrumental, and struggled to get at more "knotty, unpredictable and unruly expressions of experience" (Galani and Kidd, 2019, p. 13). The Artcasting project proposed that a useful approach would be to ask whether the articulation of engagement itself could be generative: whether it could provide a lens through which visits and artworks could be engaged with in a variety of ways by both participants and educators.

The Artcasting project

The Artcasting project involved the design, development, piloting and analysis of a methodology and a digital output in the form of a mobile app. The mobile app invited visitors to select an artwork from one of two gallery exhibitions, and create an "artcast" by choosing and describing a new imagined location and time for the artwork. Visitors could then encounter or re-encounter artcasts in those locations at a later date. The Artcasting approach generated and measured links and relationships between objects, places and people, simultaneously creating connections and evaluating the intensity of engagement with artworks and exhibitions.

The project was designed in connection with the ARTIST ROOMS research partnership,[3] and worked closely with the ARTIST ROOMS on Tour programme, co-led by Tate and National Galleries of Scotland. The two exhibitions involved in the project were *ARTIST ROOMS: Roy Lichtenstein* at the Scottish National Gallery of Modern Art (Scotland), and *Robert Mapplethorpe: The Magic in the Muse* at the Bowes Museum (England).

The project had three phases. The initial scoping phase involved analysis of existing evaluation materials and practices in use by ARTIST ROOMS and partners, semi-structured interviews with key stakeholders from ARTIST ROOMS associate galleries, National Galleries of Scotland and Tate, and funders; and design-based workshops with young people at the National Galleries of Scotland and the Bowes Museum. The design, development and piloting phase was an iterative process of creating and refining the Artcasting app, informed by evolving research questions and findings from the team's reading, experimentation, data analysis, input from participants and partner reflections and insights. The analysis and evaluation phase involved qualitative thematic coding, the development of an Artcasting data dashboard and the production of a visual representation (Miller and Ross, 2016).

The ephemerality of some speculative objects – particularly digital ones – is one of their notable dimensions. Artcasting is now a defunct digital artefact (the app was still usable on my mobile phone in 2020, but when I had to replace the

132 Speculative objects to think with

phone, it disappeared because it was no longer available in the app store to be re-downloaded). A description of the Artcasting app functions helps in understanding what it was and did. The four functions of the Artcasting process were:

1. Select an artwork: in the gallery space, once the app had been downloaded, users could choose any artwork from the two pilot exhibitions (by browsing or, in an even more experimental mode, being offered nearby artworks served through ibeacons).
2. Create an artcast: the app guided users to choose a location on an interactive map, where their selected artwork would be placed or "cast to". Users were also invited to choose a time for their artwork, and provide a short narrative of why they had chosen that specific place and time (see Figure 7.1). Once completed, this artcast would appear on the shared artcasting map, with a pin to mark its place. Artworks cast to the future would take time to arrive

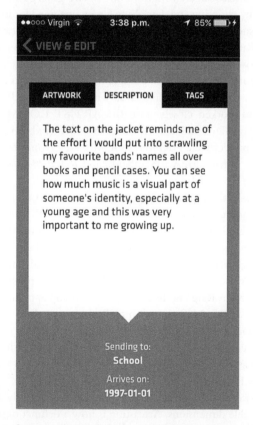

FIGURE 7.1 Text of artcast of Mapplethorpe's *Nick Marden*. Sent to the year 1997, to the sender's school in Ireland.

Artcasting and digital cultural heritage engagement futures **133**

at their destination, being marked on the map with a dotted line showing their progress.

3. Find artcasts: all shared artcasts appeared on an interactive world map, and users could browse, search for or filter other artcasts, and "re-cast" any they wanted to duplicate and send to another location.

4. Interact with artcasts: users with the artcasting app installed on a mobile device would be alerted if they went to a physical location where an artcast had been sent. Along with the ibeacons, this was the most technologically experimental aspect of the project, using geofencing and mobile devices' locative capabilities.

Artcasting demonstrated the complexity of holding different understandings of value together, but also the richness of potential outcomes when evaluation and engagement are approached in theoretically imaginative ways – in this case through the lens of mobilities theory. Mobilities theory approaches the idea of space and its material and social configurations as open to re-imagining and movement. It takes as its starting point "the combined movements of people, objects and information in all of their complex relational dynamics" (Sheller, 2011, p. 1), rather than viewing the world in terms of stable locations, individuals or institutions. The mobilities paradigm (Sheller and Urry, 2016) has had a significant impact on thinking about movement as a social and political, as well as a practical, issue (Cresswell, 2011). While mobilities theory was not extensively represented in museum studies literature at the time, it was fairly common in tourism studies (see for example Bærenholdt et al., 2004), and increasing attention was being paid to the spatial contexts of museums and galleries (Hetherington, 1997, 2010; Malpas, 2008; Geoghegan, 2010). In the context of heritage, Waterton and Watson (2013) characterise mobilities theory as offering "critiques of representational thought, a shared appreciation of the complexity of practices and a broadly relational view" (p. 552). Speaking of the museum building, Prior (2011) noted that different forms of spatial and temporal imaginings could make opportunities for unanticipated interactions, including "using museums as shortcuts, traversing the collection backwards, or playing with the limits of security" (p. 207).

Mobile devices and mobile practices were making new arrangements between cultural heritage, movement, and public and private spaces. People used mobile technology to bring place and memory together, create networked memory that could both remember the past and interact with others (Frith and Kalin, 2016). Multiple mappings of place and meaning emerge from digital mobile practices and artefacts. The Artcasting project asked: "how can such mappings be mobilised in the context of cultural heritage engagement?" (Ross et al., 2018).

Developing a conceptual connection between evaluation and mobilities was generative. The measurement of value in the context of exhibitions tended to

FIGURE 7.2 Artcasting banner at the Bowes Museum, November 2015.

focus on individual experience, development or well-being, grounded in understandings of the human subject interacting with external objects and places. Mobilities theory provided an alternative theoretical framework that shifted the site of analysis away from the psychology of exhibition visitors, or the development of audiences, and towards a richer understanding of the complex relations between the humans, technologies and spaces involved (Ross et al., 2018). Artcasting generated an approach through which galleries might engage the public more imaginatively in the capture of both qualitative and quantitative metrics, suggesting futures for engagement and evaluation that were more integrated and intertwined.

Through iterations of the Artcasting app, and supported by a range of approaches including in-gallery leaflets and prompts (see Figure 7.2), workshops and drop-in sessions (see Figure 7.3), we ultimately had 167 artcasts available for analysis, created between October 2015 and April 2016. In our analysis, we organised these into themes that reflected the primary purposes evidenced in the artcasts: personal memory and messages or gifts (Ross et al., 2018). In a second, complementary analysis, we proposed that the instability of the process and approach of Artcasting called for an additional, mobilities-informed approach, where personal responses and individual artcasts:

> can be put into relationship with one another and understood as an articulation of engagement that moves with and beyond the interpretive authority of the gallery, or any one visitor. Using the metaphor of hypermobility (double-jointedness), we can explore what Bal (2006, p. 531) means when

she describes an exhibition as a conversation where 'the event is reiterated in each visit, in each act of confrontation between viewer and show'.

(Ross et al., 2018, p. 409)

To demonstrate this, we analysed artcasts sent of a single artwork, Lichtenstein's *In the Car*, and argued that the very different locations and interpretations of the artwork confronted visitors and gallery staff with the double- (or multiple-) jointedness of the point of engagement. Artcasting became "more mobile and more meaningful as it is seen in terms of its trajectories and layers of interpretation" (p. 411).

This emergent, speculative analysis had significant implications for our project's evaluation-related findings. In addition to our thematic and mobilities analysis, we developed a dashboard for analysing the artcasts, as a way of understanding how a digital interface could allow gallery staff to review and analyse artcasts. By plugging Artcasting into an existing platform,[4] we were able to test the flexibility of the approach and build on work previously done to help visualise visitor engagement data. The development of the dashboard involved detailed discussions amongst the team about what could and should be the focus

FIGURE 7.3 Drop-in artcasting session at the National Galleries of Scotland, January 2016.
Photo credit: James Lamb.

136 Speculative objects to think with

of analytics. Starting from the position that data visualisation does not speak for itself, and that the choice of what to visualise affects what can be seen (Kinross, 1985; Kennedy et al., 2016), we considered a number of different possibilities. Ultimately, we visualised Artcasting in terms of intensity, type and geographical spread of engagement with artworks, rather than in terms of individual demographics of users. Gallery colleagues could view the destinations and casts associated with particular artworks, see the overall distance travelled of exhibitions and artworks (including filtering to see artworks within particular distances of the galleries) and explore the trajectories of artworks through time. Our focus in the dashboard visualisations on artworks, space and movement, rather than on individuals, showed how a mobilities perspective can inform evaluation, but also provoked questions about how this could map onto existing discourses and expectations about visitor experience, inspiration and engagement.

Finally, our evaluation involved a creative collaboration with artist and ethnographer Mitch Miller to produce a "dialectogram" visualisation of Artcasting, which I discuss in the next section.

Overall, Artcasting approached the notion of value by looking at alternative ways of capturing and analysing engagement, and developing speculative methods for evaluating participants' experience. Beyond this, and at the heart of the speculative approach taken, it aimed to demonstrate that innovations in cultural heritage evaluation were possible and desirable, and to support broader conversations about evidence, value and the arts. In other words, artcasting was an interesting and valuable concept, and generated rich data and insights, design reflections and approaches to engagement, but its value went beyond a specific prototype app.[5] The relocating and re-encountering of artefacts in time and space also proved to be a productively "re-usable" concept, amenable to exploring other kinds of questions (for example, about the nature of the "monument" as part of a partnership with the Edinburgh Art Festival in 2016). It was, and remains, a fruitful object-to-think-with.

Artcasting as a speculative method

Artcasting as a project and a method was speculative in two main ways. First, the development and piloting of the Artcasting app was premised on the expectation that visitors would construct their accounts of connection, desire and movement in partnership with the objects, processes, environments and social relationships surrounding the experience, and anticipated a wide range of places would be chosen for varied and often personal reasons. We proposed that Artcasting was speculative because it manifested:

> not just as an app for engaging audiences or gathering data, but also as an "object to think with": affecting visitors' encounters with art;

Artcasting and digital cultural heritage engagement futures   **137**

foregrounding ideas of movement and trajectory; to develop a digital platform that captures and retains this thinking; and influencing arts evaluation
in positive ways.

(Knox and Ross, 2016)

In design terms, Artcasting as a process could be thought of as a "cultural
probe" – a designed object or set of materials given to participants to provoke
responses that could be returned in a fragmentary form over time (Gaver, Dunne
and Pacenti, 1999). Also in common with the cultural probe was the way that
Artcasting valued uncertainty: "Far from revealing an 'objective' view on the
situation, the Probes dramatize the difficulties of communicating with strangers"
(Gaver et al., 2004).

In my work on digital co-production, I engaged with this uncertainty using
theories of hospitality[6] (Ross, 2018). My argument there was that roles of hosting and forms of co-production of digital cultural heritage meanings create
new possibilities and tensions for museums. Encounters with digitised heritage
online make a connection to the museum, through the use of these objects, and
trace a trajectory away from it, to express memories, relationships, feelings, ideas
and sensibilities. As they do, trajectories of engagement online coalesce around
objects whose meanings are shifting in the process. These tensions and uncertain-
ties of digital engagement can be understood in online contexts as a relationship
between visitor and institution which is spatially and temporally "out of joint":
museums and visitors work co-operatively, but not always together, to create
new encounters with objects. For this reason, digital co-production involves
trajectories of hosting, lines of movement that cut through the stable and fixed
boundaries of an exhibition or collection and carry their offering elsewhere, to
a guest that may never arrive in the museum, but may nonetheless be part of an
encounter with it. Users and others might also continue to re-encounter and
re-use digital objects in a future which no longer includes the original exhibition or collection. This is hospitality in the Derridean sense: what Doron (2009)
refers to as "hospitality's infinite obligation to the unknowable other" (p. 178),
and with the imbalances of power Derrida (2001) observes: "being at home
with oneself… supposes a reception or inclusion of the other which one seeks
to appropriate, control, and master according to different modalities of violence"
(pp. 16–7). Some distinctive features emerged from practices of digital co-production: the impact of multiple spaces and times, the "unknowable other", the
challenges to the stability of relationships of host and guest, and a rethinking of
hospitality (Ross, 2018).

Second, Artcasting enabled engagement with creative and inventive modes
of generating data about visitor experiences, with the aim of supporting cultural
organisations to claim greater agency in relation to the evaluation process. We
argued that there is no single or simple message that can be given to funders and

138 Speculative objects to think with

other stakeholders about the impact or value of an exhibition or programme of engagement, and that there were alternatives to evaluation methodologies that sought solely to instrumentalise or quantify impact (Ross et al., 2017). We suggested that "gallery educators need resources and approaches that help them insist on the value of divergence, multiplicity and diversity in the ways visitors make and understand connections with art" (Ross et al., 2018, p. 412). We began, too, to tackle some truisms around the kinds of data that are meaningful for evaluation, asking partners and others to consider what forms of anonymous, ephemeral data might contribute to their understanding of engagement and impact, and what creative, visual and ethnographic representations of engagement could offer. The latter was illustrated through the process of developing an Artcasting Dialectogram (see Figure 7.4).

The Dialectogram method "depict[s] places that are marginal, under threat or disappeared. [Dialectograms] borrow elements from ethnography, psychogeography and graphic art to depict the relationship we have with place, and each other" (Miller, n.d.). Mitch Miller, working closely with the research team, adapted his approach in order to capture some of the rich contexts through which people travelled to, entered and engaged with a gallery exhibition. The Bowes Artcasting dialectogram incorporated data from public artcasts, interviews with Bowes visitors, and visual resources from the gallery and exhibition. The process attempted to capture how visitors to the exhibition were using the Artcasting app:

> People were channeling ideas from the exhibition texts – for example, the 'Renaissance' feel and religious imagery of many of the photographs was echoed in the comments. Layout also had evident effects on where people clustered, how they worked their way around the room and, perhaps, how they cast.
>
> *(Miller, 2016)*

For the researchers, the dialectogram functioned as a critical map, a transformation of the more cartographical visual representations of Artcasting we were used to seeing (for instance, a digital map filled with Artcasting pins to represent the locations of the casts). As an entirely different mode of placemaking, the dialectogram was able to indicate the intensity of interest around particular artworks, how spaces can overlap and the importance of the gallery space even as it shifts and changes. Engaging with the dialectogram process was a continual slippage between location and mobility in the form of the map and the illustration. It also functioned as a generative discussion piece for the project, engaging people with the concepts of Artcasting and offering an accessible way in to some of the complex ideas associated with the research and its contribution to speculative evaluation methods for digital cultural heritage settings.

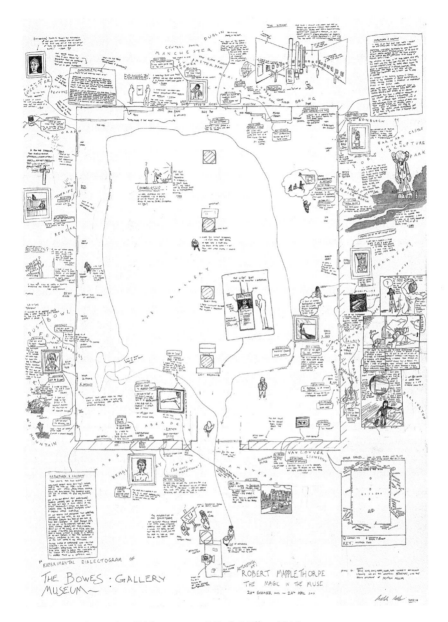

FIGURE 7.4 Artcasting Dialectogram, Mitch Miller, 2016.

Artcasting and heritage engagement futures

Buoyed by our own and others' interest in the project, and the findings that had emerged from it, the project team and other colleagues looked for ways to directly continue the work. We undertook an experimental but

140 Speculative objects to think with

short-term partnership with the Edinburgh Art Festival in 2016. We applied for "follow-on" funding to develop the concept further, but were unsuccessful. Staffing and other changes in ARTIST ROOMS meant that some of the ongoing pathways to impact we had been pursuing stalled. We were publishing and giving talks about the project, and we still got many queries about it, but over time we began to focus on other projects and priorities. Still, we thought there was more to say, and do, in the speculative space that Artcasting had generated.

In early 2018, four colleagues convened a meeting to talk about Artcasting futures – Chris Speed and me from the university, and Christopher Ganley and Màiri Lafferty from NGS. The conversation ranged widely around what we thought we could learn from Artcasting, with a view to working in low-tech ways with automation and big data in some new forms of speculative engagement at NGS. Using metaphors of the lamppost, the Sukkah (building on Doron's (2008) work), and the orphan, we sketched out three new potential gallery interventions involving visible expressions of changing motivations and questions informing gallery visits, curation of new collections that a "digital curator" would suggest connections between, and collaboratively relabelling art in real time. Looking back at notes from this discussion, none of these projects would be out of place in 2022. For instance, how engagement, and the institution's role in facilitating it, is understood has been taking some interesting turns as scholars and practitioners consider the value of interpersonalisation (Eklund, 2020; Ryding et al., 2021), emotion (Perry et al., 2017) and imagination (Bertrand et al., 2021). Methods of evaluating engagement are evolving as bio-quantified approaches such as eye-tracking grow in sophistication (Wilson-Barnao, 2020). Beyond specifically digital heritage, fascinating debates are taking place, for example around the nature of creative inspiration (Sabeti, 2017) and the tension between engagement and use in the present, and conservation for the future (Henderson, 2020; Morgan and Macdonald, 2020). However, despite their promise, our ideas did not go further at that time. There were practical reasons for this, but there is also, I think, a lesson about research impact that Michael (2021) articulates particularly well:

> Whatever one thinks of the value of one's research, it is routinely overtaken by events. Or rather, research and researcher are emergent within these larger events, and valued in ways that do not always resonate with the researcher's own valuation of their work... value itself is subject to valuation.
>
> *(p. 145)*

To illustrate this changing resonance of speculative research, I close with a few thoughts about a form of impact that is difficult to capture or value because it happens at relational or personal levels that can be hidden or invisible. Màiri Lafferty was the driving force for the 2018 Artcasting futures meeting and subsequent exchanges about it. She had been involved in the Artcasting project as our key curatorial and engagement contact at NGS, but was not part of the initial project development or named as part of the project team. However, she was invested in continuing this speculative work. We met about halfway through the project, and over time it became apparent that Artcasting was contributing something to Màiri's wider thinking that was generative, and had not been anticipated. In turn, she brought fresh insights to the final months of the project, and beyond it into many discussions since.

Later in 2018, Màiri and I were invited to talk about Artcasting to students on Dr Kirsten Lloyd's MSc by Research in Collections and Curating Practices programme at the University of Edinburgh. We presented our session twice, in 2018 and 2019, and across the two sessions our talking points included anonymity, ephemerality and data; expertise, authority, conversation and experience; narrative and context; trust; the nature of digital spaces; the role of memory in engagement with art; and how we value what audiences do and share. Both years, we also discussed the question: "How should we think about the success of the Artcasting project?". The first year, I said that the project had not achieved the success I had hoped for because of our inability to find new formal routes for continuing the work, while Màiri said that she had found it to have had a lasting impact on her own thinking and on conversations within NGS. The second year, Màiri said that she thought it had failed to live up to its promise because evaluation practice was still caught up in the same kinds of problems as before, while I said that I saw the possibility of subtle but meaningful shifts in ways of thinking as a mark of the project's success.

All of these things were, and remain, true. This project's lasting value is not fully measurable by the metrics the funder asks us to use each year to track ongoing impact. We did not get to turn Artcasting into a service (as we had once thought we might), and galleries are still asking people to fill in surveys about their visits. However, we know that Artcasting's value is embodied in a person and their practice. Màiri is now leading digital engagement work in another organisation, and her thinking is turning to different contexts of participation and interpretation. I do not know what the speculative encounters of Artcasting will lead to for her, or for me or the other project partners, in the years to come. But I recognise in a way I had not before what it can mean to do speculative work – how the uncertainty and emergence of the futures we tangled with have implications for how we should now understand what we did. The ripples of this work continue to expand, beyond what was designed for or imagined.

142 Speculative objects to think with

Summary of insights

- Mobile and digital technologies, approached creatively, can serve to unsettle assumptions and illuminate cultural heritage futures.
- Demands for evaluation need not be a stumbling block to speculative methods: evaluation itself is a rich site for speculative enquiry.
- Public participation in speculative encounters creates additional complexity and uncertainty that has to be accounted for.
- The production of coded speculative objects relies on interdisciplinarity and flexibility.
- The emergence of speculative work extends to outcomes and impact.

Notes

1 Chris Speed, Jeremy Knox, Claire Sowton and Chris Barker.
2 Arts and Humanities Research Council, grant number AH/M008177/1.
3 https://www.ed.ac.uk/edinburgh-college-art/history-art/artist-rooms/research-framework
4 The Institute of Digital Art and Technology at Plymouth University's "Qualia" dashboard (http://qualia.org.uk).
5 Indeed, at the time of the project the standalone, app-based nature of Artcasting was understood to be a feature of our development needs and the technological possibilities and constraints of the time, rather than "best practice" in the creation of museum resources that could achieve critical mass without further intervention.
6 With thanks to my colleague Dr Philippa Sheail for the research we did together in a different context that drew on hospitality theory (Sheail and Ross, 2016), including for her discovery of Claudia Ruitenberg's work on hospitality in the context of education (Ruitenberg, 2011, 2015). This combined productively with my longstanding appreciation for Edith Doron's (2009) paper about inclusion and hospitality in children's museums, still one of my favourite analyses of museum education. These and other sources of inspiration informed my digital co-production framework.

References

Alexander, J. (2014) 'Gallery one at the Cleveland Museum of Art', *Curator: The Museum Journal*, 57(3), pp. 347–362. doi:10.1111/cura.12073.
Anderson, D. (1999) *A Common Wealth: Museums in the Learning Age*. London: HM Stationery Office.
Aufderheide, P., Milosevic, T. and Bello, B. (2016) 'The impact of copyright permissions culture on the US visual arts community: The consequences of fear of fair use', *New Media & Society*, 18(9), pp. 2012–2027. doi:10.1177/1461444815575018.
Bærenholdt, J.O. et al. (2004) *Performing Tourist Places*. Farnham: Ashgate.
Bailey-Ross, C. et al. (2017) 'Engaging the museum space: Mobilizing visitor engagement with digital content creation', *Digital Scholarship in the Humanities*, 32(4), pp. 689–708. doi:10.1093/llc/fqw041.

Bal, M. (2006) 'Exposing the public', in Macdonald, S. (Ed) *A Companion to Museum Studies*. Oxford: Blackwell Publishing Ltd, pp. 525–542.

Bayne, S., Ross, J. and Williamson, Z. (2009) 'Objects, subjects, bits and bytes: Learning from the digital collections of the National Museums', *Museum and Society*, 7(2), pp. 110–124.

Belfiore, E. and Bennett, O. (2010) 'Beyond the "toolkit approach": Arts impact evaluation research and the realities of cultural policy-making', *Journal for Cultural Research*, 14(2), pp. 121–142. doi:10.1080/14797580903481280.

Bertrand, S. et al. (2021) 'From readership to usership: Communicating heritage digitally through presence, embodiment and aesthetic experience', *Frontiers in Communication*, 6, pp. 1–11. doi:10.3389/fcomm.2021.676446.

Bicknell, T. (2013) 'Best of the web winners 2013', *Museums and the Web*, 20 April. Available at: https://mw2013.museumsandtheweb.com/best-of-the-web-winners/ (Accessed: 19 October 2021).

Bonacchi, C. (2021) 'Heritage transformations', *Big Data & Society*, 8(2), pp. 1–4. doi:10.1177/20539517211034302.

Charitonos, K. et al. (2012) 'Museum learning via social and mobile technologies: (How) can online interactions enhance the visitor experience?' *British Journal of Educational Technology*, 43(5), pp. 802–819. doi:10.1111/j.1467-8535.2012.01360.x.

Cooper, C. (2019) 'You can handle it: 3D printing for museums', *Advances in Archaeological Practice*, 7(4), pp. 443–447. doi:10.1017/aap.2019.39.

Coughlan, T. et al. (2015) 'ArtMaps: Interpreting the spatial footprints of artworks', in *Proceedings of the 33rd Annual ACM Conference on Human Factors in Computing Systems*. New York, NY, USA: Association for Computing Machinery (CHI'15), pp. 407–416. doi:10.1145/2702123.2702281.

Cresswell, T. (2011) 'Mobilities I: Catching up', *Progress in Human Geography*, 35(4), pp. 550–558. doi:10.1177/0309132510383348.

Crews, K.D. (2011) 'Museum policies and art images: Conflicting objectives and copyright overreaching', *Fordham Intellectual Property, Media & Entertainment Law Journal*, 22, pp. 795–834.

Crossick, G. and Kaszynska, P. (2014) 'Under construction: Towards a framework for cultural value', *Cultural Trends*, 23(2), pp. 120–131. doi:10.1080/09548963.2014.897453.

De Souza e Silva, A. (2006) 'From cyber to hybrid mobile technologies as interfaces of hybrid spaces', *Space and Culture*, 9(3), pp. 261–278. doi:10.1177/1206331206289022.

Derrida, J. (2001) *On Cosmopolitanism and Forgiveness*. London: Psychology Press.

Dolen, J. (2013) *Copyright or Copyleft? Balancing Image Rights for Artists, Museums and Audiences*. University of Minnesota. Available at: http://conservancy.umn.edu/handle/11299/149953 (Accessed: 5 August 2022).

Doron, E. (2008) 'Building a Sukkah for the museum: From social inclusion to exilic education', *International Journal of the Inclusive Museum*, 1(1), pp. 75–82.

Doron, E. (2009) 'At hospitality's threshold: From social inclusion to exilic education', *Curator: The Museum Journal*, 52(2), pp. 169–182. doi:10.1111/j.2151-6952.2009. tb00342.x.

Drotner, K., Haldrup, M. and Achiam, M. (2021) 'Implications and perspectives for experimental museology', in Achiam, Marianne, Haldrup, Michael, and Drotner, Kirsten (Eds) *Experimental Museology*. Abingdon: Routledge.

Drucker, J. (2009) *SpecLab: Digital Aesthetics and Projects in Speculative Computing*. Chicago: University of Chicago Press. doi:10.7208/chicago/9780226165097.001.0001.

Dunn, S. et al. (2019) 'Spatial narratives in museums and online: The birth of the digital object itinerary', in Giannini, T. and Bowen, J.P. (Eds) *Museums and Digital Culture: New Perspectives and Research*. Cham: Springer International Publishing (Springer Series on Cultural Computing), pp. 253–271. doi:10.1007/978-3-319-97457-6_12.

Eklund, L. (2020) 'A shoe is a shoe is a shoe: Interpersonalization and meaning-making in museums – Research findings and design implications', *International Journal of Human–Computer Interaction*, 36(16), pp. 1503–1513. doi:10.1080/10447318.2020.1767982.

Falk, J.H. and Dierking, L.D. (2013) *The Museum Experience Revisited*. Walnut Creek: Left Coast Press.

Frith, J. and Kalin, J. (2016) 'Here, I used to be mobile media and practices of place-based digital memory', *Space and Culture*, 19(1), pp. 43–55. doi:10.1177/1206331215595730.

Galani, A. and Kidd, J. (2019) 'Evaluating digital cultural heritage "in the wild": The case for reflexivity', *Journal on Computing and Cultural Heritage*, 12(1), pp. 1–15. doi:10.1145/3287272.

Gaver, B., Dunne, T. and Pacenti, E. (1999) 'Design: Cultural probes', *Interactions*, 6(1), pp. 21–29.

Gaver, W.W. et al. (2004) 'Cultural probes and the value of uncertainty', *Interactions*, 11(5), pp. 53–56.

Geoghegan, H. (2010) 'Museum geography: Exploring museums, collections and museum practice in the UK', *Geography Compass*, 4(10), pp. 1462–1476. doi:10.1111/j.1749-8198.2010.00391.x.

Harrison, R. (2015) 'Beyond "natural" and "cultural" heritage: Toward an ontological politics of heritage in the age of Anthropocene', *Heritage & Society*, 8(1), pp. 24–42. doi:10.1179/2159032X15Z.00000000036.

Hawkey, R. (2002) 'The lifelong learning game: Season ticket or free transfer?' *Computers & Education*, 38(1), pp. 5–20. doi:10.1016/S0360-1315(01)00091-4.

Henderson, J. (2020) 'Beyond lifetimes: Who do we exclude when we keep things for the future?' *Journal of the Institute of Conservation*, 43(3), pp. 195–212. doi:10.1080/19455224.2020.1810729.

Hetherington, K. (1997) 'Museum topology and the will to connect', *Journal of Material Culture*, 2(2), pp. 199–218. doi:10.1177/135918359700200203.

Hetherington, K. (2010) 'The empty gallery? Issues of subjects, objects and spaces', *Museum and Society*, 8(2), pp. 112–117.

Hooper-Greenhill, E. (2000) *Museums and the Interpretation of Visual Culture*. Abingdon: Routledge.

Hooper-Greenhill, E. (2013) *Museums and Their Visitors*. Abingdon: Routledge.

Hsi, S. (2003) 'A study of user experiences mediated by nomadic web content in a museum', *Journal of Computer Assisted Learning*, 19(3), pp. 308–319. Doi:10.1046/j.0266-4909.2003.jca_023.x.

Hudson-Smith, A. et al. (2012) 'Experiments with the internet of things in museum space: Qrator', in *Proceedings of the 2012 ACM Conference on Ubiquitous Computing*, New York, NY, USA: Association for Computing Machinery (UbiComp '12), pp. 1183–1184. Doi:10.1145/2370216.2370469.

Ireland, T. and Bell, T. (2021) 'Chasing future feelings: A practice-led experiment with emergent digital materialities of heritage', *Museum and Society*, 19(2), pp. 149–165. Doi:10.29311/mas.v19i2.3663.

Jeffrey, S., Love, S. and Poyade, M. (2021) 'The digital Laocoön: Replication, narrative and authenticity', *Museum and Society*, 19(2), pp. 166–183. Doi:10.29311/mas.v19i2.3583.

Kenderdine, S. (2021) 'Experimental museology: Immersive visualisation and cultural (big) data', in Drotner, Kirsten, Achiam, Marianne, and Haldrup, Michael (Eds) *Experimental Museology*. Abingdon: Routledge.

Kennedy, H. et al. (2016) 'The work that visualisation conventions do', *Information, Communication & Society*, 19(6), pp. 715–735. doi:10.1080/1369118X.2016.1153126.

Kidd, J. (2019) 'With new eyes I see: Embodiment, empathy and silence in digital heritage interpretation', *International Journal of Heritage Studies*, 25(1), pp. 54–66. doi:10.1 080/13527258.2017.1341946.

Kinross, R. (1985) 'The rhetoric of neutrality', *Design Issues*, 2(2), pp. 18–30. doi:10.2307/1511415.

Knox, J. and Ross, J. (2016) '"Where does this work belong?" New digital approaches to evaluating engagement with art', in *MW2016: Museums and the Web 2016*, Los Angeles. Available at: http://mw2016.museumsandtheweb.com/paper/where-does-this-work-belong-new-digital-approaches-to-evaluating-engagement-with-art/.

Landau, F. and Pohl, L. (2021) 'Ruined museums: Exploring post- foundational spatiality', *Ephemera: Theory & Politics in Organization*, 21(1), pp. 197–228.

Malpas, J. (2008) 'New media, cultural heritage and the sense of place: Mapping the conceptual ground', *International Journal of Heritage Studies*, 14(3), pp. 197–209. doi:10.1080/13527250801953652.

Mazel, A. et al. (2012) '"I want to be provoked": Public involvement in the development of the Northumberland Rock Art on Mobile Phones project', *World Archaeology*, 44(4), pp. 592–611. doi:10.1080/00438243.2012.741813.

Melchionne, K. (2010) 'On the old saw "I know nothing about art but I know what I like"', *The Journal of Aesthetics and Art Criticism*, 68(2), pp. 131–141. doi:10.1111/j.1540-6245.2010.01398.x.

Michael, M. (2021) *The Research Event: Towards Prospective Methodologies in Sociology*. Abingdon: Routledge

Miller, M. (2016) 'An Artcasting Dialectogram – reflections from the artist', *Artcasting Project Blog*. Available at: https://www.artcastingproject.net/uncategorized/an-artcasting-dialectogram-reflections-from-the-artist/.

Miller, M. (n.d.) 'Dialectograms'. Available at: http://www.dialectograms.com/dialectograms-2/ (Accessed: 21 October 2021).

Miller, M. and Ross, J. (2016) 'Bowes Museum gallery dialectogram'. doi:10.7488/ds/1558.

Morgan, J. and Macdonald, S. (2020) 'De-growing museum collections for new heritage futures', *International Journal of Heritage Studies*, 26(1), pp. 56–70. doi:10.1080/13527 258.2018.1530289.

O'Brien, T. et al. (2010) 'Unpacking the politics of evaluation: A dramaturgical analysis', *Evaluation*, 16(4), pp. 431–444. doi:10.1177/1356389010380002.

Parry, R. (2008) 'The future in our hands? Putting potential into practice', in Tallon, L. and Walker, K. (Eds) *Digital Technologies and the Museum Experience: Handheld Guides and Other Media*. Lanham: Altamira Press.

Parry, R. (2010) *Museums in a Digital Age*. Abingdon: Routledge.

Perry, S. et al. (2017) 'Moving beyond the virtual museum: Engaging visitors emotionally', in *2017 23rd International Conference on Virtual System Multimedia (VSMM). 2017 23rd International Conference on Virtual System Multimedia (VSMM)*, pp. 1–8. doi:10.1109/VSMM.2017.8346276.

Pijbes, W. (2015) 'The battle for beauty in a virtual world: How museums can profit from the digital revolution', *Uncommon Culture*, 6(2), pp. 138–145.

Prior, N. (2011) 'Speed, rhythm, and time-space: Museums and cities', *Space and Culture*, 14(2), pp. 197–213. doi:10.1177/1206331210392701.

Roberts, L. (1992) 'Affective learning, affective experience: What does it have to do with museum education', *Visitor Studies: Theory, Research, and Practice*, 4, pp. 162–168.

Ross, J. et al. (2017) 'Artcasting, mobilities, and inventiveness: engaging Engaging with new approaches to arts evaluation', in Ciolfi, L. et al. (Eds) *Cultural Heritage Communities: Technologies and Challenges*. Abingdon: Routledge.

Ross, J. (2018) 'Casting a line: Digital co-production, hospitality and mobilities in cultural heritage settings', *Curator: The Museum Journal*, 61(4), pp. 575–592. doi:10.1111/cura.12280.

Ross, J., Beamer, A. and Ganley, C. (2018a) 'Digital collections, open data and the boundaries of openness: A case study from the National Galleries of Scotland', in *Museums and the Web*, Vancouver, Canada. Available at: https://mw18.mwconf.org/paper/digital-collections-open-data-and-the-boundaries-of-openness-a-case-study-from-the-national-galleries-of-scotland/ (Accessed: 28 November 2018).

Ross, J. et al. (2018) 'Mobilising connections with art: Artcasting and the digital articulation of visitor engagement with cultural heritage', *International Journal of Heritage Studies*, 25(4), pp. 395–414. doi:10.1080/13527258.2018.1493698.

Ruitenberg, C. (2011) 'The empty chair: Education in an ethic of hospitality', *Philosophy of Education Archive*, pp. 28–36.

Ruitenberg, C. (2015) *Unlocking the World: Education in an Ethic of Hospitality*. Abingdon: Routledge.

Ryding, K. et al. (2021) 'Interpersonalizing intimate museum experiences', *International Journal of Human–Computer Interaction*, 37(12), pp. 1151–1172. doi:10.1080/1044731 8.2020.1870829.

Sabeti, S. (2017) *Creativity and learning in later life: An ethnography of museum education*. Abingdon: Routledge. doi:10.4324/9781315676340.

Schavemaker, M. et al. (2011) 'Augmented reality and the museum experience', *Museums and the Web 2011: Proceedings*, Philadelphia.

Sheail, P. and Ross, J. (2016) '"Hospitality at a distance": Supervisory practices and student experiences of supervision in online Masters dissertations', in Cranmer, S, Dohn, N.B., de Laat, M., Ryberg, T., and Sime, J.A. (Eds) *Proceedings of the 10th International Conference on Networked Learning 2016*, Edinburgh.

Sheller, M. (2011) 'Mobility', *Sociopedia. isa*, pp. 1–12. doi: 10.1177/205684601163

Sheller, M. and Urry, J. (2016) 'Mobilizing the new mobilities paradigm', *Applied Mobilities*, 1(1), pp. 10–25. doi:10.1080/23800127.2016.1151216.

Simon, N. (2008) 'The future of authority: Platform power', *Museum 2.0*. Available at: http://museumtwo.blogspot.com/2008/10/future-of-authority-platform-power.html (Accessed: 21 May 2018).

Simon, N. (2010) *The Participatory Museum*. Santa Cruz: Museum 2.0. Available at: http://www.participatorymuseum.org/read/ (Accessed: 5 August 2022).

Stobo, V. et al. (2018) '"I should like to see them some time": An empirical study of copyright clearance costs in the digitisation of Edwin Morgan's scrapbooks', *Journal of Documentation*, 74(3), pp. 641–667. doi:10.1108/JD-04-2017-0061.

Tallon, L. and Walker, K. (eds) (2008) *Digital Technologies and the Museum Experience: Handheld Guides and Other Media*. Lanham: Altamira Press.

Waterton, E. and Watson, S. (2013) 'Framing theory: Towards a critical imagination in heritage studies', *International Journal of Heritage Studies*, 19(6), pp. 546–561. doi:10.10 80/13527258.2013.779295.

Wilson-Barnao, C. (2020) 'The quantified and customised museum: Measuring, matching, and aggregating audiences', *PUBLIC*, 30(60), pp. 208–219. doi:10.1386/ public_00016_7.

8

TELLING DATA STORIES TO EXPLORE THE FUTURE OF SURVEILLANCE

Introduction

In this chapter, I write in the midst of the circumstances I am attempting to describe. In 2022, surveillance in higher education settings has become "increasingly pervasive and fine-grained as monitoring and data-gathering technologies grow in sophistication and as the quantification and measurement of everything from outcomes to student satisfaction to engagement is increasingly valued in universities" (Collier and Ross, 2020, p. 276). Goals of quality, efficiency and transparency are provided as a rationale for the intensification of demands for, and technologies to support, ever greater visibility on the part of staff and students. The Covid-19 pandemic and rapid pivots to online teaching and assessment exacerbated issues of privacy, consent, fairness and trust that monitoring technologies were already raising. The anticipated surveillance futures of higher education are therefore provoking considerable concern amongst activists, scholars and educators, while investment continues to flow into products and services that are built on surveillance practices and platforms. The Data Stories project was developed to explore these concerns and developments through the lens of speculative storytelling, using a purpose-built, scaffolded online tool to which people could contribute anonymously. The chapter begins with an overview of current thinking about surveillance in higher education, then describes the project and its context. Through an analysis of some of the stories that have been shared through the Data Stories tool, I explore how participatory speculative fiction can work to counter digital resignation and – even through dystopian accounts of feared futures – begin to envision how things could be otherwise.

DOI: 10.4324/9781003202134-10

Surveillance in the digital university

An understanding of the complexity of surveillance, privacy and visibility is seen in recent theorising of surveillance cultures, where surveillance is increasingly understood as something more than what is done *to* people. As Lyon (2017) argues, a surveillance culture lens is a way of understanding how people "actively participat[e] in an attempt to regulate their own surveillance and the surveillance of others" (p. 824). Rather than focusing only on the exercise of top-down surveillance power by agencies and organisations of various kinds (though this continues to be of interest), attention to surveillance culture invites awareness of "citizens', consumers', travelers', or employees' experience of and engagement with surveillance" (p. 826). A particularly important feature of surveillance culture is that it functions in ways that are "not necessarily or even primarily clandestine – it is better understood as a set of relations or a sensibility, and the values aligned with it (transparency, sharing, safety) as contingent and provisional" (Bayne et al., 2020, p. 174). These relations are pervasive and often opaque, shaping the experiences of people even before they are born, including through the use of sophisticated health and behaviour monitoring technologies, and the transformation of the home through smart technologies (Barassi, 2019).

There are arguments for the value of specific technologies of monitoring and datafication that contribute to surveillance cultures in higher education. The purpose of this chapter and of the data stories project is not to analyse these arguments, but to explore the nature of surveillance cultures and their impacts, for instance on relationships, inequality, the shifting understanding of the value of anonymity and the role of privacy in the context of university education.

In higher education, relationships are affected by the way digital technologies and surveillance cultures intersect. Trust in educational relationships is undermined by surveillance practices (Ross and Macleod, 2018; Doyle, 2021), as logics of competition between institutions and amongst individuals intensify (Tanczer et al., 2019, p. 15). A hidden curriculum of datafication is that being visible, tracked and monitored without meaningful consent becomes normal and expected – what Dencik and Cable describe as "surveillance realism'" (2017), which leads to what Draper and Turow (2019) call "digital resignation". Learning technologies and spaces of all kinds – online and offline – create data trails that are a potential source of analytics and data mining. Individual participation and interaction on platforms, of whatever kind, is valuable to now-dominant platform capitalism (Srnicek, 2016), and the resource that is pouring into edtech ventures is evidence of the perceived value of educational data. Indeed, digital resignation benefits such ventures, as it leads to a situation where:

> despite individuals' worries about surveillance and data flows they cannot control, their concerns are unlikely to be accompanied by collective anger

150 Speculative objects to think with

that motivates action to change the status quo. Rather, resignation likely results in frustration that such action would be futile.

(Draper and Turow, 2019, p. 1829)

Within the university, data-driven decision-making turns activities of staff, students, partners and others into quantifiable evidence for streamlining, improving and reshaping institutions. More data and more monitoring are seen as solutions to challenges such as preventing cheating, improving student attainment and dealing with increasing student-teacher ratios. A sense of activity that cannot be seen or heard, but might still be meaningful, is being displaced in favour of learning made visible (Watson et al., 2017; Dall'Alba and Bengtsen, 2019). Along with this reality has come a powerful rhetoric against digital anonymity as a concept both in and beyond higher education, with online abuse and other anti-social behaviours laid at the feet of "faceless" individuals (or bots) who hide behind pseudonyms or avatars (Bayne et al., 2019; Curlew, 2019). This is the case even when such accusations appear to be unwarranted (Clark-Gordon, Workman and Linvill, 2017), and even though there is evidence that anonymity supports important aspects of learning in informal contexts (Sacks, Gressier and Maldon, 2021), including circumventing social expectations, managing identity and self-presentation, initiating and developing relationships and learning about the self (Ellison et al., 2016). Teachers, staff and students often do not have the choice to be invisible, partly visible or anonymous in their university lives. Added to this are the shifts that have taken place in higher education during the Covid-19 pandemic, where:

new relationships have been speedily formed and technologies introduced at an unprecedented scale. These technologies produce new effects in universities, but they also build on longstanding practices of monitoring, assessment and measurement, they entrench existing structures of power, and they continue the centralisation of management functions in higher education, displacing more collegial forms of academic governance.

(Beetham et al., 2022, p. 4)

Surveillance is bound up in issues of power and justice (Gilliard and saheli singh, 2021). Inequality in society and in education is discernable by who is made visible to whom and under what circumstances (Gilliard, 2017), but these relations tend to be obscured by imaginaries that present surveillant technologies as invitable (Logan, 2021). Transparency, Monahan (2021) argues, has from the Enlightenment era been a tool of subjugation and the consolidation of white power, and surveillance and privacy studies in higher education require further attention to these issues.

The future of privacy is tied up with questions about visibility, anonymity and openness. Cohen (2012) observes that the role of privacy is to provide shelter to "dynamic, emergent subjectivity" in the face of attempts to "render individuals and communities fixed, transparent, and predictable" (p. 1905) – and is a central quality that supports self-determination, as well as innovation through play and experimentation. She is talking about the wider social and legal context of surveillance and privacy, but her observations are useful for those thinking about the nature of surveillance in higher education. So, too, is Southerton and Taylor's (2021) warning that algorithmic forms of surveillance change how young people relate to and understand who they are and what they can do.

Alternatives for participation are conceived of and created in the space between visibility and anonymity. Decolonial theory may help to conceptualise these futures in generative ways. As Arora (2019) notes, a common understanding of marginalised people's privacy and visibility practices as "deviant" is a marker of analysis in need of decolonial thinking (p. 374). Arora recommends reconceptualising such practices:

> paying heed to the desire for selective visibility, how privacy is often not a choice, and how the cost of privacy is deeply subjective and seemingly irrational as desire and aspiration overtakes pragmatism. Subjects need to go beyond the parameters of the researcher's interests to become de-subjectified, or better yet, de-exoticized.
>
> *(p. 375)*

Milan and Treré (2019) echo this call, encouraging scholars to look to the Global South and the imaginaries of datafication that are emerging there. Other alternative modes include forms of critical disengagement, challenges to social media practices of value extraction, avoidance of controversy and strategic concealment (Bachmann, Knecht and Wittel, 2017). They also involve what Duffy and Chan (2019) call the "'renovat[ion]' of conventions of digital space" (p. 127), and new ways of thinking about and enacting authenticity. Natale and Treré (2020) point to ways technical knowledge can be subverted in the service of alternatives to intrusion and toxicity – not in the form of a temporary "digital detox", but in genuinely different forms of engagement.

Bayne et al. (2019) propose that universities need principles and frameworks that can respect the social value of anonymity, ephemerality and unreachability in educational life in a data age. However, the gap between the possible future introduction of such principles and where we are now in higher education is large. There is therefore important work that needs to be done to map, understand and critique surveillance cultures in higher education, and it is work that needs to be done collectively, to have any hope of making an impact on the flows of data, decisions and judgements that come along with them. There are challenges to this collective work, however. The perception and reality of visibility, the importance placed on institutional reputations and contemporary relations of precarity in universities mean that many people – perhaps most – have reason

152 Speculative objects to think with

to worry about the consequences of going against the grain. Students, whose data and privacy is perhaps most problematically at stake in the development and growth of new educational technologies, are rarely able to meaningfully consent to their use. At the same time, as Lupton (2020), Barassi (2019) and others note, people are aware of, interested in, and involved in relations of care and responsibility with their own and others' data, and there is therefore reason to engage in speculative, future-making work in this area. This chapter explores the speculative work of a project – Data Stories – that was designed to give voice to controversial topics around data in higher education, helping to investigate and shape sensibilities around surveillance and data ethics by engaging with hoped for, and feared, futures for learning.

Higher education after surveillance and the Data Stories project

In late 2018, Amy Collier and I began to think about creating a new network to bring together a group of academics, university leaders, students, edtech commentators and technologists to consider futures for surveillance in education. We called this network "Higher Education After Surveillance" to acknowledge the nature of surveillance within the contemporary university, its history and its importance – realities that "beyond", "against" or "without" surveillance would not capture (Collier and Ross, 2020). At the same time, we saw the network as explicitly activist, aimed at being "a springboard for critical conversations, new insights and knowledge, and to support action" to address problematic uses of surveillance and erosions of privacy in higher education (Ross, 2019a).

Inspired by the work of members of the network, for example, Gilliard's "digital redlining" concept (Gilliard, 2017), Wilson's research on learning analytics (Wilson et al., 2017), Watters' commentary on digital surveillance and care (Watters, 2020), and Gregory's work with the Worker's Observatory,[1] the group developed the idea of creating a surveillance observatory. This would gather and organise information about practices in institutions, organisations and companies associated with higher education. In addition, reflecting some members' work with speculative methods and projects like network member sava saheli singh's series of Screening Surveillance films (Screening Surveillance, 2019), we considered how to include "stories about harms, marginalisation, and hopeful directions" (Ross, 2019b). These ideas and plans led a group of network members, along with a colleague with expertise in creative writing, to apply for funding to develop the Data Stories project.

The emerging speculative turn in education futures work has involved a variety of storytelling methods (see for example the special issue devoted to speculative edtech fictions (Selwyn et al., 2020)), and interest in how the stories that people are engaging with outside formal education might inform their education futures (Priyadharshini, 2019). Story-based research methods are well established in the social sciences and other disciplines, including in the form of narrative and fictional inquiry (Clandinin and Connelly, 2000; Clough, 2002), transmedia and digital storytelling (Hancox, 2017), and in futures-focused social science fictional methods (Gerlach and Hamilton, 2003; Suoranta et al., 2022; Watson, 2021; Watson and Gullion, 2021). Surveillance as a subject of social inquiry has been the focus of a number of storytelling projects in recent years (Screening Surveillance, 2019; Cahill and Newell, 2021). The elicitation of speculative stories from or with research participants, or what has been termed Participatory Speculative Fiction (Wilson et al., 2022) and Citizen Science Fiction (Schuijer, Broerse and Kupper, 2021), also takes inspiration from participatory modes of design fiction. Participatory modes provide a response to the tendency of design fictional or speculative approaches to foreground "elite" or powerful voices (Forlano and Mathew, 2014, p. 11; Light, 2021) – those of researchers, for example. At the same time, they expose and generate "frictions" (Forlano and Mathew, 2014), when the embedded values and assumptions that structure the participatory work come into tension with participants' experiences and expertise, or the negotiated access and expectations that permit the research to take place (Duggan, Lindley and McNicol, 2017). Chapter 9 discusses these frictions further in the context of speculative methods.

The Data Stories project was funded and launched in early 2020, just before the start of the first Covid-19 lockdowns in the UK. The initial plan was to run a series of workshops with learning technologists in UK universities. People in these roles were a particularly important constituency for this work, because they were both subject to and generative of edtech imaginaries, and their position in the higher education ecosystem was a crucial one for both understanding and reconfiguring the future of surveillance. The impact of the Covid-19 pandemic meant that face-to-face co-creation workshops could not take place, and potential participants' availability was affected as universities scrambled to shift to online teaching and assessment. In April 2020, we shifted the focus of the project to the creation of an online story-writing tool, enabling participants to engage in briefer, asynchronous ways with a speculative storytelling task. From its initial purpose as a replacement for the original research plans, the Data Stories creator became something more, and different, than the research team had anticipated. Developing a self-led speculative storytelling process and implementing it in a purposefully anonymous digital environment generated insights, and stories, that are highly relevant to considering how speculative methods can be used to engage with controversies and unsettle expectations about education futures.

The project's initial questions were: 1) how can the role of surveillance in higher education be interrupted, reduced or reconfigured through speculative storytelling and co-design? And 2) what questions, narratives and issues will shape research in the ethics of data-driven higher education? A third question developed along with the Data Stories creator: what would people publicly imagine about surveillance if they were free to do so? The next section recounts

154 Speculative objects to think with

the making of the storytelling tool, and how these questions came together with a theoretical framework and a specific technological setting to generate a new speculative method.

Making a speculative Data Stories Creator

Rather than asking people to start with a blank screen, the Data Stories Creator was a scaffolded experience. We drew on Anna Wilson's grounding in Deleuzian theory and previous experience with speculative storytelling using elicitation methods (Wilson, 2020) as a starting point for producing story "seeds" based on actors and actions/interactions. An initial list of seeds came from stories written by the project team. These were developed and refined through online storytelling interviews between Anna and seven university stakeholders, mostly learning technologists, and eventually became a series of prompt questions that would be used by participants to generate "story objects". In the Data Stories Creator, users are first asked to:

> try to think about a time when you have used, or become aware of, a bit of technology (software or hardware) that was either explicitly being used for surveillance or might be used for surveillance, even if unintentionally.
>
> *(Data Stories Creator guidance)*

This example formed the foundation for responding to one or more prompt question (see Table 8.1).

Once a question was answered and saved, it became a story object that was placed in the second stage of story creation, the story map. In the map, the objects first appeared as unconnected nodes, which could be clicked and dragged around the map space, with lines added between them and labelled to indicate the relationship between them. This stage supported users to:

> re-think the actual experience or practices you described in your answers to the prompt questions, and to think about whether the actual relationships between different elements might be changed, or even reversed. Could the scrutiniser become the scrutinised? What impact would that have? Or could something that previously wasn't measured become something that is measured? Could acquiescence turn to into happy embrace, or resistance?
>
> *(Data Stories Creator guidance)*

This map then formed the inspiration and possible structure for a multimodal story, written and submitted in the "write" tab of the tool. The story could contain text, images, hyperlinks, social media objects such as tweets, GIFs and

Telling data stories to explore the future of surveillance 155

TABLE 8.1 Prompt questions for the data stories creator

Question	Rationale
Who is being scrutinised? What is being scrutinised/quantified? Who is doing the scrutinising? Who else might have access to the data? Who benefits? What are the benefits? Who is disadvantaged? What are the disadvantages?	Exploring the actors involved in the data story – those subject to and conducting scrutiny, and the focus of the scrutiny. The intended or unintended advantages and disadvantages for actors are also invited for consideration.
What technologies enable the scrutiny? Where is it taking place? Is the scrutiny regulated or unregulated?	Situating the story in a particular setting – general or specific, and identifying the relevant tools and technologies – bearing in mind that these are often not explicitly "for" surveillance. The wider context of the scrutiny, including its regulatory status, is part of the setting.
What is the purpose – e.g. monitoring, audit, resource allocation, control, comparison, correlation? What are the motives – e.g. transparency, distrust, care?	Distinguishing between stated and the implicit purposes of data practices as a prompt for considering their place and function within surveillance cultures.
Are the processes hidden or in full view? Are the processes targeted or all embracing? Are the data individualised or aggregated? Are the data identified or anonymised?	Describing the visibility and scope of processes and products of surveillance, including how personalised and overt they are.
What might trigger an action or intervention? What form might an action or intervention take?	Exploring the mechanisms of surveillance and its potential outcomes.
Is the scrutiny resisted, acquiesced to or embraced? What feelings might be aroused or associated with the scrutiny?	Imagining or articulating the affective and responsive dimensions of surveillance.

emojis. The length and style of each story was not prescribed, and stories were submitted and published anonymously, with no personal information collected, no attribution and no link to an author.

While the final story creator tool was a more-or-less polished artefact with a fixed design, its creation was a highly iterative process that involved extensive

156 Speculative objects to think with

collaboration between the research team (me, along with Anna Wilson, Amy Collier and Jane McKie) and the web developer we engaged for the project. Pat Lockley became an important member of the research team and his insights significantly informed our thinking. We relied on him to understand the potential and limitations of the platform (WordPress) and to translate our ideas into a workable interface. In turn, his questions about and experiments with functionality forced us to consider what we were trying to accomplish, and how. One major addition to the mapping element (the ability to label connecting lines between story objects) came about in this iterative way. Another feature – an option for users to add an email address to recover or later edit a story – was changed several times and then dropped to facilitate anonymity.

The data stories creator tool was launched in August 2020, and shared on Twitter, via email and amongst various networks, and in conference presentations. A few stories were published over the months following the launch, but the majority of the 31 stories online at the time of writing were published during or after workshops led by the project team. At one of these, from a group of about 25 attendees, 14 stories were published. In addition, we know of at least two people who used the story creator to generate stories for assignments on postgraduate courses (and which were not published on the data stories site, but in one case elsewhere (Collins, 2021)), and others who indicated that they wanted to use the tool as part of their teaching. Because there is no digital trace of how the questions and mapping functionality are used, and no obligation to submit stories that are written, there may be a "hidden" context of participation with the tool. This is one of the risks (or perhaps features) of working in a privacy-respecting way online.

The decision not to collect any user information created some other challenges and surprises, too. For instance, it is actually not terribly *easy* to work in this way using standard web tools. An exchange between Pat, Anna and me during the development period illustrates this. Thinking it would be useful to have some usage statistics for the site, I installed a WordPress plugin called Jetpack, which is designed in part to help monitor web site use. I did not give this much thought, as I knew this was one of the most popular WordPress plugins, and one that is heavily promoted within the WordPress backend itself. Pat quickly noticed, and got in touch to tell me about the extensive number of cookies and tracer images that Jetpack uses to gather visitor data. Without meaning to, and as someone with a reasonable sensitivity to online privacy issues, I had potentially opened future site visitors to covert tracking that they would not be able to opt out of unless I tweaked the plugin's default settings (which I did not know about).[2] The web in general – even for those living in countries covered by internet privacy policies such as Europe's General Data Protection Regulation (GDPR) – is currently a minefield of overlapping and complex systems for tracking and monitoring user activity. Mostly this is in the service of advertising in some form, and sometimes, as with us, it is about looking for ways to justify or support the existence of something one has spent time and money trying to make, and hoping to make useful and used. As I discussed in the previous chapter, evaluation of digital engagement is a thorny matter at the best of times. When research impact, external funding or other important matters are determined by use, then finding ways to measure digital footfall, if not engagement, becomes central to the case we can make for how our work matters. In analysing the impact of this project so far, we have not focused on numbers (not least because they are small), and looked instead at what the stories themselves are doing and saying, and what they might tell us about value of another kind – the freedom to tell any kind of story, to ring any kind of alarm, without fear.

Another challenging dimension to the anonymity of participation in this project is a residual discomfort about how data produced by unknown participants can be used. The web site makes clear that the stories are being made public and freely available on the web, and by definition (unless stories are published with identifying information, which we check for before approving them) no one is at risk from disclosure of information. Nevertheless, particular kinds of consent procedures for social research are deeply engrained in the practices and attitudes of researchers. Despite the long-understood complexity of the status of content on the public web (Bassett and O'Riordan, 2002), it can be difficult to feel relaxed about implicit permission when using user-generated data. These are stories that were made to be told, though, and so here I present an analysis of some Data Stories.

Stories about surveillance futures

This section introduces and analyses some of the initial stories that were produced through the data stories interface.[3] Though still small in number (26 are included for analysis here, those published up until the end of 2021), these stories capture a fascinating interplay of present concerns and issues, trajectories and imaginings. Most importantly, they capture, at a particular moment in time, some ways of thinking about surveillance futures that are important for educators and researchers. Ways of understanding surveillance in these stories are, for the most part, dystopian, with a sense of technology developments that are undesirable but unstoppable. At the same time, these gloomy imaginings carry their own energy, outrage and some hints of other possibilities.

The main characters in these stories tend to be individual students (8) or academics (8), but there are also stories told from the perspective of a student union, a cleaner, a director and several ambiguous characters experiencing aspects of surveillance culture in or beyond a contemporary or imagined university. Many of the platforms are familiar in these stories – learning management systems, online exam proctoring services, productivity or collaborative software, student

158 Speculative objects to think with

request management systems – but some of the technologies, data forms and data uses are novel. Characters in the stories experience neuro- and bio-scanning, health and wellbeing metrics and measurements, DNA-driven decision-making, competition for lecture views and a mirror that quizzes students about their first-year university experience.

While many stories are implicitly set in future or alternate timelines with technologies or processes that do not currently exist, others could very well be (and may be) happening now. A story about "people counters", for example, discusses the data-driven decision-making that determines university library opening hours based on usage; but also includes a note about hacking the video cameras that support the counters, with sinister implications for two students (*People counters at building entrances*). Another, in the horror genre, is set during a remotely invigilated examination (an emergent practice that took off hugely during the Covid-19 pandemic), with a figure appearing to be in the student's room – causing the exam to be halted – that the student cannot see (*The Invigilator*). Another student, too tired from long shifts at their job to keep up with their study, games the learning management system's engagement metrics by "click[ing] through all the activities as fast as I could without comprehending a word, selecting the 'download' button any time I had the opportunity" (from *Learning Management*). On the flip side of this story, in *Content is King* lecturers frantically "email links to their friends and family of videos they have made for their students, in the hope that their contacts will like these and their content will move up the ladder" so that they can win the university's competition for the content with the most views. A frustrated teacher uses the data at their disposal to identify and expose an obnoxious MOOC participant (*A motorboat in Ireland*). And a student receives a visit from the police after a video surveillance system identifies them as being involved in a theft off-campus (*The Fault in Facial Recognition System*). These stories are (probably) fictions, but it is not because they are technologically impossible. The authors of these stories are drawing attention to unseen or under-considered implications of existing technologies.

Stories are also told about people in precarious positions in the higher education system. Several of the fictional characters are international students, for whom the stakes of failing to be visible, or being seen to do the wrong things, are very high. Mai's story about being wrongly accused of theft touches on the racial bias of facial recognition technologies but also the despair that a student in this position might feel:

> she needs a clear profile to study in the US, or her Asian family will disown her. She started to get panicked… Mai thought she would cry soon. She was at loss. confusion.
>
> *(The Fault in Facial Recognition System)*

The impacts on international students of being suspected of wrongdoing are experienced by several characters:

> I knew that I had revised how to compose a formal letter, but my nerves were getting the better of me. "NO ONE CAN BE IN THE ROOM WITH YOU DURING THE TEST". I jumped! "Yes, yes I know!" I replied – my English was starting to suffer a bit, it was offputting having to answer these questions throughout the hardest bit of the test.
>
> *(The Invigilator)*

> I may not have time to go through everything properly now, but I sure as hell don't want to get flagged up by the 'student support' system or worse, reported to [the UK's department responsible for immigration, including student visas] as 'non-engaged'. I'm sure to have more time in a few weeks, right?
>
> *(Learning Management)*

Uneven distribution of monitoring and surveillance is reflected on in *Monitoring them*:

> Students are being monitored, not all, only those that deserve to be observed, they deserve it because they come from poor families, zones, schools, towns, countries, because their parents crossed the pond, because the data prejudices tell they tend to under perform.

And a harsh account of what is *not* seen comes in *The Watchman* – cameras shattered as police officers attack students in Delhi – a reminder, as in Mai's story, that the university is not separate from the wider society around it, and that there are limits to the safety it can or will provide.

Teachers, too, are negatively affected by surveillance in these stories – both emotionally and, in the case of a story about a Director whose role it is to monitor students' engagement in learning and "academics' engagement in monitoring students' engagement", physically through electric shocks they receive that cause them to forget the surveillance they are under (*Rules of Engagement*). Even relatively low-tech monitoring, such as productivity software that sends summaries of use, causes anxiety when work is precarious: "Knowing when you are answering emails outside work hours etc. is given under the guise of improving wellbeing, but it is really causing anxiety to know that you are being monitored so intently" (*MS office always watching*).

The intentions behind the surveillance, benign or otherwise, are not especially important to the characters in these stories. Technological interventions aimed at

160 Speculative objects to think with

supporting "wellbeing" come in for a particular trouncing, with one lecturer, going through a mental health crisis as a result of social distancing, escorted by security to the "Staff Wellbeing Centre, where he would undergo Resilience Assessment" (*The Cleaner's Tale*). Similarly threatening remedial "compulsory emotional intelligence training" or "compulsory resilience training" are possible outcomes for students and teachers who appear to overuse extension requests and extenuating circumstances (followed by job losses for the teachers if numbers do not improve) (*Emotional intelligence and resilience training*). Concepts of wellbeing and resilience, in these stories, are experienced as opportunities for punitive and non-consensual interventions that at best must be avoided or submitted to cheerfully to avoid negative consequences, as in Jodi's assurance to their smart-mirror that "I honestly think these [well-being citations] are helpful to keep me healthy and productive as a college student" (*First Year Student Experience*). Another student, subject to intensive monitoring of his involuntary reactions, posture, body temperature, heart rate and other metrics, all aimed at scoring his SEL [social-emotional learning] and other capacities, hones "an ability to fake his feelings", apparently successfully, but at great personal cost (*William Stone P267*).

In contrast to William Stone's ability to understand and manipulate the data gathered about him, another theme that recurs is that of uncertainty about the purpose and use of data. In the story *DNA-fueled universities*, the requirement for students to provide DNA samples as part of university admissions and to perhaps inform subsequent experiences is not questioned by the main character, but she does wonder about it:

> It wasn't totally clear how her DNA data would be used… Kari wondered if her DNA sample played a role in her [college placement] options… She wondered, more than once, if the personalization would someday begin to feel less like a benefit and more like a curse?

A short reflection on the creation of online collaborative workspaces laments that the main character "felt a responsibility that everyone should know who has access to what – but this became impossible to manage properly. No-one knew who could 'see' what, and what is Microsoft doing with all this data?" (*Microsoft Teams and the cost of collaboration*). And an account of conference badges with RFID chips built expresses the participants' unease: "we all just felt under surveillance and by whom or what was unclear. Whether we kept or tossed out the badges, THEY would know. We were trapped" (*Welcome to the machine*). This story encapsulates how surveillance tends to create or at least exacerbate conflicts and mistrust – between people with different roles in the university, amongst students or staff who are induced to compete with one another, and towards technology. Others take up this theme, also: a future student union, dismayed by the university's failure to protect their "reputational wellness" by providing scramblers that block neuroscanning, threatens disclosure of harms (*Urgent: re the promised model 3 scramblers*). Human teachers' lack of ability to fully know their students in an evidence-based way is justification for their removal from all but "innocuous" tasks in a future characterised by personalised education that gives you "what (it calculates that) you need, in order to satisfy the needs of society" (*Remembrance*). One of the more ambiguous stories, *Too much information*, centres on a character who upsets a new colleague by inadvertently revealing they had sensitive information about her that had been gained through some unspecified version of cyberstalking.

Examples of resistance to surveillance, with action taken at personal and collective level, are seen in a few stories – from Will's attempt to control his body's emotional signals (*William Stone P267*) to a group of democracy activists who manage to mix up speaker identities in all the recordings made at a conference to protect themselves and other at-risk speakers from government reprisals (*Altruistic Academics*). Beyond examples of explicit resistance, the use of humour also serves the function of drawing attention to absurdity in some stories. A flight of imagination about why a new centralised "extensions and special circumstances" (ESC) system is not working well involves a printer, a ladder, a pit and "ESC peat" that will eventually be used to heat the university and help it meet its carbon goals (*The ESChole*). However, more broadly, I propose that the act of recording a data story in this context is a meaningful move to resist digital resignation (Draper and Turow, 2019) and surveillance realism (Dencik and Cable, 2017).

Resisting resignation: participatory speculative fiction and surveillance futures

The speculative futures produced through the data stories tool are participatory in nature. Participants are directed towards particular ways of thinking and creating, but the scaffolding also allows for considerable variation and some unanticipated outcomes. For instance, the dystopian mood of the stories was not primarily a function of the design of the storytelling tool – we were careful to provide prompts that could be read in a number of ways, and could result in more positive accounts than we saw here. The anger and fear expressed in these stories is perhaps, instead, a reflection of the imaginaries that currently permeate accounts of technology futures, and a reflection of an inability to respond to ethical and pedagogical concerns that some technologies in higher education are producing.

These dystopias serve a function beyond revealing unease about uncertainty, loss of control, inequality, changing teacher roles and misuse of concepts of wellbeing. These worries are significant and important, and can help shape practical responses to surveillance cultures in education, including activist responses. However, perhaps just as important, accounting in speculative ways for present realities and future concerns, the data story authors open space for emotion:

162 Speculative objects to think with

frustration, fear and anger are implicit and explicit in these stories, along with defiance, suspicion and regret. As Priyadharshini (2019) argues in her work about young people's engagement with sci-fi and fantasy dystopias,

> the affects of dystopia do not work in predictable ways – they seem to indicate that hope and despair are not clearly separable in the monstrous, and that there is something to be gained from knowingly engaging with such visions of the future.
>
> *(p. 7)*

What can be gained, in the context of higher education futures, is a recognition of the scope and scale of problems that are not always acknowledged as problems, and an opening to the frustration, anger or even horror that these problems can evoke. In their work on surveillance realism, Dencik and Cable (2017) remarked on the fact that resignation was seen even in interviews with political activists working on these issues, showing how dissent and the articulation of alternatives can be constrained by imaginaries or attitudes around surveillance. They highlighted the disempowerment that comes along with perceptions of the "overwhelming nature of technological capacity to monitor and collect data" (p. 777). This, combined with a lack of meaningful ability to refuse to participate in forms of monitoring that are becoming core to the functioning of contemporary universities (see for example Brunner's (2022) analysis of international student compliance regimes in Canada), can limit what people are able to feel or say about surveillance cultures in higher education. A starting point for change to future policy and practice is therefore an individual and collective recognition of one's own position in relation to surveillance, and its possible relationships to other people's situations. This begins with making time and space for accounting for how personal, educational and institutional values intersect. Providing speculative space for such accounting creates possibilities – how large or small these are may vary, but many new worlds start with a story.

Summary of insights

- Stories can serve as engaging and versatile speculative objects.
- Providing structure and support for participatory speculative storytelling is useful for encouraging creativity and for countering digital resignation.
- Speculative technology accounts tend towards the dystopian. Designing speculative tasks to take account of this may be useful, but dystopias have a crucial place in making futures.
- Controversial topics bring risks, and digital anonymity or obfuscation can provide meaningful ways of working speculatively with risky ideas.

Notes

1 https://workersobservatory.org/about/
2 See this WordPress support forum discussion for a privacy-minded web site owner asking increasingly incredulous questions about cookie policies in this plugin: https://wordpress.org/support/topic/do-i-have-to-set-cookies-for-analytics-other-modules/
3 http://datastories.de.ed.ac.uk/datastories/allstories/

References

Arora, P. (2019) 'Decolonizing privacy studies', *Television & New Media*, 20(4), pp. 366–378. doi:10.1177/1527476418806092.

Bachmann, G., Knecht, M. and Wittel, A. (2017) 'The social productivity of anonymity', *Ephemera*, 17(2), pp. 241–258.

Barassi, V. (2019) 'Datafied citizens in the age of coerced digital participation', *Sociological Research Online*, 24(3), pp. 414–429. doi:10.1177/1360780419857734.

Bassett, E.H. and O'Riordan, K. (2002) 'Ethics of internet research: Contesting the human subjects research model', *Ethics and Information Technology*, 4, pp. 233–247.

Bayne, S. et al. (2019) 'The social value of anonymity on campus: A study of the decline of Yik Yak', *Learning, Media and Technology*, 44(2), pp. 92–107. doi:10.1080/174398 84.2019.1583672.

Bayne, S. et al. (2020) *The Manifesto for Teaching Online*. Cambridge: MIT Press.

Beetham, H. et al. (2022) 'Surveillance practices, risks and responses in the post pandemic university', *Digital Culture & Education*, 14(1). Available at: https://www.digitalcultureandeducation.com/volume-14-1.

Brunner, L.R. (2022) 'Higher education institutions as eyes of the state: Canada's international student compliance regime', *Globalisation, Societies and Education* [Preprint]. Available at: https://www.tandfonline.com/doi/abs/10.1080/14767724.2022.2037407 (Accessed: 23 February 2022).

Cahill, S. and Newell, B. (2021) 'Surveillance stories: Imagining surveillance futures', *Surveillance & Society*, 19(4), pp. 412–413. doi:10.24908/ss.v19i4.15189.

Clandinin, D.J. and Connelly, F.M. (2000) *Narrative Inquiry: Experience and Story in Qualitative Research*. San Francisco: Jossey-Bass.

Clark-Gordon, C.V., Workman, K.E. and Linvill, D.L. (2017) 'College students and Yik Yak: An exploratory mixed-methods study', *Social Media + Society*, 3(2), pp. 1–11. doi:10.1177/2056305117715696.

Clough, P. (2002) *Narratives and Fictions in Educational Research*. Edited by Sikes, P.. Buckingham: Open University Press.

Cohen, J.E. (2012) 'What privacy is for', *Harvard Law Review*, 107, pp. 210–256.

Collier, A. and Ross, J. (2020) 'Higher education after surveillance?' *Postdigital Science and Education*, 2(2), pp. 275–279. doi:10.1007/s42438-019-00098-z.

Collins, J. (2021) *The personalisation paradox: Contemplating the potential impact of AIEd on student well-being through speculative fiction*. Available at: https://edudigiculture.wordpress.com/2021/04/12/digital-essay/ (Accessed: 20 September 2021).

Curlew, A.E. (2019) 'Undisciplined performativity: A sociological approach to anonymity', *Social Media + Society*, 5(1), pp. 1–14. doi:10.1177/2056305119829843.

Dall'Alba, G. and Bengtsen, S. (2019) 'Re-imagining active learning: Delving into darkness', *Educational Philosophy and Theory*, 51(14), pp. 1477–1489. doi:10.1080/001318 57.2018.1561367.

Dencik, L. and Cable, J. (2017) 'The advent of surveillance realism: Public opinion and activist responses to the Snowden leaks', *International Journal of Communication*, 11, pp. 763–781.

Doyle, S. (2021) 'Why don't you trust us?' *The Journal of Interactive Technology and Pedagogy* [Preprint], (20). Available at: https://jitp.commons.gc.cuny.edu/why-dont-you-trust-us/.

Draper, N.A. and Turow, J. (2019) 'The corporate cultivation of digital resignation', *New Media & Society*, 21(8), pp. 1824–1839. doi:10.1177/1461444819833331.

Duffy, B.E. and Chan, N.K. (2019) '"You never really know who's looking": Imagined surveillance across social media platforms', *New Media & Society*, 21(1), pp. 119–138. doi:10.1177/1461444818791318.

Duggan, J.R., Lindley, J. and McNicol, S. (2017) 'Near future school: World building beyond a neoliberal present with participatory design fictions', *Futures*, 94, pp. 15–23. doi:10.1016/j.futures.2017.04.001.

Ellison, N.B. et al. (2016) '"The question exists, but you don't exist with it": Strategic anonymity in the social lives of adolescents', *Social Media + Society*, 2(4), pp. 1–13. doi:10.1177/2056305116670673.

Forlano, L. and Mathew, A. (2014) 'From design fiction to design friction: Speculative and participatory design of values-embedded urban technology', *Journal of Urban Technology*, 21(4), pp. 7–24. doi:10.1080/10630732.2014.971525.

Gerlach, N. and Hamilton, S.N. (2003) 'Introduction: A history of social science fiction', *Science Fiction Studies*, 30(2), pp. 161–173.

Gilliard, C. (2017) 'Pedagogy and the logic of platforms', *EDUCAUSE Review* [Preprint]. Available at: https://er.educause.edu/articles/2017/7/pedagogy-and-the-logic-of-platforms (Accessed: 1 May 2019).

Gilliard, C. and saheli singh, sava (2021) 'Introduction, themed issue: Surveillance and educational technology', *The Journal of Interactive Technology and Pedagogy* [Preprint], (20). Available at: https://jitp.commons.gc.cuny.edu/?p (Accessed: 7 January 2022).

Hancox, D. (2017) 'From subject to collaborator: Transmedia storytelling and social research', *Convergence*, 23(1), pp. 49–60. doi:10.1177/1354856516675252.

Light, A. (2021) 'Collaborative speculation: Anticipation, inclusion and designing counterfactual futures for appropriation', *Futures*, 134, pp. 1–15. doi:10.1016/j.futures.2021.102855.

Logan, C. (2021) 'Toward abolishing online proctoring: Counter-narratives, deep change, and pedagogies of educational dignity', *The Journal of Interactive Technology and Pedagogy* [Preprint], (20). Available at: https://jitp.commons.gc.cuny.edu/toward-abolishing-online-proctoring-counter-narratives-deep-change-and-pedagogies-of-educational-dignity/ (Accessed: 11 January 2022).

Lupton, D. (2020) 'Thinking with care about personal data profiling: A more-than-human approach', *International Journal of Communication*, 14(2020), pp. 3165–3183.

Lyon, D. (2017) 'Surveillance culture: Engagement, exposure, and ethics in digital modernity', *International Journal of Communication*, 11, pp. 824–842.

Milan, S. and Treré, E. (2019) 'Big data from the south(s): Beyond data universalism', *Television & New Media*, 20(4), pp. 319–335. doi:10.1177/1527476419837739.

Monahan, T. (2021) 'Reckoning with COVID, racial violence, and the perilous pursuit of transparency', *Surveillance & Society*, 19(1), pp. 1–10. doi:10.24908/ss.v19i1.14698.

Natale, S. and Treré, E. (2020) 'Vinyl won't save us: Reframing disconnection as engagement', *Media, Culture & Society*, 42(4), pp. 626–633. doi:10.1177/0163443720914027.

Priyadharshini, E. (2019) 'Anticipating the apocalypse: Monstrous educational futures', *Futures*, 113, pp. 1–8. doi:10.1016/j.futures.2019.102453.

Ross, J. (2019a) 'Higher education after surveillance: Why an international project?', *Higher Education After Surveillance*, 31 January. Available at: https://aftersurveillance.net/higher-education-after-surveillance-why-a-transatlantic-project/ (Accessed: 13 September 2021).

Ross, J. (2019b) 'Higher education surveillance observatory: Some initial thoughts', *Higher Education After Surveillance*, 9 October. Available at: https://aftersurveillance.net/higher-education-surveillance-observatory-some-initial-thoughts/ (Accessed: 13 September 2021).

Ross, J. and Macleod, H. (2018) 'Surveillance, (dis)trust and teaching with plagiarism detection technology', in *Proceedings of the 11th International Conference on Networked Learning 2018. Networked Learning*, Zagreb. Available at: http://www.networkedlearningconference.org.uk/abstracts/ross.html (Accessed: 14 December 2018).

Sacks, B., Gressier, C. and Maldon, J. (2021) '#REALTALK: Facebook confessions pages as a data resource for academic and student support services at universities', *Learning, Media and Technology*, pp. 1–14. doi:10.1080/17439884.2021.1946559.

Schuijer, J.W., Broerse, J.E.W. and Kupper, F. (2021) 'Citizen science fiction: The potential of situated speculative prototyping for public engagement on emerging technologies', *NanoEthics*, 15(1), pp. 1–18. doi:10.1007/s11569-020-00382-4.

Screening Surveillance (2019) *Blaxites*. Available at: https://www.youtube.com/channel/UCpEmA7HemoLdu-bZsr63y-Q (Accessed: 13 September 2021).

Selwyn, N. et al. (2020) 'What's next for Ed-Tech? Critical hopes and concerns for the 2020s', *Learning, Media and Technology* 45/1, pp. 1–6.

Southerton, C. and Taylor, E. (2021) 'Dataveillance and the dividuated self: The everyday digital surveillance of young people', in Arrigo, B. and Sellers, B. (Eds) *The Pre-Crime Society: Crime, Culture and Control in the Ultramodern Age*, Bristol: Bristol University Press. pp. 249–267.

Srnicek, N. (2016) *Platform Capitalism*. Oxford, United Kingdom: Polity Press.

Suoranta, J. et al. (2022) 'Speculative social science fiction of digitalization in higher education: From what is to what could be', *Postdigital Science and Education*, 4 (pp. 224–236). doi:10.1007/s42438-021-00260-6.

Tanczer, L.M. et al. (2019) 'Online surveillance, censorship, and encryption in academia', *International Studies Perspectives*, 21, pp. 1–36. doi:10.1093/isp/ekz016.

Watson, A. (2021) 'Writing sociological fiction', *Qualitative Research*, p. 1468794120985677. doi:10.1177/1468794120985677.

Watson, A. and Gullion, J.S. (2021) 'Fiction as research: Writing beyond the boundary lines', *Art/Research International: A Transdisciplinary Journal*, 6(1), pp. i–vi. doi:10.18432/ari29609.

Watson, C. et al. (2017) 'Small data, online learning and assessment practices in higher education: A case study of failure?', *Assessment & Evaluation in Higher Education*, 42(7), pp. 1030–1045. doi:10.1080/02602938.2016.1223834.

Watters, A. (2020) '*All Watched Over by Machines of Loving Grace': Care and the Cybernetic University, Hack Education*. Available at: http://hackeducation.com/2020/05/27/machines-of-loving-grace (Accessed: 8 June 2020).

Wilson, A. et al. (2017) 'Learning analytics: Challenges and limitations', *Teaching in Higher Education*, 22(8), pp. 991–1007. doi:10.1080/13562517.2017.1332026.

166 Speculative objects to think with

Wilson, A. et al. (2022) 'Telling data stories: Developing an online tool for participatory speculative fiction. in press', in *SAGE Research Methods: Doing Research Online*. London: SAGE. https://us.sagepub.com/en-us/nam/sage-research-methods-doing-research-online

Wilson, A.N. (2020) *Pedagogies of Difference and Desire in Professional Learning: Plugging in to Shared Images*. Newcastle: Cambridge Scholars Publishing.

PART 3

Keeping learning futures moving

9
SPECULATIVE METHODS AND DIGITAL FUTURES RESEARCH

Introduction

Speculative approaches to researching education and learning futures can be productive and engaging. In addition, they help maintain a creatively critical stance to complex questions and issues; navigate multiple and competing visions for learning futures; engage imaginatively with the rapidly shifting terrain of digital education by defamiliarising situations and pointing to new trajectories and possible futures; and maintain space for curiosity, critique, doubt, unintended consequences and emergent properties of technologies in use. To make the most of their potential, they need to be grounded in and responsive to their particular context, as well as attuned to the not-yetness of the futures they are exploring. The interplay of groundedness and unfamiliarity, responsibility and risk, creates a generative space for speculative research.

Those coming newly to this kind of work might well be asking: how? There is no single answer to that question, because a speculative method is produced with and through the matters it addresses. There are many ways to enact speculative methods, as we saw in Chapter 4 and throughout Part 2 of the book, so strict adherence to specific steps is not called for. Instead, this chapter outlines and discusses some key aspects of researching learning futures using speculative methods. It is aimed at giving researchers a practical resource for designing their own speculative approaches to education futures. It highlights methodological issues, challenges and possibilities, and provides a foundation for using speculation as part of a thoughtful, critical approach to working with digital futures for learning.

A speculative research design for education futures research will most likely need: a futures question, an "object-to-think-with", an audience to engage

DOI: 10.4324/9781003202134-12

170 Keeping learning futures moving

with and a way to capture responses and other materials generated through the research. The chapter begins with a discussion of each of these four elements and moves on to consider ethics and truth claims in speculative research. Along the way, we will re-encounter some of the thorny issues around complexity, speculation and thinking about the future that were introduced in the opening chapters of the book, and discuss how to engage those matters in practice. Finally, taking the representation of self in new digital spaces as an example of an emerging learning issue, I will walk through a design for a speculative project that could engage with this issue. By the end of the chapter, you should have a starting point for developing your own speculative research project.

Asking questions about the future

Engaging with the literature on speculative research looking for examples of research questions can be puzzling. Wilkie et al. (2017) come closest to explaining why when they note that "a shift to the speculative register forces one to come to terms with the constructive nature of a process that resists pre-defined research questions and risks asking alternative questions" (p. 13), and they observe that the speculative register involves "devising questions and research techniques that may engender the emergence of novel and inventive approaches" (p. 113). Coleman (2017) suggests that speculative methodologies themselves may pose, but not necessarily answer, questions. A question may therefore not serve as an organising principle for a speculative research project in the same way that a research question or a hypothesis would in other research designs.

I want to suggest, though, that curiosity about the future, and the questions that can flow from this, is a good starting point for a speculative project and an important part of "inventive problem making" (Michael, 2012). Here, curiosity means sensitivity to a situation which is either on the horizon or missing from current thinking around a topic or practice. In his most recent book, Michael describes this as attention to the "sub-topical" (2021): "those aspects of sociomaterial life that by and large remain invisible but may, with judicious attention and a few practical suggestions, serve in enabling inventive problems" (p. 15). Futures questions amenable to speculative methods are not concerned with prediction or "firmative" (Uncertain Commons, 2013) facts of the future, but with opening up possibilities and defamiliarising current understandings: they foreground less-visible forces in learning or education. A futures orientation in research questions can be expressed in concepts like re-imagining, re-framing or re-thinking, and in asking how things "can" or "could" happen. In his work on climate transitions, Hopkins (2020) argues that "what if" questions are powerful tools for opening up imagination, and these can be useful for speculative work as well. Michael (2021) suggests three particular approaches to developing "prospective" research questions: "noticing and asking", "remembering and reflecting" and "posing and querying" (p. 31).

The openness of a question (as opposed to a hypothesis, for example) is important to what a speculative approach can accomplish, and it is useful to consider the nature of questions themselves. A question, according to Gorichanaz (2019), orientates the asker to the world and brings them towards the unknown. Ideas about the future contain assumptions, understandings and ways of being that are rooted in particular presents. The development of a futures question takes into account both the unknown and the present orientation and situation of the context and the questioner, and this helps ground a speculative project's not-yetness in a productive way.

Posing a speculative futures question can be challenging for digital education researchers. There is a tendency for education and digital education research proposals to seek answers to questions of effectiveness (even if implicitly), as we saw in Chapter 3. Investigating whether one technology is better than another (for some particular purpose), or whether learning or teaching improves as a result of a change (for some definition of improvement), requires questions that are rooted in a positivist paradigm of comparison and measurement. A speculative futures question, on the other hand, cannot tell us much about what is "best" but instead what might be possible. Building on Biesta's (2007) critique of the "what works" agenda in education research, it requires thought about what, and whom, those possibilities might serve. Asking about the future may generate framings that would not reflect what is currently happening, or even be considered likely or possible. Arguably this is no less realistic than research questions or hypotheses that simplify complex educational interactions and assemblages enough to measure and identify causes of change (Gough, 2012).

The process of framing a digital futures question can take time. In addition to a good understanding of the context to be explored, engaging with learning or education policy reports (including but not limited to those with a focus on technology or the near future), science and technology news, science fiction representations of communication, knowledge and identity and even social media discussions can be excellent sources for ideas. Importantly, these resources need not be current – past representations of and ideas about the future can be highly generative (Sandford, 2019). The framing itself may change as the work progresses – neither the question nor the method is fixed or stable in speculative work, as we have seen. So, holding your question fairly lightly is a good habit to get into as your project gets underway.

Objects-to-think-with

Speculative research needs something with which participants or respondents can engage – an "object-to-think-with". The phrase comes from Seymour Papert,[1] who used it to describe his development of a programming language and a computational thinking device for children – Logo, and the Turtle. Papert described the Turtle as "a model for other objects, yet to be invented"

172 Keeping learning futures moving

(Papert, 1980, p. 11), and an object-to-think-with as an object in which there is "an intersection of cultural presence, embedded knowledge, and the possibility for personal identification" (ibid). He also saw the computer itself in this way (p. 23), and this insight was developed further by Sherry Turkle in her foundational work on human-computer relationships (2005). For digital education purposes, an object-to-think-with will often be a technology- or computing-related one, so this history is particularly relevant.

Speculative objects-to-think-with have the complex epistemological, temporal and performative dimensions discussed in Chapter 4. The goal of producing these objects is not to minimise or resolve complexity, but to provide an accessible "way in" to exploring it. For instance, discussing an emerging digital education trend in terms of its likely trajectories (as many futuring methods do) could mask the relationship between past, present and future that is shaping it. A speculative object that has been designed to keep matters open or to generate critical provocations, on the other hand, might deliberately work with that temporal confusion by highlighting absences or histories (real or imagined) (Nooney and Brain, 2019).

There are two main ways an object-to-think-with comes into being in a speculative futures project. One is that it is produced by the researcher or research team with a view to offering it to participants to engage with (or in some cases for the researchers themselves to work with). This kind of object is both an instrument and, often, an outcome of research. This dual purpose can create complexities in the research, especially if parts of the project's methods are dependent on working prototypes. It also, however, gives the researcher or research team a good deal of control in producing objects that are informed by theory they want to explore, aimed at addressing the research question in specific ways, and potentially (dependent on time, skills and funding) technologically sophisticated or innovative. They might be playful and imaginative, for instance informed by design fiction or other speculative design approaches. They might involve research with participants to scope their functionality or key issues they will address, but the creation of the object itself, in this case, is in the hands of the researchers (for example, the design of the Teacherbot in Chapter 5 and Artcasting in Chapter 7).

The other main way to generate objects-to-think-with is to give participants a means through which to create them themselves. Participatory design processes can be planned with the explicit goal of producing objects (which could be low-tech wireframes, stories or models, or more sophisticated coded or otherwise functional objects). It is also possible to produce tools for participants to use to generate speculative objects (like the data stories creator discussed in Chapter 8). The main distinction between these two types of object generation processes is *whose* speculative work is foregrounded. In the case of researcher-produced objects, the speculative work is done first, then offered to participants to respond to, creating an exchange around the object which may be imaginative, challenging or surprising, but is constrained to some extent by the rules of engagement established by the object itself. In the second type of object generation, the speculative energy comes from participants (with some degree of support and guidance from the researchers). We might think of this mode of speculative object creation as "speculative prompting", since the researchers will frame the engagement rather than producing the object themselves.

The extent to which objects-to-think-with are open to interpretation may vary considerably. The object, having been created, produces certain realities and closes off others. A speculative object might be challenging in terms of the issues it raises or the way it frames them, but directive in terms of what participants can do or how they can interact with it. On the other hand, an object might be mysterious, not include all information, or be unstable in its functioning. Whether prompting or creating speculative objects, it is worth considering how clear the vision for the object is, or needs to be, in order to generate the desired engagement or processes.

A pragmatic consideration is whether the object or prompt will require specialist skills to create or use, and how you might access the resources needed. For example, if you want to create an engaging video narrative as part of a design fiction, do you have the technical and creative skills to make this? The Artcasting, Teacherbot and Data Stories interactive tools were created in collaboration with technical partners who were able to code the prototype platforms. This is possible with funded projects (even small ones – the Data Stories project was initially undertaken with a budget of £5,000), but for masters or doctoral research, or in some research settings, other approaches might be necessary. There are DIY methods for coding some kinds of interactive objects, for example, Twitter bots.[2] Workshops and interactive activities that take a low-tech approach – sketching, modelling and so on – might be more feasible than working prototypes. Taking the production requirements of your approach into consideration early on will help you design a project that is achievable with the resources you have.

Another consideration is that software development timescales are notoriously unreliable. Depending on a working prototype for subsequent data collection can generate unexpected issues. This is not to discourage you – the benefits of building something that really works (for some definition of working) can be worth the pressure it can put on project deliverables, not least because the decisions made in the process can be extremely informative and generative, as can glitches that occur (Bodden and Ross, 2021). However, it comes with risks as well, and for some projects, the risks may outweigh the benefits and call for a lower-tech approach to generating or prompting objects-to-think-with.

Participation in a speculative encounter

When participants are enrolled in speculative research, the speculative object-to-think-with, which might in its own right take considerable time to design and create, or might be produced in a participatory way, is put into a context in

174 Keeping learning futures moving

which it can be used, or can serve as a provocation, irritation or invitation. The speculative object and its design, along with the responses to it, form the data from this method, so the identities and expectations of participants or respondents need to be carefully considered, along with the ethics of the approach to the object. For example, with teacherbot (Chapter 5), the research team were clear about who we would engage with – the participants on EDCMOOC – but needed to plan in detail how the bot would be introduced to and engage with the participants. Would we identify the teacherbot as a bot, or not? (We did.) This is important in all research involving participants, but especially where speculative objects are put into "live" learning environments. I will discuss this more in the next chapter in relation to teaching, but for educational researchers, too, designing with participants in mind is a key dimension of speculative method.

The involvement of participants is common with speculative methods, but some speculative research approaches are explicitly theoretical in nature, where the object-to-think-with is centred and no participatory work is undertaken. For examples of more object-focussed approaches, I recommend Lury and Wakeford's edited collection on inventive methods (2012). For an example of such work focused on digital education, Knox's tweeting book (2014) is worth exploring.

Returning to the discussion of "discursive closures" (Markham, 2021) in Chapter 4, it is vital to consider how the imaginaries participants bring with them will impact on their ability to engage with speculative work. Markham notes that it is difficult to imagine genuinely different futures, especially in relation to technology, where external forces are seen to dominate possibilities. She argues that anticipatory logics do not just create closures, they also become patterns that "continually strengthen the dominant frames of inevitability and powerlessness" (p. 384). She proposes that focused and activist interventions might be effective in helping to facilitate participatory future-making in research that is not just ideologically reproductive. This is one reason why design fictions are often narratively rich, with high production values and functional, or at least convincing, objects or technologies. For example, a nine-minute film called "A digital tomorrow" (Nova, 2012), created as part of a research project about gestures, postures and digital rituals, works to situate its novel technologies in an everyday setting that would be familiar to many viewers, and to emphasise the frustrations and accommodations necessary to co-exist with the technologies it proposed. The critical insights of the researchers have, here, been used to draw attention towards some specific possibilities and suggest impacts.

Having produced an object or prompt that takes its intended users or audience into account, the design of the engagement itself may take many forms, so requires considerable thought. Zine sharing (Ward-Davies et al., 2020), playlist creation (Lamb, 2017) and live interviewing (Hickey-Moody and Willcox, 2019) have been effective approaches for speculative encounters, but arts-based research and other creative and participatory methods often involve creative design

Speculative methods and digital futures research   **175**

workshops, and such workshops are fairly common in accounts of speculative research as well (Priyadharshini, 2019; Breines and Gallagher, 2020; Nijs et al., 2020; Renold, Edwards and Huuki, 2020). In these workshops, participants are together for a set length of time to engage with objects, topics and questions and generate data in the form of responses to speculative objects, design ideas or designed objects or processes.

With objects that take a self-contained digital form, more naturalistic forms and spaces of engagement are possible, including via asynchronous online participation, in cultural venues, and in various kinds of learning settings. Guidance and information can be made available within the object itself, and a large percentage of people carry mobile phones and other devices with internet access capabilities (for example, in 2021 88% of adults in the UK and 85% in the US owned a smartphone (Pew Research Center, 2021; Statista, 2021)). These engagements can be flexible and reach people in more spontaneous ways, which can be highly generative but also as Michael (2012) points out, open the research to events that are beyond what was anticipated. These "misbehaviours", he points out, are often:

> sanitized not least by being ignored – put down to the perversity of the public or the inexperience of the researcher... Yet... such examples of misbehaviors can still act affectively as irritants, haunting the analytic frame: a rumbling of the repressed, so to speak.
>
> *(p. 534)*

Michael argues that a speculative design attempts to make space for such misbehaviour by actively looking for and engaging the "absent-present other" (p. 544). This is another place where complexity emerges within a speculative project. Instead of sanitising participation that does not fit the frame, the frame expands – this is what Michael means when he talks about "inventive problem-making". The next section includes some discussion of how "haunting" of the analytic frame can be worked with, as data from speculative engagements is captured and analysed.

Capturing and analysing speculative data

The nature of the data generated through a speculative engagement will depend on the form the research takes, but should be considered from the outset of the project. This point may be controversial, as Springgay and Truman (2018) note that methods should not be for collecting data, but used to: "agitate, problematize, and generate new modes of thinking-making-doing" (p. 211). My view is that a flexible methodological approach is not at odds with planning ways to record what may happen. Indeed, data will emerge through responses to speculative objects or prompts (participant-generated data), and in aspects of the designed objects themselves and the process that produced them.

176 Keeping learning futures moving

In some cases, the responses to the speculative object can be integrated into the object itself – as in the case of an app that captures data about interactions within it, an object that is created by participants, or a Twitter stream involving a bot. Creating an interactive digital object like an app means making many decisions about what data should be gathered. It is routine now for digital devices and services to collect traces of use, including demographic, geographic and engagement data, but this does not mean these decisions are simple or inconsequential. Just because you can does not mean you should, as the saying goes, and some attempts at data collection can backfire: for example, if they are overly complex or ask for too much personal information, people may decline to participate.

In other cases, responses need to be captured for analysis via other approaches – for example, making a video or audio recording of a workshop; asking participants to keep a written or photo diary of their interactions with the object; or conducting interviews or surveys. Incorporating qualitative methods into a project with a speculative component can enrich the research, giving insight into how participants experienced the object-to-think-with that may not be apparent from observation. However, participant experience is not necessarily a primary focus of the research – if it is not, then other forms of data generation will be more appropriate.

One aspect of this is the object itself and how it came to be: treating the speculative object as both an instrument and an outcome of the research. Design processes may constitute a significant contribution to knowledge, and many academic journals focus on research design and methods and can be a good home for such work. Even if you are not sure this will be the case, it is worthwhile to keep notes about the design process accordingly, including key design decisions, sketches, mind maps, photographs and fieldnotes. I have often included this kind of material in talks about speculative projects.

Analytic approaches to speculative data will be varied, sometimes even within a single project. The analysis needs to respond to the question, the object and the audience. This does not need to happen at the end, or only once. For instance, in the Artcasting project, we looked at the data from artcasts using a qualitative thematic analysis approach, but then attempted to apply mobilities theory analytically, in a process devised specifically for that data, and through the production of a visual artwork (the dialectogram) that challenged the visual dominance of the map. The whole project was a process of finding ways to think about engagement and evaluation futures, and from the earliest interviews with museum and gallery professionals, all the way through to our "hypermobility" analytic approach (Ross et al., 2018), our responses to the data we were generating *took shape*. Equally, insights from these moments and movements of analysis shaped the design and further analytic decisions.

To achieve something productive from speculative analysis requires continual imaginative engagement. As Parisi (2012) explains, drawing on Whitehead, the

Speculative methods and digital futures research **177**

"stubborn reality of objects" is both a ground and a launchpad for experimental futures thinking:

> A speculative method… will demand of imagination to outrun direct observation, venturing towards the limits of the observable where thought becomes experimental and experiential of the future. In sum, a speculative device is truly a probe-head working in two ways. On the one hand, it depends on the authority of facts – and therefore it cannot overlook the stubborn reality of objects – and yet it cannot cease to transcend the existing analysis of facts to which it returns, after a short journey, mutated.
>
> *(p. 237)*

Digital education and learning research has in recent years explored and developed a very wide range of analytic approaches, including topological (Decuypere and Simons, 2016), posthumanist (Bayne, 2016; Gourlay, 2020) and field visualisation (Davies, Eynon and Salveson, 2021). These and other methods can be appropriate for a speculative research project. Speculative analysis requires a sensibility of experimentation and iteration. Such an experimental sensibility, running through the design and execution of a speculative project, brings significant and generative challenges – not least in the ethical domain. I now move on to discuss some of the ethical considerations of working in this way.

The ethics of speculative approaches

When considering ethical issues in relation to speculative research, there is no need to completely reinvent the wheel: matters of informed consent, confidentiality, power and the researcher's role, and the principles of proportionality and non-harm in participation are all foundational to this kind of work. There are some particular ethical considerations that come from working in a speculative way, however, and I will focus on three of these here: dealing with positionality, balancing risk and responsibility and responding to unintended consequences. All of these are best thought about through a theoretical lens of relationality, as Springgay and Truman (2018) suggest when they define methods as "becoming entangled in relations", or as "speculative eventing" (p. 204).

First, as discussed at earlier points in the book and in this chapter, orientations to the future, including the production of speculative prompts or objects for futures research, are necessarily partial and informed by the position of their creators. Research is never value-free (Eisner, 1992), including when the uncertainty and complexity of futures work is involved (Adam and Groves, 2007). For these reasons, researcher positionality has an important role in producing and enacting speculative methods – see for example Eseonu and Duggan's (2021) dialogue about Afrofuturism and cultural appropriation in co-produced research. How researchers deal with positionality varies considerably between research paradigms: from attempting to design it out (in positivist research) to inspecting the researchers' self and reporting on bias (in interpretivist research) to seeking to trace the impacts of different kinds of relationality (in posthumanist or post-representational research). Reflecting the complex temporalities of futures work and the relational and complexity-informed understanding of learning put forward in this book, Haraway (1997) and Barad (2007)'s "diffractive" rather than "reflective" sensibilities are useful – "being attentive to how differences get made and what the effects of these differences are" (Bozalek and Zembylas, 2017, p. 112). Reflexivity overemphasises self-awareness and risks falling into a "representational trap" (ibid, p. 116) of dualisms, which creates limitations for speculative methods. A diffractive approach helps ensure that speculative research is enacted with attention to context and difference. Speculative work can "clarif[y] the importance of our positionality and our engagement with ethics and how to materialise this as a central part of our material practices" (Levick-Parkin et al., 2020, pp. 210–11). Such attention and clarification is a key dimension of a speculative approach to learning futures.

Second, speculative methods, including in "live" learning contexts, must tread a fine line between risk-taking and responsibility. Speculative work can be wild and imaginative, but researchers must also take seriously its potential role in interrupting and reconfiguring learning futures, not only in theory, but in practice. This brings us back to Adam and Groves' (2007) core arguments about futures work, where they highlight the responsibilities of future-makers to engage with the consequences and impacts of knowledge practices and their "potential destinies" (p. 180). These impacts are not linear, but emerge from relations of complexity. What that looks like will be different in different contexts, but researchers must take seriously the futures their speculative work bring into being. It may be fun, but we are not (just) playing, and the futures we make will have effects for our participants, readers and ourselves. This seriousness relates to the matter of truth claims, which I will discuss in the next section.

Finally, an ethical approach to speculative work means acknowledging that it can and will have unintended consequences. This is valuable, from a knowledge creation standpoint, but how researchers inhabit uncertainty and respond to glitches is an ethical matter. We are not in a position to fully control what happens in a speculative experimental space, but we also cannot throw up our hands. We have to be ready to respond to what happens. Sometimes that may mean interrupting or redirecting what is happening, and sometimes it may mean rethinking what we were aiming to do and letting the entanglement lead in new directions.

Speculative research and truth claims

All "designerly" ways of doing research involve creative making in some form (Sanders and Stappers, 2014), and speculative research is no exception. As we have seen, these are not methods that can be implemented by following a straightforward

Speculative methods and digital futures research **179**

recipe. They have to be designed in relationship to the question they are seeking to illuminate or the topic they seek to develop new questions around. This is not in fact very different from other ways of approaching research, as Crotty (1998) points out when he notes that, while we should learn from our engagement with established methods or methodologies, "in a very real sense, every piece of research is unique and calls for a unique methodology. We, as the researcher, have to develop it" (p. 13). However, the creativity and emergence of speculative methods do raise important questions about how to evaluate what emerges from them, and what sorts of truth claims we as researchers can make. It is not enough to merely describe speculative approaches as "non-replicable" in a methods section, for example – we need to say what they *are*, and why they are worth doing. This is an ethical issue as well as a practical one: resources of time, energy, insight, materials and participation should be mobilised towards research that can matter.

I have previously suggested that Tracy's (2010) "big tent" criteria for quality in qualitative research are useful in framing conclusions and further questions generated through speculative methods – "(a) worthy topic, (b) rich rigour, (c) sincerity, (d) credibility, (e) resonance, (f) significant contribution, (g) ethics, and (h) meaningful coherence" (p. 839). These criteria can help researchers make claims for the value of surprise, complexity, aesthetic merit, sparking curiosity and interconnection. These criteria need to be approached critically to ensure that the generative qualities of the speculation are foregrounded and valued in analysis and reports of findings. Nevertheless, they are useful precisely because they provide goals but are not prescriptive about means – they are "universal but not fixed" (Gordon and Patterson, 2013, p. 693). By working through this framework, educational researchers might find helpful building blocks for conceptualising and justifying the value of methods which do not, as yet, exist. This creates space for exploring the quality of the research described in this book.

Such exploration has to actually happen, though. To develop our work in this area, we need to take speculative methods seriously and subject our work and the work of others to constructive critique. As speculative methods continue to be developed and deployed in educational research, conversations about what they offer and how their findings should be valued need to develop, too. Researchers should ask how the consequences of futures being produced through their speculative methods are to be considered (Facer, 2021), including whether specific speculative entanglements have been examined for their implications for theory and practice.

An example speculative project: inventive self-presentation

To make more tangible the elements of speculative research discussed in this chapter, I close by undertaking a speculative deep-dive into my present moment – in this case, at the end of 2021 and early 2022. By doing so, I aim to show what this approach may offer to researchers who are looking at current events

180 Keeping learning futures moving

and emerging claims and thinking about how to engage critically with them. The project I propose in this section is not one I currently intend to undertake (though I do think it would be well worth doing). It has some topical links with other work in this book, most particularly the data stories project described in Chapter 8, which examined surveillance cultures in higher education. This imagined project is about spaces of potential agency within surveillance cultures, and what they might be able to generate.

In autumn 2021, a perfect storm seemed to be brewing. The edtech sector and universities had encountered significant resistance to intensive forms of techno-monitoring during the Covid-19 pandemic, for example, remote invigilation (also known as remote proctoring), but logics of surveillance and data extraction were becoming increasingly normalised in understandings of online learning and teaching (Beetham et al., 2022). These echoed data cultures in wider society, as apps and devices for the self-monitoring of activity, sleep, eating, health and screen time proliferated and the data from them were aggregated, shared, compared and gamed; as workers in the growing gig economy faced ever more invasive surveillance; and as the control and scrutiny of citizens took on increasingly datafied and predictive forms. Awareness of being seen, measured and judged, long a feature of online interpersonal relationships, was extending to relationships with devices, platforms and services, whether chosen or compelled.

Workers and learners in high-tech contexts were among the groups suffering from "Zoom fatigue" brought on by the pivot, 18 months previously, to online video communications as a result of the Covid-19 pandemic. Mediated self-presentation, increasingly "live", now involved ring lights and virtual backgrounds, along with the already-pervasive culture of the flattering selfie, the humblebrag and the curation of experiences and opinions for sharing with complex and overlapping publics. Political and social activism online could result in prolonged and vicious abuse by hostile digital mobs of bots and trolls. Attempts to control one's visibility, interactions and reputation became a draining "side hustle" for many people. Researchers began to focus on data ethics and practices of video conferencing platforms and companies, and issues of individual control and agency over their digital representations and data flows (Thornton, 2021b).

Meanwhile, the social media platform Facebook was facing a growing backlash to its extractive, manipulative and possibly illegal data practices around the world, and it responded in part by announcing a change of name and a shift of focus. Its new focus: the "metaverse", a virtual, immersive spatial version of the internet first named in 1992 by the science fiction writer Neal Stephenson in his dystopian novel *Snow Crash*. Microsoft and others followed suit, releasing trailers of business-attired avatars scribbling on virtual whiteboards in an immersive version of Teams. Cryptocurrency proponents and investors saw opportunities in the prospective virtual economies of the metaverse. The experiences from early virtual worlds such as Second Life indicated that there would be real money in the buying and selling of virtual goods, "skins" and space, and the concept of

Speculative methods and digital futures research **181**

"non-fungible tokens" or NFTs became intertwined with discussions of meta-verse economics. The energy and resource implications of all of this were under-stood, but calls for shifts to slower, convivial technology approaches (Kerschner et al., 2018) were being swamped by dreams of expansion into a different digital landscape, a new and unspoiled territory (Cohen, 2007).

So: here we are – a moment in time, or at least one researcher's take on it. This researcher spent the early years of her academic career developing the meta-phor of the mask as a way of thinking about aspects of online reflective practices in higher education. Masks are used for performance, discipline and protection, among other things (Ross, 2011), and I am lured to pick up the mask again, to see what can be done with it now.

I start with a speculative question: **how could inventive forms of digital self-representation function in learning spaces?** This question assumes that learners might in the future be in a position to create and project virtual learning selves that they have control over, and aims to explore what impacts that might have. It takes the concept of "freedom to learn" from earlier educational theory (Rogers and Freiberg, 1994; Macfarlane, 2016) and reimagines it for a post-digital context where multiple self-representations, across social settings, platforms, ser-vices and devices, are common but not often treated playfully or inventively. Bayne (2010) theorised the potential for self-representation to be pedagogically uncanny in generative ways, exploring "different modes of disaggregation and re-aggrega-tion online, working creatively with the fragmented, spectral texts and presences which constitute the network" (p. 10), and this is the kind of generative explora-tion this question aims to provoke. Inventive representation could involve data selves as well as visual, verbal and other representations. The project would start from the position that disconnection is not the only – or indeed always the best – option for producing new digital learning futures (Natale and Treré, 2020), and explore the extent to which self-representation and even identity is performative (Goffman, 1969; Butler, 2006). Working speculatively with students, it examines how this performativity could be part of a productive educational engagement.

The nature of participation in this project will have a major impact on what the object-to-think-with is like, so I considered this next. To facilitate engage-ment with inventive digital selves, I propose to focus on mediated learning contexts, and look to online distance learning programmes with interactive or collaborative components (not self-paced, individual study). There are increasing numbers of such programmes at universities around the world, so I would look to engage with students from undergraduate and postgraduate programmes at universities in a variety of places – for example, the US, Nigeria, South Africa, New Zealand and Columbia. Students on participating programmes would be invited to take part in a short professional development course on a generative topic – for instance, intercultural digital communication.

For ease of imagination, I am going to assume a budget for the project. The budget would be spent in two ways. One: to develop the course materials, in

182 Keeping learning futures moving

partnership with the participating universities. The aim would be to create an online course that would be interesting to students and offer them something useful for their future education and work lives. Two: to produce a course space where students could tailor their self-presentation in fine-grained and iterative ways for specific purposes. This course space would constitute the object-to-think-with – perhaps with a playful "transformation booth" or similar as a way of foregrounding this activity. Self-presentation might take many forms, drawing on projects such as *Zoom Obscura* (Thornton, 2021a), technologies from gaming platforms like voice modulation and avatar creation, as well as lower-tech forms of representation in text (through pseudonyms, for instance) or data outputs like learning analytics (Knox, 2017). Each stage of the course might involve experimenting with different representations, including creative and artistic ones. Throughout, participants would be offered guidance on modifying or imagining new representations. The course would end, not with a big reveal of participants' "true selves", but with everyone returning to and further adapting the learning identity they found most interesting.

Data could be generated through images, observational studies of interactions on the course site, interviews and written or recorded participant diaries reflecting on the possibilities and limitations of working with different kinds of representations of self, for instance an online adaptation of Lupton and Watson's (2020) zine-making activity.

At this early stage in the project ideation process, this is enough – to generate conversations with potential partners, refine the question and approach, develop a proposal for funding if necessary, and move things along. As we have seen, inevitably complexity and glitches would come along with enacting such a project, and a speculative sensibility will have a role to play in those moments of potential future-making as they unfold.

What does your speculative digital learning futures project look like? The final section of this chapter offers a set of questions to help you think this through.

Conclusion

This chapter has sketched out elements of a speculative project, including questions, objects, audiences and data. It has highlighted issues of ethics and truth claims, and I close with some questions to help you develop a speculative research orientation to digital learning futures:

To generate a question: What vision of the future is dominant in your field at this time? What idea of the future are you just becoming aware of? What idea of the future of your field now seems foolish or outdated? Following Michael (2021), what is the most mundane or obvious example of a technological trend in practice, and what is potentially interesting about it? What do you take for granted about the trajectories of a particular technology, device, platform or piece of software? What would someone a few years along that assumed trajectory be wondering? What would the opposite of that situation look like?

Speculative methods and digital futures research **183**

To produce an object-to-think-with: How could you or others materialise some aspect of your question? What would help others make something of it? How much or little information does the object or prompt need to contain? What resources and skills do you have to produce it? What is the simplest way it could be made? What is the most imaginative or strange way? Who needs to do the speculative work, and who needs to respond to it? How can you support object-creation for others? What are the ethical implications of engaging people with this object? How much flexibility can be built in to the object or prompt to account for things not going as planned?

To engage participants or an audience: Whose perspectives are missing from discussion of your topic? How will you introduce and support engagement with the speculative object or prompt? What discursive closures might participants be most likely to encounter, and how could you help circumvent these? What purposes might participation serve for your audience? Do you want people to respond, create, debate, ask new questions? Do you need qualitative data about audience experiences? Will participants engage with one another, and if so, how? What traces might engagement leave, and how will you capture these?

To analyse data: What new questions, unanticipated outcomes or glitches emerged from your project? What are the strange or troublesome "outliers"? How can you incorporate analysis iteratively through the project? How can the project design respond to what you find as you go? What creative forms of analysis might be possible to help you treat your data speculatively – visual, collaborative, algorithmic, narrative or otherwise?

Speculative methods cannot be relied upon to generate a particular kind of learning future, or practical solutions to anticipated problems in education. What they can do is offer new ways of looking at issues, and they can surface issues that may not be otherwise visible. The "not-yetness" of digital education and its futures needs such methods, and the responsible and relational approaches to the future that they involve.

Notes

1 As with most things computing-history-related, I have Hamish Macleod to thank for what I know of Papert's work.
2 For example: Cheap Bots Done Quick (http://cheapbotsdonequick.com) which helps create Twitter bots.

References

Adam, B. and Groves, C. (2007) *Future Matters: Action, Knowledge, Ethics*. Boston, the Netherlands: Brill.
Barad, K. (2007) *Meeting the Universe Halfway: Quantum Physics and the Entanglement of Matter and Meaning*. Durham: Duke University Press. doi:10.1215/9780822388128.
Bayne, S. (2010) 'Academetron, automaton, phantom: Uncanny digital pedagogies', *London Review of Education*, 8(1), pp. 5–13. doi:10.1080/14748460903557589.

Bayne, S. (2016) 'Posthumanism and research in digital education', in *The SAGE Handbook of E-learning Research*. London: SAGE Publications Ltd, pp. 82–99. doi:10.4135/9781473955011.

Beetham, H. et al. (2022) 'Surveillance practices, risks and responses in the post pandemic university', *Digital Culture & Education*, 14(1). Available at: https://www.digitalcultureandeducation.com/volume-14-1.

Biesta, G. (2007) 'Why "what works" won't work: Evidence-based practice and the democratic deficit in educational research', *Educational Theory*, 57(1), pp. 1–22. doi:10.1111/j.1741-5446.2006.00241.x.

Bodden, S. and Ross, J. (2021) 'Speculating with glitches: Keeping the future moving', *Global Discourse*, 11(1–2), pp. 15–34. doi:10.1332/204378920X16043719041171.

Bozalek, V. and Zembylas, M. (2017) 'Diffraction or reflection? Sketching the contours of two methodologies in educational research', *International Journal of Qualitative Studies in Education*, 30(2), pp. 111–127. doi:10.1080/09518398.2016.1201166.

Breines, M.R. and Gallagher, M. (2020) 'A return to Teacherbot: Rethinking the development of educational technology at the University of Edinburgh', *Teaching in Higher Education*, pp. 1–15. doi:10.1080/13562517.2020.1825373.

Butler, J. (2006) *Gender Trouble*. New York: Routledge.

Cohen, J. (2007) 'Cyberspace and/as Space', *Columbia Law Review*, 107(1), pp. 201–256.

Coleman, R. (2017) 'Developing speculative methods to explore speculative shipping: Mail art, futurity and empiricism', in Wilkie, A., Savransky, M., and Rosengarten, M. (Eds) *Speculative Research: The Lure of Possible Futures*. Abingdon: Routledge, pp. 130–144.

Crotty, M. (1998) *The Foundations of Social Research: Meaning and Perspective in the Research Process*. London: Sage.

Davies, H.C., Eynon, R. and Salveson, C. (2021) 'The mobilisation of AI in education: A bourdieusean field analysis', *Sociology*, 55(3), pp. 539–560. doi:10.1177/0038038520967888.

Decuypere, M. and Simons, M. (2016) 'Relational thinking in education: Topology, sociomaterial studies, and figures', *Pedagogy, Culture & Society*, 24(3), pp. 371–386. doi:10.1080/14681366.2016.1166150.

Eisner, E. (1992) 'Objectivity in educational research', *Curriculum Inquiry*, 22(1), pp. 9–15. doi:10.1080/03626784.1992.11075389.

Eseonu, T. and Duggan, J. (2021) 'Negotiating cultural appropriation while re-imagining co-production via Afrofuturism', *Qualitative Research Journal*, 22(1), pp. 96–107. doi:10.1108/QRJ-06-2021-0060.

Facer, K. (2021) *Futures in Education: Towards an Ethical Practice*. UNESCO. Available at: https://unesdoc.unesco.org/ark:/48223/pf0000375792 (Accessed: 12 May 2021).

Goffman, E. (1969) *The Presentation of Self in Everyday Life*. London: Allen Lane.

Gordon, J. and Patterson, J.A. (2013) 'Response to Tracy's under the "big tent" establishing universal criteria for evaluating qualitative research', *Qualitative Inquiry*, 19(9), pp. 689–695. doi:10.1177/1077800413500934.

Gorichanaz, T. (2019) 'Questioning and understanding in the library: A philosophy of technology perspective', *Education for Information*, 35(4), pp. 399–418. doi:10.3233/EFI-180230.

Gough, N. (2012) 'Complexity, complexity reduction, and "methodological borrowing" in educational inquiry', *Complicity: An International Journal of Complexity and Education*, 9(1). Available at: http://ejournals.library.ualberta.ca/index.php/complicity/article/view/16532 (Accessed: 24 December 2014).

Speculative methods and digital futures research **185**

Gourlay, L. (2020) *Posthumanism and the Digital University: Texts, Bodies and Materialities.* London: Bloomsbury Publishing.

Haraway, D.J. (1997) *Modest−Witness@Second−Millennium.FemaleMan−Meets−OncoMouse: Feminism and Technoscience.* London: Psychology Press.

Hickey-Moody, A. and Willcox, M. (2019) 'Entanglements of difference as community togetherness: Faith, art and feminism', *Social Sciences*, 8, pp. 1–21. doi:10.3390/socsci8090264.

Hopkins, R. (2020) *From What Is to What If.* London: Chelsea Green Publishing.

Kerschner, C. et al. (2018) 'Degrowth and technology: Towards feasible, viable, appropriate and convivial imaginaries', *Journal of Cleaner Production*, 197, pp. 1619–1636. doi:10.1016/j.jclepro.2018.07.147.

Knox, J. (2014) 'The "Tweeting Book" and the question of "non-human data"', *TechTrends*, 59(1), pp. 72–75. doi:10.1007/s11528-014-0823-9.

Knox, J. (2017) 'Data power in education: Exploring critical awareness with the "Learning Analytics Report Card"', *Television & New Media*, 18(8), pp. 734–752. doi:10.1177/1527476417690029.

Lamb, J. (2017) 'Speculative research feat. Slick Rick', *DR JAMES LAMB*. Available at: http://www.james858499.net/6/post/2017/11/speculative-research-feat-slick-rick.html (Accessed: 19 August 2021).

Levick-Parkin, M. et al. (2020) 'Beyond speculation: Using speculative methods to surface ethics and positionality in design practice and pedagogy', *Global Discourse*, 11(1-2), pp. 193–214. doi:10.1332/204378920X16055409420649.

Lupton, D. and Watson, A. (2020) 'Towards more-than-human digital data studies: Developing research-creation methods', *Qualitative Research*, pp. 463–480. doi:10.1177/1468794120939235.

Lury, C. and Wakeford, N. (2012) *Inventive Methods: The Happening of the Social.* London: Routledge.

Macfarlane, B. (2016) *Freedom to Learn: The Threat to Student Academic Freedom and Why It Needs to Be Reclaimed.* London, United Kingdom: Taylor & Francis Group.

Markham, A. (2021) 'The limits of the imaginary: Challenges to intervening in future speculations of memory, data, and algorithms', *New Media & Society*, 23(2), pp. 382–405. doi:10.1177/1461444820929322.

Michael, M. (2012) '"What are we busy doing?": Engaging the idiot', *Science, Technology, & Human Values*, 37(5), pp. 528–554. doi:10.1177/0162243911428624.

Michael, M. (2021) *The Research Event: Towards Prospective Methodologies in Sociology.* Abingdon: Routledge.

Natale, S. and Treré, E. (2020) 'Vinyl won't save us: Reframing disconnection as engagement', *Media, Culture & Society*, 42(4), pp. 626–633. doi:10.1177/0163443720914027.

Nijs, G. et al. (2020) 'Fostering more-than-human imaginaries: Introducing DIY speculative fabulation in civic HCI', in *Proceedings of the 11th Nordic Conference on Human-Computer Interaction: Shaping Experiences, Shaping Society. NordiCHI '20: Shaping Experiences, Shaping Society*, Tallinn Estonia: ACM, pp. 1–12. doi:10.1145/3419249.3420147.

Nooney, L. and Brain, T. (2019) 'A "speculative pasts" pedagogy: Where speculative design meets historical thinking', *Digital Creativity*, 30(4), pp. 218–234. doi:10.1080/14626268.2019.1683042.

Nova, N. (2012) *A Digital Tomorrow.* (Curious Rituals). Available at: https://vimeo.com/48204264 (Accessed: 9 November 2021).

Papert, S.A. (1980) *Mindstorms: Children, Computers, and Powerful Ideas.* New York: Basic Books.

Parisi, L. (2012) 'Speculation: A method for the unattainable', in Lury, C. and Wakeford, N. (Eds) *Inventive Methods: The Happening of the Social*. Abingdon: Routledge, pp. 246–258.

Pew Research Center (2021) 'Demographics of mobile device ownership and adoption in the United States', *Pew Research Center: Internet, Science & Tech*. Available at: https://www.pewresearch.org/internet/fact-sheet/mobile/ (Accessed: 9 November 2021).

Priyadharshini, E. (2019) 'Anticipating the apocalypse: Monstrous educational futures', *Futures*, 113, pp. 1–8. doi:10.1016/j.futures.2019.102453.

Renold, E.J., Edwards, V. and Huuki, T. (2020) 'Becoming eventful: Making the "more-than" of a youth activist conference matter', *Research in Drama Education: The Journal of Applied Theatre and Performance*, 25(3), pp. 441–464. doi:10.1080/13569783.2020. 1767562.

Rogers, C.R. and Freiberg, H.J. (1994) *Freedom to Learn*. 3rd edn. New York: Merrill.

Ross, J. (2011) 'Traces of self: Online reflective practices and performances in higher education', *Teaching in Higher Education*, 16(1), pp. 113–126.

Ross, J. et al. (2018) 'Mobilising connections with art: Artcasting and the digital articulation of visitor engagement with cultural heritage', *International Journal of Heritage Studies*, 25(4), pp. 395–414. doi:10.1080/13527258.2018.1493698.

Sanders, E.B.-N. and Stappers, P.J. (2014) 'Probes, toolkits and prototypes: Three approaches to making in codesigning', *CoDesign*, 10(1), pp. 5–14. doi:10.1080/1571 0882.2014.888183.

Sandford, R. (2019) 'Thinking with heritage: Past and present in lived futures', *Futures*, 111, pp. 71–80. doi:10.1016/j.futures.2019.06.004.

Springgay, S. and Truman, S.E. (2018) 'On the need for methods beyond proceduralism: Speculative middles, (in)tensions, and response-ability in research', *Qualitative Inquiry*, 24(3), pp. 203–214. doi:10.1177/1077800417704464.

Statista (2021) *Ownership of Smartphones in the UK 2021*, Statista. Available at: https://www.statista.com/statistics/956297/ownership-of-smartphones-uk/ (Accessed: 9 November 2021).

Thornton, P. (2021a) *How to…Zoom Obscura*. Edinburgh. Available at: https://zoomobscura.files.wordpress.com/2021/04/how_to_zoom_obscura-3.pdf (Accessed: 27 October 2021).

Thornton, P. (2021b) *Zoom Obscura: Creative Interventions for a Data Ethics of Video Conferencing Beyond Encryption*. (Controversies inthe Data Society 2021). Available at: https://media.ed.ac.uk/media/Pip+Thornton+-+Zoom+ObscuraA+creative+ interventions+for+a+data+ethics+of+video+conferencing+beyond+encryption/ 1_mjdbkb4s (Accessed: 27 October 2021).

Tracy, S.J. (2010) 'Qualitative quality: Eight "big-tent" criteria for excellent qualitative research', *Qualitative Inquiry*, 16(10), pp. 837–851. doi:10.1177/1077800410383121.

Turkle, S. (2005) *The Second Self: Computers and the Human Spirit*. Cambridge: MIT Press.

Uncertain Commons (2013) *Speculate this!* Durham, NC: Duke University Press.

Ward-Davies, A. et al. (2020) 'Post studio methods: Being scicurious as a site for research', *Journal of Artistic and Creative Education*, 14(2). Available at: https://jace.online/index. php/jace/article/view/486 (Accessed: 7 August 2021).

Wilkie, A. et al. (2017) *Speculative Research: The Lure of Possible Futures*. London: Routledge.

10
SPECULATIVE PEDAGOGIES AND TEACHING

Introduction

This chapter shifts from a focus on speculative research methods to a focus on incorporating speculative approaches into formal and informal learning settings. I concentrate here on futures teaching that relates to education as a field and discipline, but the chapter is less about what is being taught and more about how. It draws on literature and examples from a range of fields, and I hope that educators will find insights they can translate to their own disciplinary context. The observations here are aimed at teachers and facilitators, but instructional designers, learning technologists, academic advisors and community practitioners will find aspects of use as well.

The key pedagogical and design issues raised here have some intersections with the issues highlighted in the last chapter: issues of participation, prompts and objects-to-think-with will be discussed again, but with a different emphasis. There are aspects of teaching speculatively that are distinctive because of the need for speculative pedagogies to generate beneficial outcomes for specific people's learning (in addition to being ethical and meaningful). The issue of consent is different in teaching than in research, as learners may have signed up for a course or programme of study but not specifically to engage in speculative work. Their ability to opt out may be limited, but in many cases, there is also time and space available to engage in a more in-depth way with a speculative approach.

The chapter begins with a discussion of course design, and how and why this might be undertaken in a speculative way. It moves on to discuss teaching strategies for supporting learners' own speculative work. Following this, I highlight the matter of assessment of speculative artefacts and make some observations about informal and lifelong learning. Finally, I share insights from the creation

DOI: 10.4324/9781003202134-13

188 Keeping learning futures moving

of a new postgraduate programme in Education Futures, and a specific example of speculative course design on that programme. By the end of the chapter, you should have some ideas that will help support your development of speculative teaching methods for futures work.

Speculative course design

In recent decades, design thinking has emerged in many fields and sectors, including education. It has moved beyond the designed "object" to services, interactions and experiences (Norman, 2013, p. 19). Instructional design and learning design, as well as design-based research, are now common terms in education, with specific goals including providing educators with models and tools to consistently produce "high quality, effective and innovative technology-enhanced learning" (Bower and Vlachopoulos, 2018, p. 981). Cross and Conole (2009) define learning design, broadly, as activities that support and guide pedagogic practices and processes, and that are documented to enable reflection and communication. However, as we saw in Chapter 3, design-based research, which aims to generate "transfer" of education research to practice (Anderson and Shattuck, 2012), struggles to engage productively with the complexities of context, agency and purpose in education. It may also, as Carvalho and Goodyear (2018) argue, fail to take into account that learning is located in the processes of activities that cannot be designed in advance, only influenced, because: "Learning cannot be designed. People learn in and through their own (emergent) activity, including through thinking, making, arguing, writing and reflecting. Learning outcomes are very varied in kind" (p. 34).

This is consistent with a relationality-informed definition of learning, with its focus on disturbance, difference, irritation and dis- and re-integration, discussed in Chapter 3. A relational view offers a way to look at design differently. Escobar (2018) explores the concept of "ontological design", which rejects the subject/object divide and emphasises the "radical innovative potential of design", particularly in relation to issues of sustainability and how to (re)design the human for a "future of futures". He argues that design un/does the world and its subjects in particular ways and calls design, at its foundation, "a conversation about possibilities" (p. 110). He asks: "Can design contribute to fulfilling the historic, perhaps vital, task of catalyzing forms of collective intelligence that attend to the kinds of choices confronting us, including design's own role in creating them?" (p. 109). This question frames education design sensibilities and ways of knowing in a more speculative register. Speculative design (or Critical Speculative Design) challenges a focus on problems and solutions in favour of the emergent relationality of "problematics" that are not amenable to being solved (Fox, 2018). How might this inform course design for exploring digital education futures?

One example of where speculative approaches might elicit productive course designs for futures work is in the matter of learning objectives. Gough (2013) critiques the concept of "constructive alignment" – where curriculum and learning outcomes are expected to directly correspond – for neglecting the complexity of education. Drawing on multiple examples of complexity, and complexity reduction, in the sciences, he argues that complexity thinking can move beyond instrumental understanding of educational inputs and outcomes. Indeed, it is in the "gaps" between inputs and outputs where learning might best be understood to take place. Some educators challenge instrumentality by involving learners in co-constructing learning objectives, but Gough offers another option, which he calls "deconstructive nonalignment" (in place of "constructive alignment"). This interprets curriculum as "story" and "text" that can be used as a focus for speculation and critique. Gough notes that this approach need not dispense with learning objectives altogether, but can provide more room for manoeuvre, for "even if a curriculum is planned to function as a simple system we can choose to interpret it as an element of a complex system – as part of a living agential space rather than a 'dead' mechanical space" (p. 1223).

The second implication for speculative course design is in how wicked problems are introduced and addressed. There are no definitive solutions to such problems, and different stakeholders will see their components differently. McCune et al. (2021) observe that teaching wicked problems in higher education contexts requires supporting students to develop ways of thinking and practicing that are interdisciplinary, recognise relationships between elements, seek out diversity of views and develop personal values. These are relational qualities, and not primarily curriculum-focused. Speculative course design, then, creates meaningful space and time for working with open-endedness, struggle and difference. This may bring advantages, as Osborn et al. (2019) found that students are able to learn to take multiple perspectives, think holistically and communicate complex ideas to wider audiences – all capacities aligned with goals of liberal arts education in the US.

Gaspar (2018), discussing her process for creating anthropological exercises for students, noted that her own, and students', engagement with "otherness" was a feature of her speculative course design:

> I was designing them speculatively - not just because the plans were open and I had to rely on a considerable amount of improvisation, but because I was creating the conditions for these openings. In other words, these exercises were speculative not just because I was exposing students to the other, but because the other (that which was unknown to me in first place) was being produced through the very pedagogical opportunities created.
>
> *(p. 86)*

As these educators have found, speculative approaches to wicked problems are relevant to the design of courses, but also to supporting learners' own futures work, and I move on to discuss this now.

Supporting futures work

The teaching approach in a course designed speculatively will, as we have seen, need an openness to surprise and emergence, and in the "live" setting of the course there are many places and times where this can occur. To take a simple example, the questions teachers pose to students, if they are in the spirit of speculative work, cannot have answers that are already known or expected. This rules out many questions commonly asked of students in formal educational settings. Writing about school teaching, Lowenberg Ball and Forzani (2009) note that the kind of question required in this setting is very different from questions in everyday life – teachers often have to ask questions they already know the answers to, and the only unknown is whether students will answer correctly, or how they will answer if not. The questions asked of students in universities are often more open, but are nonetheless framed by beliefs about what they need to know and how they need to evidence this knowledge. A futures question, approached speculatively, can have knock-on effects in terms of time, curriculum and assessment. Atkinson (2020) describes speculative pedagogies as "reactive", and emphasises the suddenness of how educational encounters might come to matter for learners, evoking "a politics and ethics of the suddenly possible" (p. 58). Without dismissing established forms of practice and knowledge, Atkinson foregrounds the role of teachers and learners as "critical inquirers and speculative innovators enabling potentials for a world to come, a world that is not yet known" (pp. 65–6).

This echoes Ruitenberg's (2015) discussion of hospitality in education, where she argues that "the task of education is to welcome newcomers into the old world, the world as it is, and not to predetermine for newcomers what they may want to do with that world as they receive it" (p. 3). To fulfil this task, she asks teachers to rethink the meanings of hospitality and their own roles in such exchanges – moving beyond a model of teacher as host and student as guest. Learners' creative and critical engagements with courses can produce new speculative futures for themselves and for others (as we saw in Chapter 6). Fiesler (2021) distinguishes between analysing speculative work (such as science fiction) and creating or building on it, and reflects on the success of more creative tasks on an information ethics and policy course. She notes that one basis of this success is that it is fun for students, and generates interest and excitement about technology and agency in the present day as well as in the future.

The strange temporalities of speculative work also have something distinctive to offer to futures work. Osborn et al. (2019) describe their Pilgrimage Model of speculative education as a kind of "retrofuturology" where imagining technology futures, drawing on the study of history, becomes useful in the present. Carstens (2020) theorises this kind of temporal shifting as an "uncanny" scrambling, where: "it is only in the otherness of their radical spectrality or ghostliness that material objects, things, bodies or events allow us to approach them and know

Speculative pedagogies and teaching **191**

them. Pedagogy occurs in this equivocal space between sensing, thinking, and knowing" (p. 78). Working in such creative, equivocal and reactive ways respects the complexity of digital learning futures, and learners are often capable of and willing to do this in educational settings that are well supported, and where the ethics of risk-taking have been thought through and discussed. The next section outlines some of the ethical dimensions of speculative pedagogies.

Participation, ethics and assessment

An ethical principle of accountability to learners can usefully underpin speculative pedagogical work. Accountability in this context takes at least two forms. First, teachers are increasingly being encouraged to recognise their own positions and how these may inform their curriculum and pedagogical choices, for example in the context of decolonising practice (Hayes, Luckett and Misiaszek, 2021). This can help push speculative work towards "critical" rather than "naïve" representations of the future, in Gonzatto et al.'s (2013) terms, and model how to understand futures work as contingent and contextual. As discussed in Chapter 9, a diffractive approach to relations of otherness in knowledge production can contribute to accountability in speculative methods.

Second, supporting people to engage productively with speculative approaches, especially if they are encountering this way of working with futures and complexity for the first time, is crucial. Teaching with speculative objects, or engaging students with speculative approaches, needs planning to ensure that challenging experiences of risk and uncertainty can be navigated. In particular, high-stakes dimensions of the work such as assessment, or asking learners to publicly share their creative work, need ideally to happen in a context of trust and clarity about expectations. A tension between responsibility and planning on the one hand, and risk and emergence on the other, was discussed in the last chapter in relation to research ethics, and it is equally tricky in a teaching context.

For instance, the way that innovative or creative student work is assessed (or not) gives a strong signal about what is valued. The complexity of producing high-quality creative work should not be underplayed, as colleagues and I argued in research about multimodal assessment:

> [these assessments] are sometimes viewed by students as relatively small and inconsequential parts of the class, particularly if the assessment value is low in comparison to more traditional assessment forms, such as essays or exams.
>
> *(Ross, Curwood and Bell, 2020, p. 301)*

Where speculative work is not formally counted, and where students need to (or choose to) devote considerable time and effort to speculative artefacts or

192 Keeping learning futures moving

processes, the work involved can be out of sync with expectations and time commitments for a course.

Beyond that, the need for accountability described in the previous section translates, in assessment terms, to a need for clarity in setting expectations and how students' work will be judged. My own experience of doing this has involved an increasingly detailed assignment brief, formative feedback on a related task and a peer feedback exercise that engages students with the assessment criteria their own work will be considered against (see Chapter 6).

It is not uncommon for discussions of creative or inventive pedagogies to neglect to discuss assessment. In part, I think this reflects discomfort with the power relations involved in assessment, especially when teachers are committed to working in ways that are responsive, imaginative and attuned to complexity. Of the small body of literature that discusses speculative pedagogy, only Osborn et al. (2019) discuss methods of feedback and assessment in detail. Different types of assessed work are highlighted, including project updates (assessed by group critique), written reflections, reports to instructors (assessed by desk critique and instructor notes) and exhibition success in relation to constraints. Example exhibition contributions themselves are given in the paper appendix, and include catalogue copy, artworks, posters and augmented, digital, interactive and multi-sensory interpretation. The diversity of the projects themselves posed issues for assessment and led to a framing of feedback in terms of how students had achieved "learning goals" including how they engaged in an iterative process of critique and response to their exhibition contributions, professionalism and communication (p. 360). The assessment also included evaluation of "improvement in technical proficiency" (judged on "improvement and growth rather than an externally defined level of expertise") (p. 362).

Nooney and Brain (2019) outline the tasks they set for students: an in-class pitch, an annotated bibliography, the creation and presentation of the artefact to class and a design rationale paper (p. 224), and describe these elements, including class critiques on presentations, where students get feedback that guides them in selecting their final artefact concept. The authors do not discuss assessment criteria or the assessment process, but again the iterative process is highlighted.

Beyond these two articles, assessment is not discussed, and I raise this as a gap in the emerging literature on speculative pedagogies, and encourage other teachers and educational researchers to publish on their practice in this area.

Informal learning, speculatively

The majority of this chapter has implicitly foregrounded teaching in formal contexts. I turn now to highlighting some key aspects of facilitating speculative encounters in informal, community or cultural learning contexts: hybridity and co-creation.

Speculative pedagogies and teaching **193**

The spaces of informal learning appear to be becoming more hybridised, which as Nørgård (2021) points out is not merely a pragmatic but also a theoretical shift towards postdigital ways of thinking about and experiencing learning, for instance through "learning interactions that unfold as a coherent experience of being in multiple places at once" (p. 1715), and by "bringing new species of learning environments into existence through cross-fertilization or cross-breeding existing ones" (ibid). She argues that hybridisation in a lifelong learning context:

> highlights the challenges and opportunities which transpire from the dissolution, fusion or transgression of boundaries between on-line and off-line, on-site and off-site, synchronous and asynchronous, formal and informal, vocational and recreational learning.
>
> *(p. 1717)*

And, she identifies new "species" of learning interactions that might come to be for, with and in the public. This is a rich space for speculative work. Indeed, as discussed in Chapter 1 in the context of the "learning is earning" scenario, speculation of various kinds is well underway: a key question is, whose stories will be told in developing informal learning futures? Considerations of the spaces of informal learning, and how those spaces may blur or intersect, is part of understanding learning as complex and as sparked, but not defined, by objects, tasks, activities, nudges, environments, timescales and so on. For this reason, it has been and remains extremely challenging to measure the impact of cultural engagement, or to pinpoint the source of transformative experiences. One implication of this for facilitating speculative informal learning activities is that learning outcomes from such activities can never be fully known – not only not in advance, but probably not in hindsight, either. However, there are other things that matter. Experimenting with space and time, for instance as the research team of the "SciCurious" project (Ward-Davies et al., 2020) did in their speculative zine-making activities, can generate hope and playfulness through their open-endedness.

The relationship between speculation, uncertainty and hope is traced also by Pringle (2012), who argues that speculative work with young people in gallery contexts is important to facilitate the potential for art to "communicate, to console, to uplift and to challenge" (p. 111), and for a relationship to develop between viewers and artworks. However, such experiences require facilitators who can work with unpredictable or emergent outcomes, and ask questions and make decisions that follow the consequences of such emergence. To enable this, she discusses the centrality of making space that is "speculatively audacious", "permissive space for ideas and questions to materialise and dialogue to develop" (p. 118) and where people can "celebrate, pull together, dismantle and redistribute knowledge" (p. 119). This form of dialogic, permissive space is best

194 Keeping learning futures moving

grounded in a particular context, as Rousell and Hickey-Moody (2020) argue. They discuss a speculative method of community arts engagement exploring belonging, belief, community life and local environments with young people that starts "with the aesthetic potentials and sensibilities that surround you and form the immediate grounds for experience" (p. 86). This in turn can cultivate new kinds of co-creation and experimentation with "alternative forms of life and relations of care" (p. 100). Co-creation, as discussed above, creates a responsibility to attune to and foreground what participants are doing or might do (Renold, Edwards and Huuki, 2020). The ability of those engaged in informal speculative encounters to opt out or to make themselves heard should not be assumed, but should be cultivated.

Futures teaching case study: culture, heritage and learning futures

In early 2019, a group of academics at the University of Edinburgh were appointed to develop new postgraduate programmes for the then newly-created Edinburgh Futures Institute (EFI). These programmes were to be on topics including future democracy, society, education, creativity, justice, health and sustainability, and one or two leads were appointed for each programme. I joined EFI in 2019 as the lead for the future education programme, now called the MSc in Education Futures. In mid-2020, James Lamb, a lecturer in Education Futures, joined as co-lead.

EFI was created as an interdisciplinary institute led from the arts, humanities and social sciences and designed to bring these disciplines into sustained dialogue with data science, engineering, natural sciences and medicine. Its

> ethos and commitment to co-production stem from the University's historic principles of the 'democratic intellect' ... [and] civic responsibilities of the University in working with and for its wider communities, and the importance of opening up education to all who can benefit.
>
> *(Edinburgh Futures Institute, 2021)*

Its initial focus on Data Driven Innovation informed the design of the new programmes.

Postgraduate education at EFI was designed to innovate in two main ways: through interdisciplinary teaching, and through a "fusion" model of course and programme delivery. The interdisciplinarity of the programmes was secured through the development of courses by people from a range of subject areas, by requiring all students to study interdisciplinary core courses in data and creative skills, and by making elective courses from across the institute available to all EFI students. Though its design pre-dated the pivot to hybrid teaching during the Covid-19 pandemic, the fusion model nevertheless offered a response to the demands of higher education during a pandemic: a highly technologised physical campus space combined with policies that allow students to access courses in person on campus, or online at a distance (and to combine modes throughout their study).

The Education Futures programme built on this foundation and was designed to "prepar[e] students from across a range of learning contexts to critically consider educational possibilities for the future, and how educational knowledge, organisations and agents can positively shape societies" (programme specification documentation, May 2021). The two main areas of focus for the programme centred on what education may be like in the future, and what it will be for. It was designed to be "sector agnostic" and to appeal to people working or aspiring to work in formal education, education policy and leadership, informal and community learning, training organisations or in private, government and voluntary sectors.

This account focuses on a course I devised and am designing at the time of writing, on the role of heritage thinking in developing visions of the future of lifelong and informal learning. The Culture, Heritage and Learning Futures course attempts to tackle the problem of how to take responsibility for the future and counter the tendency to treat it as a site of colonisation: "filled with anything, with unlimited interests, desires, projections, values, beliefs, ethical concerns, business ventures, political ambitions" (Adam and Groves, 2007, p. 12). Sandford (2019) proposes that heritage thinking can counter these "empty futures" by offering a "view from somewhere" that can be "richer, offer more scope for participatory approaches, and be less at risk of being instrumentalised as means rather than ends" (p. 71). The course tests this proposition by engaging students with heritage thinking approaches and speculative methods. The focus for the course is on informal and lifelong learning, an area of policy and practice that has in its own right been argued to have been colonised in recent decades by a hidden agenda of "creating malleable, disconnected, transient, disciplined workers and citizens" (Crowther, 2004, p. 127). Alongside introducing and discussing key themes relating to lifelong learning, the course shows students how visions of the future of knowledge and society have appeared in art, architecture and other heritage objects and collections, and how to critically "read" such objects for narratives of the future. Equipped with these skills, students will generate their own speculative story from the future. The learning objectives for the course are for students to be able to:

1. critically reflect on how education futures have been represented;
2. understand and analyse potential roles of cultural heritage in envisioning rich futures for informal and lifelong learning, and apply this to the creation of imagined futures;
3. demonstrate understanding of speculative methods and techniques, and skill in using these to develop and critically analyse stories of learning futures.

196 Keeping learning futures moving

Considering these in terms of constructive alignment, the course is designed around examining representations of future learning, working with heritage thinking approaches and using speculative methods to generate a story (the assignment). Considering what deconstructive non-alignment might offer, the "living agential space" (Gough, 2013, p. 1223) of the course may generate some surprises in terms of how students might interpret "heritage" in their own social and cultural contexts, and how disciplines like art history and library science, for instance, might shed light on the course topics. For example, in an early discussion with colleagues from the Centre for Research Collections at the University,[1] we explored the idea of "perpetuation" in terms of how artists and curators think about the lifespan of artworks and the meanings they may come to hold, and "regeneration" of objects and artworks that take on new forms over time.

As I write this, the course is about six months away from running for the first time. I am considering lifelong learning themes for year one, including learning in social movements, and learning from and through creative practice. Bringing heritage thinking, lifelong learning futures and speculative method together in one short course – and accounting for the wide variety of backgrounds that participants in the course will have – I am anticipating an "emergent set of relations" or "problematic" (Fox, 2018, p. 157) that may need considerable flexibility to account for. In this case, a speculative pedagogy that is "reactive" (Atkinson, 2020) to a world that is not yet known must leave space for students to tell stories that may (as with the open educational resources discussed in Chapter 6) go well beyond what I can currently imagine. Students' own use of speculative methods may bring some uncanny (Carstens, 2020), retrofuturistic (Osborn et al., 2019) surprises, too. The task of assessing these, as discussed above, will require a careful balance between structure, iterative development of shared expectations, and an openness to the unexpected.

Conclusion

The way educators personally and collectively frame the task at hand in making courses can generate more or less productive possibilities for teaching about education futures. My argument, building on the issues and ideas raised in this chapter, is that speculative approaches can be generative both in the design of courses and learning engagements, and in supporting students to be creative and critical in their future-making.

Speculative pedagogies are informed by problematics and complexity in ways that are related to speculative research methods, but distinctive in their orientation to what matters – finding ways to take the lead from the priorities of learners. This requires flexibility, a willingness to work in open-ended ways, and a responsive and responsible understanding of whose futures are in play and how to create space for more kinds of not-yetness in framing those futures. Working with children and young people, as a number of educators cited in this chapter have done, brings the question of "whose futures?" into particularly sharp focus, but this is a question for all educators in their futures work with learners.

I have said less about digital education and technology futures in this chapter than in others, so I close with a few reflections on why speculative pedagogies can make good approaches in this field. As discussed in earlier chapters, digital futures for learning are very often presented as inevitable, for good or for ill – with a growing role predicted in the short- and medium-term for devices, analytics, computational thinking and online forms of writing and collaboration. Education, in this near future, is understood as playing a preparatory role for contexts where machine learning and ubiquitous connectivity will continue to expand, and technological skills will be needed for productive employment, while digital literacies will become increasingly vital for democratic engagement in post-truth societies. Counter-futures of ecological breakdown, resource constraint and ongoing climate crisis are sometimes presented as lower-tech, but usually in an assumed context of collapse and reversal, a return to pre-digital ways of being. A hybrid, inventive and perhaps even convivial technological landscape for education, what this could look like and what it would be like to learn and work in, is not currently being very much discussed or envisioned. The implications of slower, older edtech – edtech within limits, as Selwyn (2021) describes it – are not yet being seriously anticipated. Speculative pedagogies that give space to learners to explore and work creatively with possible digital futures have a role to play in educating around wicked problems and the meanings of those futures for the present.

Note

1 Many thanks to Julie-Ann Delaney and Liv Laumenech for this discussion and their excellent input, as well as to Sarah Ames, Helen Vincent and Màiri Lafferty at the National Library of Scotland, and Callum McGregor and Shari Sabeti at the University of Edinburgh, for stimulating conversations as this course came into being.

References

Adam, B. and Groves, C. (2007) *Future Matters: Action, Knowledge, Ethics*. Boston, the Netherlands: Brill.

Anderson, T. and Shattuck, J. (2012) 'Design-based research a decade of progress in education research?' *Educational Researcher*, 41(1), pp. 16–25. doi:10.3102/00131 89X11428813.

Atkinson, D. (2020) 'Inheritance, disobedience and speculation', in Burgess, Lesley and Addison, Nicholas (Eds) *Debates in Art and Design Education*. Abingdon: Routledge, pp. 57–71.

Bower, M. and Vlachopoulos, P. (2018) 'A critical analysis of technology-enhanced learning design frameworks', *British Journal of Educational Technology*, 49(6), pp. 981–997. doi:10.1111/bjet.12668.

Carstens, D. (2020) 'Toward a pedagogy of speculative fabulation', *Critical Studies in Teaching and Learning*, 8(SI), pp. 75–91.

198 Keeping learning futures moving

Carvalho, L. and Goodyear, P. (2018) 'Design, learning networks and service innovation', *Design Studies*, 55, pp. 27–53. doi:10.1016/j.destud.2017.09.003.

Cross, S. and Conole, G. (2009) 'Learn about learning design'. Part of the OU Learn about series. Available at: http://www.open.ac.uk/blogs/OULDI/wp-content/uploads/2010/11/Learn-about-learning-design_v7.doc.

Crowther, J. (2004) '"In and against" lifelong learning: Flexibility and the corrosion of character', *International Journal of Lifelong Education*, 23(2), pp. 125–136. doi:10.1080/0260137042000184174.

Edinburgh Futures Institute (2021) *About us, Edinburgh Futures Instistute*. Available at: https://efi.ed.ac.uk/about/ (Accessed: 18 November 2021).

Escobar, A. (2018) *Designs for the Pluriverse: Radical Interdependence, Autonomy, and the Making of Worlds*. Durham, United States: Duke University Press.

Fiesler, C. (2021) 'Innovating like an optimist, preparing like a pessimist: Ethical speculation and the legal imagination', *Colorado Technology Law Journal*, 19(1), pp. 1–18.

Fox, T. (2018) 'Problematic milieus: Individuating speculative designs', in Filimowicz, M. and Tzankova, V. (Eds) *New Directions in Third Wave Human-Computer Interaction: Volume 2 - Methodologies*. Cham: Springer International Publishing (Human–Computer Interaction Series), pp. 155–173. doi:10.1007/978-3-319-73374-6_9.

Gaspar, A. (2018) 'Teaching anthropology speculatively', *Cadernos de Arte e Antropologia*, 7(2), pp. 75–90. doi:10.4000/cadernosaa.1687.

Gonzatto, R.F. et al. (2013) 'The ideology of the future in design fictions', *Digital Creativity*, 24(1), pp. 36–45. doi:10.1080/14626268.2013.772524.

Gough, N. (2013) 'Towards deconstructive nonalignment: A complexivist view of curriculum, teaching and learning', *South African Journal of Higher Education*, 27(5), pp. 1213–1233.

Hayes, A., Luckett, K. and Misiaszek, G. (2021) 'Possibilities and complexities of decolonising higher education: Critical perspectives on praxis', *Teaching in Higher Education*, 26(7–8), pp. 887–901. doi:10.1080/13562517.2021.1971384.

Loewenberg Ball, D. and Forzani, F.M. (2009) 'The work of teaching and the challenge for teacher education', *Journal of Teacher Education*, 60(5), pp. 497–511. doi:10.1177/0022487109348479.

McCune, V. et al. (2021) 'Teaching wicked problems in higher education: Ways of thinking and practising', *Teaching in Higher Education*, pp. 1–16. doi:10.1080/13562517.2021.1911986.

Nooney, L. and Brain, T. (2019) 'A "speculative pasts" pedagogy: Where speculative design meets historical thinking', *Digital Creativity*, 30(4), pp. 218–234. doi:10.1080/14626268.2019.1683042.

Nørgård, R.T. (2021) 'Theorising hybrid lifelong learning', *British Journal of Educational Technology*, 52(4), pp. 1709–1723. doi:10.1111/bjet.13121.

Norman, D. (2013) *The Design of Everyday Things: Revised and Expanded Edition*. Boulder, United States: Basic Books.

Osborn, J.R. et al. (2019) 'The pilgrimage project: Speculative design for engaged interdisciplinary education', *Arts and Humanities in Higher Education*, 18(4), pp. 349–371. doi:10.1177/1474022217736510.

Pringle, E. (2012) 'From trance-like solipsism to speculative audacity?: Young people's learning in galleries today', in Burgess, Lesley and Addison, Nicholas (Eds) *Debates in Art and Design Education*. Abingdon: Routledge, pp. 111–120.

Renold, E.J., Edwards, V. and Huuki, T. (2020) 'Becoming eventful: Making the "more-than" of a youth activist conference matter', *Research in Drama Education: The Journal of Applied Theatre and Performance*, 25(3), pp. 441–464. doi:10.1080/13569783.2020.1767562.

Ross, J., Curwood, J.S. and Bell, A. (2020) 'A multimodal assessment framework for higher education', *E-Learning and Digital Media*, 17(4), pp. 290–306. Doi:10.1177/2042753020927201.

Rousell, D. and Hickey-Moody, A. (2020) 'Speculative and symbolic forms of expression: New practices in community arts education', in Burgess, Lesley and Addison, Nicholas (Eds) *Debates in Art and Design Education*. Abingdon: Routledge, pp. 82–104.

Ruitenberg, C. (2015) *Unlocking the World: Education in an Ethic of Hospitality*. Abingdon: Routledge.

Sandford, R. (2019) 'Thinking with heritage: Past and present in lived futures', *Futures*, 111, pp. 71–80. doi:10.1016/j.futures.2019.06.004.

Selwyn, N. (2021) 'Ed-tech within limits: Anticipating educational technology in times of environmental crisis', *E-Learning and Digital Media*, 18(5), pp. 496–510. doi:10.1177/20427530211022951.

Ward-Davies, A. et al. (2020) 'Post studio methods: Being scicurious as a site for research', *Journal of Artistic and Creative Education*, 14(2). Available at: https://jace.online/index.php/jace/article/view/486 (Accessed: 7 August 2021).

11

KEEPING LEARNING FUTURES MOVING

Key messages from this book

There is a tendency to treat predictions about technology and its consequences for education and learning as either incontrovertible or meaningless: but they are neither. The future is not an empty vessel to be filled with whatever we desire or fear, and nor is it predetermined or fixed. Using speculative approaches, we can tune in to a sensibility of interest in the processes of making futures and the unpredictability of their outcomes. This is not so different from an interest in learning itself, when viewed through a lens of complexity. Learning cannot be designed (Carvalho and Goodyear, 2018) and "what works" is not universal but particular to a setting and purpose (Biesta, 2007), but what we do as we work towards meaningful pedagogy and new insights into education matters. Similarly, the futures we make through speculative methods and pedagogies may be partial, messy and provisional, but they matter.

As I have argued throughout this book, there is a need to work with digital learning futures in ways that offer an explicit counterpoint to fixed orientations (Facer, 2016) and uncritical predictions. Methods and pedagogies that take account of the relationality and indeterminacy of the future can form such a counterpoint. Returning to Facer's (2016) argument for the "potential for novelty in the future" (p. 70), working speculatively is a practice of engaging with possibilities, and following some to see where they lead.

This book has outlined a speculative approach to working with digital learning futures that is principled and imaginative, responsible and creative. The case studies in Part 2 aimed to show in detail what this can look like, but not to constrain the types of questions that readers might ask in their own settings. Overall, what I have proposed is that speculative approaches can provide

DOI: 10.4324/9781003202134-14

teachers, researchers, learners, policymakers, technologists and others with lively and critical visions to help counter instrumental, colonising or empty versions of the future. They are responsive, dynamic ways of keeping the future and our ideas about it moving. This final chapter ties together key messages from the book and offers some ideas about how to go forward with speculative methods and pedagogies.

In Chapter 4, I described three qualities of speculative method: temporality, epistemology and performativity. Working with speculative approaches needs awareness of and attunement to these qualities, and these can be captured in three key messages, which are at the heart of this book's contribution.

1. **The interplay of past, present and future produces speculative approaches**. Working explicitly with this interplay helps to situate and ground even the most whimsical work – not necessarily in "reality", but in responsibility. Attention to where questions and visions of the future come from and how they can be situated can break problematic loops where predicted futures are endlessly deferred or reconfigured. Interrupting what we are "busy doing" (Michael, 2012) in favour of sensitivity to the temporal strangeness of working with futures may slow things down, require a fresh start, or trip us into the unexpected. Speculative questions, objects and engagements need time and space for interruptions and surprises.

2. **The futures made by speculative approaches are creative and imaginative**. Speculative accounts like the ones explored in this book differ from instrumental descriptions of the future of education and learning by being knowing and explicit about their inventiveness. Speculative approaches do not attempt to predict, do not weigh up the balance of probabilities or analyse trends. They can be challenging in both research and teaching contexts because they also do not claim to know in advance what they will produce – hypotheses and learning outcomes sit uneasily with a speculative approach. They may instead be nonaligned (Gough, 2013), messy (Law, 2004) or glitchy (Bodden and Ross, 2021).

3. **Speculative approaches produce realities**. A speculative approach is attuned to the realities it creates: their liveliness and their ambiguity. Just because these are invented and inventive does not mean they are not real, that they do not have consequences. Sociotechnical and edtech imaginaries shape educational policy, practice, investment and theory in a range of ways. A story, an object, an experience can add weight to already established or emerging futures, or produce a future that had not been thought of. Working with participants or audiences to perform particular futures does things: but not always things that were anticipated. There is a riskiness to speculative work – it may set futures into motion, and those futures may not be what anyone intended.

202 Keeping learning futures moving

To explore the implications of these three key messages, I close by returning to a few important ideas that have shaped the development of the approaches described in the book.

First, **the relationality of learning needs approaches that can account for its complexity**. In both methodological and pedagogical terms, speculative approaches are productive for working with the future as a social practice, as a medium for imagination, and as a site of ongoing not-yetness. As we attempt to navigate the limitations of "best practice" and the impacts of sociotechnical imaginaries, digital education contexts are shaped by forces that are political, temporal, social, technical, economic and cultural. Learning is not a tidy or methodical process, but takes place in flows of disturbance, difference, disintegration and re-integration (Biesta, 2005). Speculative approaches can result in real outcomes where they enter these flows. Most powerfully, they can change how possibilities are brought into being and how people see the choices open to them. This, as Osberg (2010) argues, is the unique and affirmative role of education as a place of "experimental engagement with the possibility of the impossible" (p. 168).

However, the outcomes of such experimental engagement are not predictable. Teachers and researchers, learners and participants, may enter into a speculative situation with possibilities in mind, but find others in the relations that emerge. For this reason, a speculative approach is not only a starting point for work but a sensibility that carries through it. Springgay and Truman (2018) refer to the "speculative middle" in research, a space of openness, incorporeality, virtuality and temporal strangeness. This "speculative middle" does not negate the possibility of methods, they argue, but does compel a shift from thinking in terms of data collection to understanding methods as a form of relational entanglement. Other things besides methods, such as aesthetic objects, may also become agents of speculative relationality (Georgis and Matthews, 2021).

Second, **speculative research questions or pedagogical structures need space for unanticipated or surprising experiences or insights**, and time for "creative or inventive problem making" (Michael, 2012, p. 537). Gaining an understanding of the complexity of learning requires creative approaches, and that creativity, as we have seen, may emerge at unexpected times. Taking time at different stages of the work to consider and reconsider what is being produced and making space for changes of direction are key aspects of working speculatively. As new questions or ideas are encountered, a speculative stance will not be too quick to treat these as distractions or judge them as "out of scope", but will try to move towards them. This may be easier in some settings than others, but even in a formal teaching context, as bell hooks (1994) maintained, transgressing boundaries requires room for spontaneity and excitement, flexible agendas and attunement to shifts in direction.

Sometimes the impacts of speculative approaches such as the ones discussed in this book are to unsettle assumptions, produce space for broader conversations than had previously been had, and to show that such troubling can be desirable. This means the value of a speculative encounter can go beyond a single project or course and create new ways of working, and it also means that metrics of "impact" that funders and institutions rely on may not fully (or even partially) capture shifts in trajectory or new possibilities that have emerged. A fracture in the experience of the everyday, for students, participants, research partners and others, can expose larger fault-lines and different configurations than had been realised, and rushing to quantify, summarise or move on can be counterproductive to the new worlds and different futures that have been glimpsed.

Third, **speculative approaches bring risk to research and teaching situations**. Instrumental or closed futures are about reducing or managing risk; speculative futures dwell in possibility and uncertainty. Speculative not-yetness provides a kind of antidote to the conviction with which education and its futures are often presented. Such conviction does not serve us very well in the context of learning and digital education, but the alternative can feel risky. The surprises we made room for may not be the ones that emerge, and there are many threats to future health, prosperity and justice that our best educational endeavours may not be equal to. Failure of various kinds is an option. If there is confidence to be had in our methods and pedagogies, it is in the worth of working creatively with the uncertainty of the future, not in the likelihood that we will solve wicked problems or prepare ourselves or others for what is not yet. Building relationships that can weather this degree of risk, and can change course to account for more interesting or important meanings and moments that emerge through speculative encounters, is what can enable new approaches to flourish in teaching and research. Things may happen in the course of speculative work that have to be accounted for – glitches that require a response, anxieties that come from doing new kinds of relational or knowledge work in high-stakes settings, meanings that become contested through the unpredictability of strangers. In other kinds of teaching or research, such things might be repaired or perhaps ignored. In speculative teaching or research, they have to become part of "vectors of risk and creative experimentation" (Wilkie et al., 2017, p. 5) of possible futures.

Finally, **working speculatively means acknowledging that representing knowledge differently creates different futures.** I hope it has been apparent throughout this book that, while the specific shape and substance of futures that are being predicted, worked with or envisaged are important, it is just as important to think about *how* these ideas of the future are produced and how they come to be accepted. Speculative methods and pedagogies are best worked with self-consciously in this respect: to explicitly recognise that they produce futures and to look diffractively at the knowledge practices that are shaping them and the futures that emerge.

Speculative approaches, being creative and explicitly working between temporalities, can be of use precisely because of the partiality and provisionality of their visions. The questions asked and the approaches taken in the projects

204 Keeping learning futures moving

described in this book are specific to a place, a time, and a context. As far as possible, I have described how they came to be, and some of the historical, political and practical factors that influenced them. That in itself has been a productive exercise, and I highly recommend it to others working speculatively on learning futures topics. Further, as methods attuned to complexity and emergence, they are able to dwell in not-yetness – a space between expectation and uncertainty that characterises futures work in the digital education sphere. They do not need to be "right" by reducing complexity or predicting new technological breakthroughs. Their rightness comes from engagement with futures in ways that keep them open, moving and able to be worked with further, by others with a stake in them.

What next?

Developing interdisciplinary, creative representations and forms of analysis can generate new possibilities from within the midst of the questions, theories or topics being explored. The questions themselves might reflect not-yetness in productive ways. How to tell what topics or issues are in need of speculative future-making is in some senses at the heart of the matter of speculative approaches. While there are possibly better and worse questions to ask of the future at any particular time, more kinds of future-facing questions are rather urgently needed and can, in their own right, make a significant contribution to unsettling unhelpful, instrumental assumptions about education, learning and technology.

There are always good questions that are not currently being asked, or "subtopical" questions, as Michael (2021) describes them. For example: Selwyn (2021) prompts us to ask "what if" our future education takes place in the context of fewer or older devices, more considered use of material resources, and a general trend towards "degrowth" in education – what would this mean for educators, learning technologists, digital education researchers? This question might not have made sense even a few years ago, but it is now not only rich with possibilities for speculative explorations, but also increasingly urgent for us to attend to. Attempting to work with problems that are not yet acknowledged as problems, or possibilities that are not yet seen as possibilities, is something that speculative approaches are well-suited to do. In addition, objects, as well as ideas, can become "issufied" through controversies (Marres, 2012, p. 297), and speculative analysis (for instance, topological approaches) can work generatively with the emergence of concerns and the spatial and temporal configurations they produce. How questions are operationalised with audiences, participants or learners is an area that requires thought and planning. As Markham (2021) found, inviting people to be creative, or to imagine freely new technological futures, may not counter a sense of inevitability, for example around surveillance (Dencik and Cable, 2017). More "radical scaffolding" (Markham, 2021, p. 384) may be needed to refuse cynicism and resignation in favour of imagining new relations of care and responsibility in digital learning contexts.

In attempting to work with the future, there are also questions we (as educators and researchers) need to ask of ourselves. How are we to take responsibility for worlds within and beyond our imaginations? How are we to understand the role of digital education in the sorts of challenging futures we are currently asked to envision? To answer, we need to include in our thinking not only unasked questions, but a nuanced view of whose voices, and whose futures, we are capable of inquiring about and including. Taking account of flows of power between teachers and students, researchers and researched, and within the complex positionality of participatory work of all kinds is part of our responsibility as researchers and educators. The relationships created and revealed within speculative practices, however playful they may sometimes be, are also serious about the future, responsible to the present and thoughtful about the history of our field. This means that the tensions and contradictions and complexities of our work are not there to be resolved – they *are* the work. It also means that the futures we work with are highly contingent, and there will always be a need for new discussions and questions as new realities come into being. A speculative method or pedagogy can create openings and closures simultaneously, and critically questioning the dynamics of voice and engagement is part of what keeps futures moving, not fixed. All visions of the future are views from somewhere. Amongst many implications, this means considering the extent to which our work contributes to the colonisation of the future (Milojević, 2005).

Through a thoughtful approach to the impacts speculative work may have on learners and participants, such work can be pedagogically and epistemologically generative. It can offer new ways of being towards the future that are rich with possibility. Indeed, I think that the speculative approaches discussed in this book have done more than orientate me to research and teaching in the particular ways I have discussed. They have also led me to understand speculation quite broadly, as a lively, freewheeling and questioning quality of contact among people, technologies and texts. Where that quality of contact exists, there is the potential for working creatively with uncertainty and emergence.

Hope for the future in challenging times

We can use a speculative stance to engage in the debates that will inform learning in the coming decades. However, we cannot always predict the terms of those debates. For instance, over the past few years, online distance learning has become entwined in the public imagination with unwanted but necessary mitigations of the Covid-19 pandemic – an alternative when "real life" became fraught with danger, illness and death. Like a mask, an online class is currently seen by many as an emergency measure for terrible times, to be discarded as soon as possible. The campus, always implicitly treated as the guarantor of an "authentic" educational experience (Bayne et al., 2014), is now explicitly referred to in terms such as "centre of gravity" (all-staff email from University of Edinburgh's director of strategic change, September 2021), and we are urged to get back there for the good of our students, our research and our collaborative ethos. The digital work educators undertook during the first two pandemic years is framed in terms of loss and struggle. The coming years, if predictions of waves of illness and variants prove accurate (Scientific Advisory Group for Emergencies, 2022), may see a shift in this idea – for instance, towards fusion modes of teaching of various kinds. But there is no guarantee, and futures that looked possible a few years ago, where there is more widespread appreciation for "distance as a positive principle" (Bayne et al., 2020), may be further away than we had hoped.

The thing is, though: hope is a practice, not an attribute. We can engage with education as a hopeful practice, one that can be grounded in "attention to the relational nature of the many worlds in which we all live together" (Veletsianos and Houlden, 2020, p. 858). Utopias, as hard as they may be to come by and sustain, are important because of their "capacity to embody hope rather than simply desire" (Levitas, 2013, p. 108). That capacity can be nurtured through speculative practice that engages with problems and challenges, acknowledges partiality, gaps and silences, but still works *towards* something. Tara Fenwick, writing about adult education, defines hope as defying inevitability (Fenwick, 2006, p. 16), and of all the things speculative approaches can do, it is this that I think matters most. At its defiant, immediate, "audaciously hopeful" and "wide awake" (p. 21) best, speculative work has an energy that can help in troubled times.

Hopeful relations can also be found in challenging, critical and even dystopian future-making. Articulating or designing from ambiguity, loss or anger is also a form of care in a world that sometimes seems to reward detachment. I invite you to consider what forms of future-making are necessary and meaningful where you are, to keep working creatively with the messy and provisional futures around you, and making the case for why they matter. At the same time, let us all keep looking out for and listening to those who are working with futures that sit beyond our own speculative grasp. This is a challenge to be tackled not just once, but over and over – a call to embody a speculative quality of contact that refuses to settle around agreed or comfortable ways of understanding education's futures.

References

Bayne, S. et al. (2020) *The Manifesto for Teaching Online*. Cambridge: MIT Press.

Bayne, S., Gallagher, M.S. and Lamb, J. (2014) 'Being 'at' university: The social topologies of distance students', *Higher Education*, 67(5), pp. 569–583. doi:10.1007/s10734-013-9662-4.

Biesta, G. (2005) 'Against learning. Reclaiming a language for education in an age of learning', *Nordisk Pedagogik*, 25, pp. 54–66.

Keeping learning futures moving **207**

Biesta, G. (2007) 'Why "what works" won't work: Evidence-based practice and the democratic deficit in educational research', *Educational Theory*, 57(1), pp. 1–22. doi:10.1111/j.1741-5446.2006.00241.x.

Bodden, S. and Ross, J. (2021) 'Speculating with glitches: Keeping the future moving', *Global Discourse*, 11(1–2), pp. 15–34. doi:10.1332/204378920X16043719041171.

Carvalho, L. and Goodyear, P. (2018) 'Design, learning networks and service innovation', *Design Studies*, 55, pp. 27–53. doi:10.1016/j.destud.2017.09.003.

Dencik, L. and Cable, J. (2017) 'The advent of surveillance realism: Public opinion and activist responses to the Snowden leaks', *International Journal of Communication*, 11, pp. 763–781.

Facer, K. (2016) 'Using the future in education: Creating space for openness, hope and novelty', in Lees, H.E. and Noddings, N. (Eds) *The Palgrave International Handbook of Alternative Education*. London: Palgrave Macmillan UK, pp. 63–78. doi:10.1057/978-1-137-41291-1_5.

Fenwick, T. (2006) 'The audacity of hope: Towards poorer pedagogies', *Studies in the Education of Adults*, 38(1), pp. 9–24. doi:10.1080/02660830.2006.11661521.

Georgis, D. and Matthews, S. (2021) 'The trouble with research-creation: Failure, play and the possibility of knowledge in aesthetic encounters', *International Journal of Qualitative Studies in Education*, pp. 1–17. doi:10.1080/09518398.2021.1888164.

Gough, N. (2013) 'Towards deconstructive nonalignment: A complexivist view of curriculum, teaching and learning', *South African Journal of Higher Education*, 27(5), pp. 1213–1233.

hooks, bell. (1994) *Teaching To Transgress*. Abingdon: Routledge.

Law, J. (2004) *After Method: Mess in Social Science Research*. Psychology Press.

Levitas, R. (2013) *Utopia as Method*. London: Palgrave Macmillan UK. doi:10.1057/9781137314253.

Markham, A. (2021) 'The limits of the imaginary: Challenges to intervening in future speculations of memory, data, and algorithms', *New Media & Society*, 23(2), pp. 382–405. doi:10.1177/1461444820929322.

Marres, N. (2012) 'On some uses and abuses of topology in the social analysis of technology (or the problem with smart meters)', *Theory, Culture & Society*, 29(4–5), pp. 288–310. doi:10.1177/0263276412454460.

Michael, M. (2012) '"What are we busy doing?" Engaging the idiot', *Science, Technology & Human Values*, 37(5), pp. 528–554. doi:10.1177/0162243911428624.

Michael, M. (2021) *The Research Event: Towards Prospective Methodologies in Sociology*. Abingdon: Taylor & Francis.

Milojević, I. (2005) *Educational Futures: Dominant and Contesting Visions*. Abingdon: Routledge. http://ebookcentral.proquest.com/lib/ed/detail.action?docID=181960

Osberg, D. (2010) 'Taking care of the Future? The complex responsibility of education and politics', in Osberg, D. and Biesta, G. (Eds) *Complexity Theory and the Politics of Education*. Leiden: BRILL. doi:10.1163/9789460912405.

Scientific Advisory Group for Emergencies. (2022) *Viral Evolution Scenarios, 10 February 2022*. GOV.UK. Available at: https://www.gov.uk/government/publications/academics-viral-evolution-scenarios-10-february-2022

Selwyn, N. (2021) 'Ed-Tech within limits: Anticipating educational technology in times of environmental crisis', *E-Learning and Digital Media*, 18(5), pp. 496–510. doi:10.1177/20427530211022951.

Springgay, S. and Truman, S.E. (2018) 'On the need for methods beyond proceduralism: Speculative middles, (in)tensions, and response-ability in research', *Qualitative Inquiry*, 24(3), pp. 203–214. doi:10.1177/1077800417704464.

Veletsianos, G. and Houlden, S. (2020) 'Radical flexibility and relationality as responses to education in times of crisis', *Postdigital Science and Education*, 2(3), pp. 849–862. doi:10.1007/s42438-020-00196-3.

Wilkie, A., Savransky, M. and Rosengarten, M. (2017) *Speculative Research: The Lure of Possible Futures*. Abingdon: Routledge. doi:10.4324/9781315541860.

INDEX

Note: Figures are indicated by *italics* and tables by **bold**. Endnotes are indicated by the page number followed by "n" and the note number.

accountability: diffraction 178; ethical principle of 191; issue of responsibility 32–33, 50, 178, 201, 205
Adam, B. 32, 38, 178
Adams, V. 26–27
affirmative speculation 57
ambiguity 12, 43, 63, 74n1, 201, 206
anticipation 26–28
Artcasting project 16, 68, 125–127, 173, 176; analysis and evaluation phase 131; app-based nature of 142n5; dialectogram 138, *139*; ephemerality, of speculative objects 131–132; functions of *132*, 132–133; and heritage engagement futures 139–141; in-gallery leaflets 134, *134*; mobilities theory 133–135; as speculative method 136–139; workshops and drop-in sessions 134, *135; see also* digital cultural heritage
artificial intelligence (AI) 92, 98
assessment: multimodal 191; OERs 109–110; online teaching and 148, 153; Participation, ethics and 191–192; peer and authentic 108; power dynamics around 104; of speculative artefacts 187
assemblage 40
augmented reality 129
automation, Teacherbot project and 87–89

Barad, K. 13, 40, 178
Barnett, R. 46–47
Bayne, S. 93, 151, 181
Biesta, G. 42–43, 45, 171; evidence-based practice 44
big data 30
Bloch, E. 47
blockchain technologies 4–5, 17n2, 112
Bodden, S. 90
bridging techniques 64

Cable, J. 149, 162
Citizen Science Fiction 153
Clarke, A.E. 26–27
cognitive technologies 113–114
Cohen, J.E. 150–151
Coleman, R. 170
Collier, A. 152
complexity 15; contingency 40–43; digital education research 44–46; dimensions of 49; indeterminacy 40–43; not-yetness 46–49; open educational resources 117; overview of 38–39; relationality 40, 42–43; speculative approaches 50–51; of surveillance 149; theory 39, 50
complexity congruent approaches 39
complex relational web 43
compositional methodology 13, 62

210 Index

constructive alignment 189, 196
contingency 40–43
Covid-19 pandemic 28; digital pivot in
8–9; higher education during 150;
online distance learning 148, 205;
speculative event 59; techno-monitoring
during 180
Cox, A.M. 67–68, 97
critical education futures research 11–12
critical engagement, with future 31–34
critical thinking, in educational settings 114
Crotty, M. 179
culture, heritage and learning futures
194–196

data-driven decision-making 30–31,
150, 158
data stories project 16, 148, 173, 180; higher
education after surveillance and 152–154;
speculative data stories creator 154–157,
155
deconstructive nonalignment 189, 196
Dencik, L. 149, 162
design-based research 44, 188
design fiction 67
Dewey, J. 56, 71
dialectogram method 138, *139*
digital cultural heritage: engagement and
practice 126–131, 140; humanities
research 124–125; in museums and
galleries 125; *see also* Artcasting project
digital education futures 8, 33, 74, 80,
107, 152, 195
digital education research 6, 44–46
digital engagement 126–127; online
engagement 128–130; technology-
mediated engagement, in museum
127–128; value and evaluation 130–131
Digital Futures for Learning course
107–109, 119–120
Digital Futures Open Education
Resources 109
digital resignation 149–150
digital technologies, in learning futures 8
discourse analysis methods 23
discursive practices, defined 23
Doron, E. 137
Dourish, P. 24, 60
Drucker, J. 62; speculative computing 125

EDCMOOC *see* E-learning and Digital
Cultures MOOC
Edinburgh Futures Institute (EFI) 194

edtech imaginaries 25, 28, 201; open
educational resources 111–115
Edublocks 3, 4
educational imaginaries 24–25
educational technology 6–10
Edwards, R. 38, 105, 118
E-learning and Digital Cultures MOOC
(EDCMOOC) 84–87, 89–92, 174; *see
also* Teacherbot project
epistemology, and speculative method
61–62
ethics, of speculative approaches 177–178,
191–192
European CEPEH project 98
evaluation of heritage engagement
130–131, 133–135, 137–138
evidence-based practice 44
experimental and quasi-experimental
research 45
Eynon, R. 10

Facer, K. 11–12, 14, 32–33, 50, 200
Fenwick, T. 42, 206
Fiesler, C. 72, 190
financial speculation 57
firmative speculation 57, 170
fusion model 194–195
future-making tactics 15; anticipation
and mobilising, in present 26–28;
critical engagement 31–34; data-driven
future-making 30–31; overview of
22–23; promissory organisations 28–29;
sociotechnical and edtech imaginaries
23–26

Gallery, Library, Archive and Museum
(GLAM) 124
Gilliard, C. 152
Gonzatto, R.F. 60, 191
Goodyear, P. 9, 188
Gough, N. 117, 188–189
Gourlay, L. 105
Groves, C. 32, 38, 178

Haraway, D.J. 66, 178
Harrington, C. 66, 69
Hickey-Moody, A. 71, 194
higher education after surveillance
152–154
hypermobility analytic approach 176

imaginative speculation 56
Inayatullah, Sohail 31–32

indeterminacy 40–43
informal learning 9–10, 42–43, 192–193, 195–196; *see also* lifelong learning
Institute for Advanced Play 58
Institute for the Future (IFTF) 5
interdisciplinary teaching 119, 189, 194
"interventions in automated teaching" project *see* Teacherbot project
inventive method 62, 174
inventive problem making 57, 170, 175, 202

Jasanoff, S. 24
Jill Watson project 97–98

Law, J. 13, 40, 63
Learning Analytics Report Card (LARC) project 68
learning futures: educational technology and 6–10; multiple and critical futures 10–12; overview of 3–6; speculative approaches 12–15
Learning is Earning 3–5
Learning, Media and Technology 67
Ledger technology 3–4
Levitas, R. 32, 206
lifelong learning 42–43, 193, 195–196; *see also* informal learning
Lupton, D. 152, 182
Lury, C. 13, 61–62
Lyon, D. 149

Mackenzie, A. 31
MacLure, M. 24, 44
Markham, A. 65, 67, 174, 204
Massive Open Online Courses (MOOCs) 83, 85–87, 89, 91–95, 99, 99n2, 100n3, 105
McCune, V. 43, 189
methodological inventiveness 43
Michael, M. 57, 62–63, 65–67, 90, 140, 170, 175, 182, 204
Miller, M. 138
mobile technology 127
mobilities theory 125, 133–135
MOOCs *see* Massive Open Online Courses
MSc Digital Education programme 85, 108–109
MSc Education Futures 194–195
multimodal assessment 191
Murphy, M. 26–27
museum ethics 41

Natale, S. 151
non-digital education, defined 6
Nooney, L. 72, 192
not-yetness 59; of digital education 46–49, 51n3; of sociotechnical landscape 70

objects-to-think-with 171–173
OERs *see* open educational resources
online informal learning 10
online teaching, at scale and automation 85–87
open educational resources (OERs) 16, 104; assignment in 109–111, 117–118, 120; complexity 117; course structure **111**; digital futures for learning 107–109, 118–120; edtech imaginaries 111–115; licensing and design of 121n5; openness, practices and continuum of 105–107, 118; workplace learning futures 115–117, *116*
open education conference 106–107
Osberg, D. 50, 57, 202
Osborn, J.R. 71, 119, 189–190, 192
Ovens, A. 39

Papert, S.A. 171–172
paradigm proliferation 45
Participatory Speculative Fiction 153
Pilgrimage model 71–72; of speculative education 190
Pilgrimage project 71, 119
Plummer-Fernandez, M. 62–63
Poli, R. 26–27
Pollock, N. 28
postdigital theory 117, 193
Pringle, E. 71, 193
Priyadharshini, E. 68–69, 162
probabilistic methods 30
proliferation 31, 45, 49
promissory organisations 28–29
prototype-building workshops 69
prototypes, ask participants to generate 68

queer theory 41, 48, 60, 90
Quennerstedt, M. 49

Raby, F. 57
Reimagining Our Futures Together (UNESCO) 10–11
relationality 40, 42–43, 92, 133, 177, 188, 202
research landscape, in digital education 66–71

212 Index

retrofuturology 71
Rosengarten, M. 12
Rousell, D. 71, 194
Ruitenberg, C. 190

Sandford, R. 195
Savransky, M. 12–13, 61–62
Selwyn, N. 15, 25, 67, 87, 116, 197, 202, 204
social imaginary 24
social science fiction 67
sociomateriality 39–40
sociotechnical imaginaries 24–25, 28, 201
space of agency 40–41
speculation, anticipation *vs.* 27
speculative approaches 33, 169–170;
Artcasting project 136–139; complexity 50–51; course design 188–189;
data stories creator 154–157, **155**;
development of 202–203; enactments of 57–58; engagement 17, 63–65;
engagement, data generation 175–177;
epistemology and 61–63; ethics 177–178, 191–192; formal learning 17, 187;
informal learning 17, 187, 192–194;
inventive self-presentation 179–182; key messages 201; methods and pedagogies 12–15, 200–201; "object to think with" 171–173; OERs *see* open educational resources; overview of 187–188;
participants in 173–175; performativity 65–66; qualities of 59; research design 169–170; research landscape, in digital education 66–71; research questions 170–171; surveillance futures and 161–162; Teacherbot *see* Teacherbot project; teaching with 71–74; temporality and 59–61; truth claims 178–179; virtual reality 60–61; work analysis 190–191, 204, 205
speculative audacity 56
speculative computing 125
Speculative.edu project 73
speculative enactments 64

speculative fiction 67
speculative objects, researchers building 68
speculative outputs/analysis 70
Springgay, S. 59, 61, 175, 177
Staley, D.J. 8, 58
Stengers, I. 48, 90
story-based research methods 152–153
St. Pierre, E.A. 13, 34n1
student-generated open educational resources (OERs) *see* open educational resources
surveillance: cultures in higher education 180; data stories project *see* data stories project; in digital university 149–152; realism 149, 162; speculative futures 161–162; stories about futures 157–161; technological interventions 114, 159–160

Teacherbot project 16, 68, 84, 173, 174;
automation and 87–89; content analysis 93; futures 95–99; glitches 90–95; social network analysis 93
technological utopianism, accusations of 32
technology-mediated engagement, in museum 127–128
Tracy, S.J. 179
Treré, E. 151
Truman, S.E. 59–60, 61, 175, 177, 202
Turow, J. 149
Twitter bot 87–88, 93–94

Veletsianos, G. 46, 58, 106, 206
virtual reality (VR) 60–61

Wakeford, N. 62
Watters, A. 25, 152
Wilkie, A. 12, 62–63, 88, 170
Williamson, B. 28, 113
Williams, R. 28
Wilson, A. 152, 154
workplace learning futures 115–117, *116*

Zoom Obscura project 182